# Development and Advocacy

# Oxfam GB

Oxfam GB, founded in 1942, is a development, relief, and campaigning agency dedicated to finding lasting solutions to poverty and suffering around the world. Oxfam believes that every human being is entitled to a life of dignity and opportunity, and it works with others worldwide to make this become a reality.

From its base in Oxford, England, Oxfam GB publishes and distributes a wide range of books and other resource materials for development and relief workers, researchers and campaigners, schools and colleges, and the general public, as part of its programme of advocacy, education, and communications.

Oxfam GB is a member of Oxfam International, a confederation of 12 agencies of diverse cultures and languages, which share a commitment to working for an end to injustice and poverty – both in long-term development work and at times of crisis.

For further information, visit www.oxfam.org.uk

# Development and Advocacy

Selected essays from *Development in Practice*

Introduced by
Maria Teresa Diokno-Pascual

A Development in Practice Reader

Series Editor:
Deborah Eade

Oxfam

First published by Oxfam GB in 2002

© Oxfam GB 2002

ISBN 0 85598 463 5

A catalogue record for this publication is available from the British Library.

Available from Bournemouth English Book Centre, PO Box 1496, Parkstone, Dorset,
BH12 3YD, UK
tel: +44 (0)1202 712933; fax: +44 (0)1202 712930; email: oxfam@bebc.co.uk

and from the following agents:

*USA*: Stylus Publishing LLC, PO Box 605, Herndon, VA 20172-0605, USA
tel: +1 (0)703 661 1581; fax: +1 (0)703 661 1547; email: styluspub@aol.com

*Southern Africa:* David Philip Publishers, PO Box 23408, Claremont 7735, South Africa
tel: +27 (0)21 674 4136; fax: +27 (0)21 674 3358; email: orders@dpp.co.za

For details of local agents and representatives in other countries, consult our website:
http://www.oxfam.org.uk/publications.html
or contact Oxfam Publishing, 274 Banbury Road, Oxford OX2 7DZ, UK
tel. +44 (0)1865 311 311; fax +44 (0)1865 312 600; email publish@oxfam.org.uk

The Editor and Management Committee of *Development in Practice* acknowledge the support
given to the journal by affiliates of Oxfam International, and by its publisher, Carfax,
Taylor & Francis. The views expressed in this volume are those of the individual contributors,
and not necessarily those of the Editor or publisher.

Printed by Information Press, Eynsham

Oxfam GB is a registered charity, no. 202 918, and is a member of Oxfam International.

# Contents

# Contributors

**Ian Anderson** works in international structured finance and is Chair of Oxfam International and Vice-Chair of Oxfam Hong Kong.

**Jennifer Chapman** is a freelance researcher and consultant who is an associate of the New Economics Foundation (NEF) in London.

**A. M. R. Chowdhury** is the Director of the Research and Evaluation Division of the Bangladesh Rural Advancement Committee (BRAC) in Dhaka.

**Maria Teresa Diokno-Pascual** leads the Freedom From Debt Coalition in the Philippines, a broad-based movement which served as a model for Jubilee 2000, later known as Jubilee Plus.

**Deborah Eade** has worked in the development NGO sector for 20 years and is Editor of the journal *Development in Practice*.

**Michael Edwards** is Director of the Governance and Civil Society, Peace and Social Justice Programme at the Ford Foundation in New York. At the time of writing, he worked for The Save the Children Fund (UK) in London.

**Thomas Fisher** leads the community finance team at the New Economics Foundation (NEF) in London and has a special interest in non-farm rural livelihoods.

**Cees J. Hamelink** is Professor of International Communication at the University of Amsterdam, Editor-in-Chief of *Gazette: The International Journal for Communication Studies*, and Honorary President of the International Association for Mass Communication Research.

**Dot Keet** is a Senior Researcher at the Centre for Southern African Studies at the University of the Western Cape, a member of the Alternative Information and Development Centre in Cape Town, and an activist in Jubilee 2000 (SA).

**Gerd Leipold** advises NGOs on campaigning and organisational development. He is trained as a physicist and physical oceanographer and was previously director of Greenpeace Germany and director of the disarmament campaign of Greenpeace International.

**Carmen Marcuello** works at the Department of Economics at the University of Zaragoza in Spain.

**Chaime Marcuello** works in the Department of Sociology at the University of Zaragoza in Spain.

**Paul Nelson** is Assistant Professor in the Graduate School of Public and International Affairs, University of Pittsburgh, and previously worked for 15 years as a policy analyst for several US-based NGOs.

**Warren Nyamugasira** is the Director of the Advocacy Centre for Strategic Change in Uganda, and has worked in the NGO development sector for more than 20 years. At the time of writing, he was working for World Vision International in Rwanda.

**K. Pushpanath** works for The Save the Children Fund (UK) in Vietnam. He represented Oxfam GB in Malawi and Zambia at the time of writing.

**Mohammad Rafi** is Senior Research Sociologist in the Research and Evaluation Division of the Bangladesh Rural Advancement Committee (BRAC) in Dhaka.

**Larry Reid** has been active in Central America solidarity groups since 1983, both in Canada and in the region. More recently, he has been involved in fair-trade issues and is a member of the board of TransFair Canada.

# Preface

## Deborah Eade

*'Communication is the nervous system of internationalism and human solidarity.'* (Juán Carlos Mariategui, Lima, 1923)

The realisation that development and humanitarian relief projects will never, in and of themselves, bring about lasting changes in the structures which create and perpetuate poverty and injustice is nothing new. Back in the 1960s and 1970s, debates raged about whether the satisfaction of 'basic needs' comes first, or whether 'social change' is the only way to address the underlying structures that prevent these needs from being met. The emergence in the early 1990s of advocacy programmes and public-policy departments within mainstream development and relief NGOs reflected the growing sense that the 'needs versus change' dichotomy was a false one, that progress is uneven and incremental, and that sustainable change requires a range of inputs at many different levels, from the household and local community right through to the boardrooms of global institutions.[1] The new orthodoxy was that work to change the policy environment, and to promote specific policies, should thus inform and be informed by efforts to bring about tangible improvements in the daily lives of those who are living in poverty and whose basic rights are abused. This strategy is not one of seeking to achieve spectacular success through NGO advocacy alone, but of taking an integrated approach to the pursuit of social and economic justice for all. Thus, contributions to this volume describe modest but significant achievements, while also revealing something of the painstaking work that underpins them.

But just as there are profoundly conflicting views of what 'development' means, as well as how best to achieve it, so there are many differing approaches to advocacy. In both areas, there may be yawning gaps between what an agency says it believes and does, and the way in which it actually behaves. An obvious example is that of an organisation's declared commitment to promoting gender equity or cultural diversity, despite the fact that it has a male-dominated leadership and a top–down form of management. When that same organisation takes the moral high ground in public and seeks in its advocacy work to tell others how they should manage their affairs, these gaps can become dangerous credibility deficits.

Research recently undertaken by ActionAid (Chapman and Wameyo 2001) gives some insight into the spectrum of advocacy options, not all of them mutually compatible. What the research does make clear, however, is that although advocacy is self-evidently of a political nature (both in itself, and in terms of what it seeks to achieve), agencies seldom appear much clearer about their politics than they are about which development theory they espouse. Yet no number of campaigns or high-level lobbying activities will add up to a coherent political platform, any more than thousands of projects will constitute a theoretical standpoint on development.

The perceived disjunctures between rhetoric and reality in the field of advocacy work have exposed NGOs to increasing criticism, particularly since the much-publicised anti-globalisation demonstrations in Geneva, Seattle, and Prague. The fact that some critiques are intended to deflect or diminish the impact of NGO advocacy work does not in itself render them invalid. Indeed, NGOs' apparent failure to check that their own houses are in order before launching public attacks on major institutions has sometimes rendered them easy targets — as, for instance, in a piece published in *The Economist*, entitled 'Angry and effective':

> The increasing clout of NGOs, respectable and not so respectable, raises an important question: who elected Oxfam, or, for that matter, the League for a Revolutionary Communist International? Bodies such as these are, to varying degrees, extorting admissions of guilt from law-abiding companies and changes in policy from democratically elected governments. They may claim to be acting in the interests of the people — but then so do the objects of their criticism, governments and the despised international institutions. ... Who holds the activists accountable?[2]

In fairness, and as this volume attests, disquiet about aspects of NGO advocacy was already being voiced by those more sympathetic to the NGO community long before the issue began to hit the headlines (see, for example, Sogge *et al.* 1996, especially Chapter 5, and Michael Edwards' contribution to this volume). It is therefore worth highlighting some of the concerns raised most frequently about NGOs that lobby *on behalf of* others.[3]

## Some uncomfortable questions

### Legitimacy

From where do NGOs draw legitimacy for their advocacy work? Being 'pro-poor' is not enough – especially since, as NGOs themselves argue, 'the poor' are not an undifferentiated mass of identical interests and aspirations. Does their assumed proximity to 'the poor', usually in a donor or aid-related capacity, give NGOs any right to represent them? As three seasoned NGO-watchers put it: '[c]laiming the right to speak out simply because an NGO has projects or contacts on the ground is unlikely to be acceptable to a sceptical audience in the media, among other observers, and – most importantly – a more critical local population' (Edwards, Hulme, and Wallace 1999:15).

### Accountability

To whom are NGOs accountable for their choice of advocacy goals and strategies? What voice do their diverse constituencies (donating public, official donors, local interlocutors, or intended beneficiaries, as well as trustees and staff) have in shaping an NGO's advocacy programme? Whose view prevails when there are disagreements among the different stakeholders? Can the intended beneficiaries appoint (or dismiss) their NGO advocate? Or decline to be 'represented' by an NGO on, for instance, the issue of labour standards, on which trade unions have greater legitimacy? If an NGO displaces another representative body, it risks both weakening civil society and also depoliticising the issue, since many companies would prefer their behaviour to be monitored by an international NGO, rather than by a unionised workforce.

### Effectiveness

How is the effectiveness of NGO advocacy work evaluated, and by whom? Unless its (long-term) impact can be measured, how can an NGO assess which resources should be dedicated to it? What is to stop an NGO being seduced by the very institutions that it seeks to influence? Where does the 'insider' tactic of constructive engagement stop, and cosy co-existence or outright co-option begin – and who is to decide when that line has been crossed?[4] This issue is now critical, as NGOs switch their attention from the familiar targets of the IMF and the World Bank to focus on specific companies, precisely because the corporate sector is anxious to show that it is responding to criticism of its social or environmental record by 'respectable' NGOs.[5] A low-cost but high-profile 'greenwash' tactic will protect their reputations but enable the companies to carry on business as usual.

> Many companies, corporate foundations and business associations or partnerships liberally apply the label 'sustainable development' to initiatives or activities that in practice amount to fairly minor interventions to improve environmental management systems or eco-efficiency ... Many ... also focus narrowly on one particular aspect associated with corporate responsibility – for example, environmental protection – and ignore others, such as labour conditions and indigenous rights. (Utting 2000:16)

### Content

It is easy for NGOs to criticise and protest against what they don't like, but what concrete alternatives can they propose? And do they have the specialist knowledge as well as the comprehensive vision necessary to do so? Where does the buck stop if an NGO's specific policy recommendations in one context have negative implications for poor people elsewhere, or over time? (As Jennifer Chapman and Thomas Fisher show in their contribution to this volume, the carpet-weaving trade illustrates how an over-simplistic understanding of the full situation can, in the absence of other measures, worsen the situation of child labourers and their families.)

## The dangers of self-promotion

Tensions have always existed between an NGO's legitimate fund-raising needs and the means that it uses to meet them, particularly in relation to the mass media. Today, however, aid agencies jostle for television footage or interview sound-bites, since without this constant projection of their 'brand' they fear losing not only their market share but also their influence in the policy arena. Thus, 'the aims of corporate communication have increasingly encroached on the territory reserved for advocacy for development' (Winter 1996: 26). In order to pursue a strategy of 'naming and shaming' the institutions whose policies they hold responsible for causing or exacerbating needless suffering — be it the IMF, a military government, or a sportswear company — an NGO not only needs to be sure of its facts, but must also have an impeccable reputation. Ideally, it also needs to be a respected household name.

We would highlight three dangers that can arise if self-promotion is conflated with what it projects as disinterested altruism. First, if an NGO falls into the trap of devising advocacy campaigns *in order* to raise its profile (as well as keeping the income flowing) – AIDS this year, child soldiers the next – it risks trivialising the issues, as well as instrumentalising its relationships with its Third World 'partners' : selecting and/or manipulating the partner organisations to fit its own agenda. Second, if an NGO feels it must always have something to say on any matter of public concern, it risks not only undermining its own credibility but also crowding out expert (and potentially more persuasive) 'niche' organisations. And third, the projection of simple campaign messages (albeit complemented by expert behind-the-scenes lobbying) that are simultaneously appeals for cash seldom enhances public understanding; yet without a groundswell of well-informed support for change, institutions will remain largely impervious to NGO advocacy efforts. One commentator argues as follows.

> Leaders must be prepared to enter into dialogue with a worried citizenry on how to allocate limited resources. And they must discuss these matters with the public as equals, not as audiences to be manipulated nor as ignoramuses to whom leaders impart a small fraction of their superior knowledge. (Daniel Yankelovich, cited in Winter 1996: 24)

Despite the complexities described in this volume by Dot Keet, the Jubilee 2000 campaign is an innovative and very exciting example of how to develop an advocacy agenda in a way which empowers everyone involved: concentrating first on informing local public opinion on the debt crisis, in order to mobilise people into a global movement which would in turn enable its members to lobby authoritatively at the very highest level.

## The question of legitimacy

At this point, it is worth recalling the origins of the word 'advocate'. Derived from the Latin for 'someone called to one's aid', the word generally refers to a legal representative, such as a barrister, who is paid to work on behalf of a client. A secondary meaning applies to someone who argues for a cause or recommended course of action. In the former case, the advocate's legitimacy depends on his or her professional expertise and ability to argue the client's case persuasively. In other words, clients do not speak up unless required to do so. If they are not satisfied with the performance of their representative, clients may replace their advocates. In the second meaning, the advocate's legitimacy is not *assumed* to be based on expertise, although it may well be. For instance, a local aid worker who is involved in the rehabilitation of war victims might advocate condemning a convicted war criminal to death, in the belief that healing cannot begin until people feel that justice has been done. A colleague might oppose the death penalty in any circumstances and argue that to execute the criminal will serve to perpetuate a culture of violence. Both are entitled to their *opinions*, and both can legitimately press for their views to be heard. By the same token, in weighing up the two opinions, a third party would want to know whether they are genuinely disinterested, or motivated by partisan convictions. In this sense of the term, advocacy is value-based rather than expert-driven.

NGO advocacy rests on both sources of legitimacy, which it tends to conflate. As quintessentially value-driven organisations, NGOs quite rightly invoke their moral mandate to advocate for causes they believe in, even if they do not claim specialist expertise. However, the political nature of advocacy requires NGOs to demonstrate their accountability to their multiple constituencies; and their credibility therefore depends not only on their knowledge of the subject matter but also on genuine dialogue with those whom they seek to represent. This is no easy matter, and it is hardly surprising that few NGOs have the mechanisms in place to be as downwardly accountable as they should be, or the resources to maintain a high level of specialist knowledge over time.

As this anthology from *Development in Practice* shows, critiques of NGO advocacy have come from many quarters, and certain NGOs are making serious efforts to grapple with the issues. More significantly, however, transnational popular movements are now realising the potential of electronic communications to define their own advocacy agendas and strategies. The structural challenge to conventional NGO advocacy will come not from the resident sceptics or armchair critics, but from emerging forms of social organisation and political struggle that do not depend on or want NGO mediation: the traditional arbiters of how advocacy should be done are simply being by-passed in this wave of secular protestantism. If NGO advocacy is to carry authority in the future, it must move decisively away from what might be termed *paternalistic advocacy* (whereby Northern NGOs corner the international forums, and Southern organisations provide the raw material for their lobbying campaigns), to what ActionAid calls *participatory advocacy*, whereby civil-society organisations are drawn into efforts to broaden the political space within which the voices of the poor can be expressed and heard; and *people-centred advocacy*, whereby people negotiate for their rights on their own behalf. The role of the Northern NGO will then be to act in solidarity – sharing its resources where it can, helping when it is invited to do so, and generating a climate of support for pro-poor policy change within its own immediate constituency.

In her introductory essay to this volume, **Maria Teresa Diokno-Pascual** of the Freedom from Debt Coalition in the Philippines demonstrates the enormous odds against the voices of poor people being heard in the places where decisions that most affect them are made. Development NGOs often used to say that they were working for their own extinction. Whether any institution can actually do this is questionable, but the spirit of this claim was that NGOs believed that the attainment of their goals would render them redundant. It is time to revive this aspiration in relation to advocacy: success would then be measured by the extent to which NGOs (North or South) had opened doors for those who were denied access to the institutions that shaped their lives, helped them to organise their own advocacy agendas — and then stepped aside.

## Notes

1 There is a long history of NGOs whose *raison d'être* was to campaign on behalf of a cause: Anti-Slavery International (formerly the Anti-Slavery Society) is an early example, Amnesty International or Greenpeace are more recent ones. But we refer in this essay to NGOs which have taken on advocacy *in addition* to their traditional role of funding and/or undertaking development and relief activities.

2 *The Economist*, 25 September 2000, in a Business Special from an unnamed reporter based in Washington DC. The writer's arguments against NGOs and political organisations are misleading, however. Their legitimacy is not based on whether or not they are elected, but grounded in the Universal Declaration of Human Rights, which confers freedom of opinion and expression, including the right to receive and impart ideas, freedom of peaceful assembly, freedom of association, and the right to take part in public life.

3 For the purposes of this essay, we exclude those organisations which advocate on behalf of their members, such as consumer unions, labour unions, and various kinds of self-help organisation. These are of course not immune from the problems described here, but they do have formal structures of accountability, and their representational status is relatively clear.

4 Chapman and Wameyo (2001:10) cite criticisms that international NGO advocacy readily becomes 'a debating exercise between members of a "New Managerial Class" in which NGO professionals debate with other members of the same global class in

the international financial institutions. The critique raises the concern that NGO staff based in the industrial capitals, with class origins and academic training similar to those of the World Bank staff, can force policy-making processes open to their own participation, without ensuring access for excluded communities.'

5  Interestingly, the author of *The Economist* article makes the same observation, but from the perspective of embattled organisations being forced by the lunatic fringe to deal with critics whom they perceive to be at the tamer end of the spectrum: 'The activists have also raised the profile of "backlash" issues — notably, labour and environmental conditions in trade, and debt relief for the poorest countries. This has dramatically increased the influence of mainstream NGOs, such as the World Wide Fund for Nature and Oxfam. Such groups have traditionally had some say (albeit less than they would have wished) in policymaking. Assaulted by unruly protesters, firms and governments are suddenly eager to do business with the respectable face of dissent.'

# References

Chapman, Jennifer and Amboka Wameyo (2001) *Monitoring and Evaluating Advocacy: A Scoping Study*, London: ActionAid.

Edwards, Michael, David Hulme and Tina Wallace (1999) 'NGOs in a Global Future; Marrying Local Delivery to Worldwide Leverage', Background Paper to a conference of the same title, hosted at the University of Birmingham, UK, 10–13 January 1999.

Sogge, David with Kees Biekart and John Saxby (1996) *Compassion and Calculation: The Business of Private Foreign Aid*, London: Pluto Press.

Utting, Peter (2000) *Business Responsibility for Sustainable Development*, Geneva 2000 Occasional Paper 2, Geneva: UNRISD.

Winter, Anne (1996) *Is Anyone Listening? Communicating Development in Donor Countries*, Geneva: UN NGLS.

# Development and advocacy

## Maria Teresa Diokno-Pascual

In June 1999, while at the British Parliament to attend a panel discussion organised by Christian Aid on the World Bank/IMF Heavily Indebted Poor Countries initiative ('HIPC'), I had a brief exchange with the Secretary of State responsible for the Department for International Development, who was one of the speakers at this affair. I had been told that the minister, Clare Short, was most sympathetic to the NGOs who had been calling for improvements in the HIPC proposals. It therefore came as a shock to hear her tell the audience that it was useless to demand the de-linking of structural adjustment from HIPC. She added that countries in the Third World needed structural adjustment, and therefore it would be foolish to insist that debt reduction be undertaken in these poor countries without it.

Since I come from a country which has gone through ten structural adjustment loans from the World Bank and more than 30 years of IMF stabilisation lending without much success in achieving sustainable growth and in reducing poverty, I thought I should challenge this view. When the opportunity came for the audience to raise questions or comments, I asked the Secretary of State: what weight would she give to voices from the South, to the opinions of people like me from countries of the South, who say that we don't like structural adjustment and what it has done to our people? Would those voices matter?

I did not expect to get a tongue-lashing. The minister held firm to her position that structural adjustment was needed in countries like mine, adding words to the effect that since I had supported a corrupt dictatorship in my country (referring, I presume, to the Marcos dictatorship[1]), then I deserved structural adjustment. The format of the panel discussion did not allow me to respond. To be honest, had I been given the opportunity, I do not know what I would have said. This was the first time I had ever been told that structural adjustment was the answer to a corrupt and brutal dictatorship that I had never supported in the first place. Besides, history will attest that the World Bank and other international creditors had propped up the Marcos regime, particularly in its twilight years, knowing full well how corrupt it was. But it seemed to me that this spokeswoman of the British government was disturbed by my question and needed to invalidate it somehow. And her rejoinder carried a message that was far more disturbing: no, your voices *don't* matter.

Whose voices do matter when you are inside the rather imposing walls of the British Houses of Parliament, or, for that matter, any such venue in the developed world? How much importance should we give these places, considering the distance between them and the poor in our countries? I do not doubt the strategic value of being able to intervene at a level where major decisions are made which affect millions of nameless, faceless lives. But I tend to see these venues as part of a much broader terrain, in which many unceasing struggles take place simultaneously, involving a range of individuals and movements within a country and across borders of North and South. What is important to stress, however, is that no amount of power, influence, and effective advocacy can take the locus of the struggle away from those hardest hit by the decisions of the powerful. But very often it is these struggles that tend to be overlooked and forgotten in the world of development advocacy.

Don't get me wrong. It takes a lot of confidence and courage to speak up before government ministers of the North, in a language they understand and in a place more familiar to them than to oneself. It takes much more knowledge and imagination to present to them a reality that they are too privileged ever to experience for themselves. (I know this because, while I can hardly count myself among the rich in my country, I have been spared the kind of deprivation that can be very raw and violent to its victims among the poor.)

At the end of the day, the untiring work we have put in only makes sense if it has strengthened people's movements on the ground. This is where we must be honest with ourselves, sparing no criticism. How much of our advocacy work is based on the dehumanising experience of the poor? How much of our advocacy work is relevant and meaningful to their lives? Do we bother to make the connections, especially for advocacy issues that are not easy for ordinary people to relate to but which do have an impact upon them? How serious are we in our efforts constantly and consistently to enrich our knowledge and experience with what is happening in the communities of the poor, with what often gets least exposed to the public eye? How open are we to these realities? How relevant *are* we?

The group to which I belong, the Freedom from Debt Coalition, is one of the few radical bodies in the Philippines that have continued to thrive despite the recent factionalism in the movements of the Left.[2] Its members not only come from a broad range of social sectors, but also span most of what we call the progressive forces in the country. Building unity on issues and strategies is a difficult task, especially in the midst of the re-defining and re-organising that accompanies a group's breaking away from former comrades. All of this is taking place at a time when the free-market ideology dominates mainstream thinking and economic policy. One can thus appreciate the demands on our member organisations in the context of a country which is being drawn very forcefully into the neo-liberal policies that come with World Bank and IMF structural adjustment and stabilisation programmes.

We must strengthen our unity on alternative policies and strategies. We had a relatively easy time uniting on a critique of the proposed reforms, but formulating concrete alternatives is always more difficult, particularly for a coalition. I am convinced, however, that alternatives *do* exist, and many of them are there simply waiting to be recognised, appreciated, and propagated. We will find them, the closer we get to the ground.

I keep saying this because advocacy work tends to locate itself close to the centres of power, away from the marginalised. In the Philippines that means Metro Manila, a rich enclave which cannot completely hide the poverty that abounds within, but where the income opportunities, wealth, and power are highly concentrated. One can get steeped in the lobbying and advocacy work that one needs to do with the decision makers in Congress and in the Executive Branch, and occasionally the Judiciary. Yet we have learned in the Freedom from Debt Coalition that none of these institutions and their members will pay serious attention to us without our having done the groundwork —education, mobilisation, organisation — among our own members. Having the political expertise and the capacity to draw on the technical expertise of others is important. Having the skill to discuss and argue with the powerful at a high level of debate is also important. But all that is meaningless without vibrant and dynamic movements on the ground.

Dealing with government ministers and Members of Congress in our own country is a tedious and often frustrating task. In the Philippines, to be elected into office a candidate must have money in unlimited quantities, and constant publicity. (The host of a television and radio talk show, whose own reputation for honest reporting has come into question, garnered the greatest number of votes in the nationwide senatorial campaign last May.) Scruples and principles will not get you elected. It does not even matter if the candidate has a campaign platform, much less what kind of platform it is. To a jaded eye, voting is a way for the urban poor to earn money, especially when no jobs are available. It is serious business for the political candidates.

When the campaign is over, those elected turn their focus to recouping their huge investment, or at least that of their financial backers among the élite. Again there are no scruples here. In this world of globalising markets, everyone, especially the politician, has a price. At the height of the debates surrounding the Bill that would privatise the State-owned National Power Corporation and restructure the electricity industry, what struck me the most was how few Members of Congress made an effort to study the proposed reforms and understand all of their very serious implications. The Chair of the energy committee of the House of Representatives constantly told the Freedom from Debt Coalition that the proposed reforms were too technical for us to grasp. (I suppose he just wanted us to trust him, who was known to lose five million *pesos* in one night of gambling.) We ignored his bluff and took up his challenge.

We studied the reforms as best as we could, tapping the Internet for information from Europe and the USA, where reforms in the power sector had already been instituted. We talked with fellow activists on debt from Pakistan and Indonesia about the contracts between the State-owned power companies in our respective countries and the private investor-owned independent power producers. We kept going back to our members with the new information and analysis that we were able to uncover. We used all forms of media available to us. We carried on our protest within and outside Congress, outside the headquarters of the Asian Development Bank, in meetings with the new President's Cabinet,[3] and on the streets.

We surprised the politicians with our understanding and critical analysis. And yes, we did offer alternatives, even though these were hastily rejected by all officials of the executive and legislative branches. (We were accused of being communist and of being impractical when we suggested that if the assets of the State-owned power company were to be sold, then they might as well be sold to consumers and workers, in order to democratise ownership in the country.[4]) In the end, money and powerful lobby groups — multilateral creditors included — determined how the politicians would vote, and they voted in favour of big capital.

Our ministers must heed another voice, and that is often the voice of the creditors. While the politicians are out to recover their money, and to enrich themselves further, the World Bank, the Asian Development Bank, and the IMF, together with bilateral 'donors', have each drawn up their strategy for lending to the Philippines. A vital part of this strategy is the package of policy reforms that accompany their loans, co-ordinated of course among themselves. Nowadays these strategies even come with the added legitimacy of having gone through some kind of 'civil society' participation.

Never mind that the Philippines went through a currency crisis only recently.[5] Never mind that the World Bank pushed the country to liberalise its capital accounts and make itself vulnerable to short-term capital. Never mind that the IMF agreed with the central bank authorities to maintain an overvalued *peso* and subsequently high interest rates to keep footloose capital coming in. Never mind either that private-sector borrowers, encouraged by the overvalued *peso* and the high cost of borrowing, shifted to short-term dollar loans – only to find themselves in deep trouble when the *peso* crashed. Despite all these factors, the message of the multilateral creditors simply remained more of the same: *Liberalise more! Deregulate more! Privatise more!*

The pressure exerted by the creditors on government is tremendous. It is compounded by the fact that the economy remains in crisis, and that the deposed government of Joseph Estrada left behind huge fiscal deficits to be tackled by his successor, Gloria Macapagal-Arroyo. In the case of the Power Sector Reform Bill, for example, the newly proclaimed President Arroyo had said she was in no hurry to pass it and wanted instead to review all options available to her government. However, shortly thereafter, she announced that the Bill had to be ratified by Congress and signed into law as soon as possible. Her government forced its passage through soon after the May elections. Yet the President could not hide her dissatisfaction with the Bill: at the very moment when she signed it into law, she said that it needed to be amended.

The only plausible reason for her to sign a law she was not fully confident about was that the passage of this Bill was a condition for the release of some US$950 million in loan funds from multilateral and bilateral creditors. Ironically, the money has not been released at the time of writing (July 2001), because the creditors want to review and approve the law's implementing rules and regulations. In fact, the Asian Development Bank, the main lender in this regard, is sitting as an observer in the committee that is drafting the implementing rules.

The message of the British government spokesperson and the compelling hand of the multilateral creditors clearly show us where power actually resides in our world today. Which brings me to my final point about development advocacy: it is first and foremost about communicating a perspective from a strange, often unseen world: the realities of the unempowered and disempowered. But it is also about struggle – to assert the legitimacy and primacy of these perspectives, and to shift the balance of power in favour of the poor.

*Maria Teresa Diokno-Pascual*
*Freedom from Debt Coalition*
*Quezon City, Philippines*

## Notes

1. Ferdinand E. Marcos was elected President of the Philippines in 1965 and re-elected for a second and final term in 1969. He declared martial law in 1972, arrested key members of the political opposition, and curtailed civil and political rights. His military dictatorship ended in 1986, when he was forced to leave the country after a non-violent uprising known as People Power I.

2. In the early 1990s, major divisions occurred within the communist movement of the Philippines. The repercussions continue to be felt to this day. For example, member organisations associated with one bloc withdrew their membership of the Freedom from Debt Coalition. New left-wing groups have since emerged, and continue to reorganise and redefine themselves.

3. On 21 January 2001, Gloria Macapagal-Arroyo was sworn in as President of the Philippines, following the resignation of Joseph Estrada, who was accused of committing graft, economic plunder, and perjury, following allegations in October 2000 by Luis Singson, governor of Ilocos Sur province, that he had personally benefited from illegal gambling. The Freedom from Debt Coalition was invited to a meeting with President Arroyo's finance minister in February 2001, to discuss the Power Bill.

4. This was a serious proposal, not just a propaganda ploy. Consumers in the Philippines not only pay for the electricity they actually consume, but also for the idle capacity of the privately owned plants and for the enormous debts of the State-owned power company. In short, they are the real source of investment capital.

5. In mid-1997, following the crash of the Thai *baht*, the Philippine *peso* plunged after portfolio investors withdrew their money from the country. The Asian currency bug moved on to infect Malaysia, Indonesia, and South Korea, before affecting Russia and then Latin America.

# NGOs and advocacy:

how well are the poor represented?

## Warren Nyamugasira

A growing number of non-government organisations (NGOs), North and South, have intensified their advocacy work in an attempt to surmount the constraints placed on their development efforts by the global powers that be — both economic and political — which they allege serve interests other than those of the poor. They have come to the sad realisation that, although they have achieved many micro-level successes, the systems and structures that determine power and resource allocations — locally, nationally, and globally — remain largely intact. Therefore, they need to find ways to 'scale up' their influence upon these determinants, so that their small-scale successes have greater and more lasting impact (Sutherns, 1996).

Until the 1980s, greater impact was thought to come about through replicating successful projects, or what Clark (1992) refers to as the 'additive' approach. However, many strategy-minded NGOs find expansion by replication too slow and resource-stretching, especially as those restricted resources are declining. They seek to move into the 'faster lane' of positive and strategic social change by influencing attitudes, policies, and practices of the decision-makers at critical levels (op. cit.). In their advocacy work, such NGOs 'have assumed the role of ambassadors for the World's poor' (op. cit., p. 195). They see part of their mission as being to represent the political concerns of the poor, injecting the voice of the traditionally voiceless into international decision-making, facilitating the two-way flow of information, and helping to make the world's political and economic institutions more broadly accountable.

However, achievements by NGOs in these areas are, at best, mixed. Some do argue that enormous successes have been won. Caldwell (1990), for example, contends that 'the growth of NGOs during the past century has changed the character of international relations, broadening their scope, multiplying the number of participants, and sometimes outflanking the formal protocols of international diplomacy'. The North–South Institute would seem to agree when it argues that the education and advocacy role of Canadian NGOs over 15 years may have been their most significant activity and contribution, having had a more lasting effect than the millions of dollars they used in programmes in the developing world in the same period (op.cit., p.7).

According to Clark (op.cit., p.197), the combined influence of NGOs and public opinion has initiated major policy changes by Northern governments on several issues, including the production of a code of conduct for the marketing of baby milk, the drafting of an international essential drugs list, concerted action on international environmental issues such as global warming and rain-forest destruction, and affording special debt-relief to the poorest countries. Edwards (1993, p.166) adds to this list, citing developments in the food régime of refugees and displaced persons, and modifications in 'structural adjustment packages' to take more account of social impact, among others. Quoting Clark, he concludes that 'if it were possible to assess the value of all such reforms, they might be worth more than the financial contributions made by NGOs'.

Edwards, however, is more circumspect, and argues that most achievements have been at the level of detailed policy and/or on issues where NGOs have not encountered strong interest-group pressures. According to him, little progress has been made at the level of ideology and global systems. Furthermore, progress on more fundamental issues, such as the conservation of the environment and the impact of structural adjustment on the poor *en bloc*, appears less impressive on closer inspection. While there have been superficial responses, the basic ideology and structures have remained largely intact. Where changes have occurred, they may have been damaging in their impact on women and children. And there is no conclusive evidence that changes have been due to NGO pressure, except in a few instances. Finally, 'NGOs have failed to build an international movement for development' (Edwards, p.167).

## The new division of labour

To enhance the effectiveness of their advocacy, NGOs have evolved a new division of labour. Northern NGOs are relinquishing the more operational roles to concentrate on ideas, research, empowerment, and networking (Clark, 1992). They are increasingly focusing their efforts on development education, advocacy, and information flows, and challenging policies of their governments and of the corporations and multilateral institutions that are perceived to block, undermine, or co-opt 'genuine' development initiatives. They are leaving the 'hardware' — the time-bound, geographically fixed projects, such as building schools or health centres, or installing oil mills and so on — to their Southern counterparts. They are also assigning to these the advocacy task of addressing the forces emanating from the national or sub-national political economy. Northern NGOs prefer to concentrate on forces of an international character, such as the structure of the world trading system, financial and investment flows, energy consumption, technological innovation, and intellectual property, and the policies of multilateral and bilateral donor agencies. 'The increasing international-ization of decision-making in economic and political fields, and the limited accountability of global institutions, have increased the power of these interests' (Edwards, p.163) and made the task very urgent. Nevertheless, it should be acknowledged that most NGOs are still relatively weak on advocacy, not yet having the stature, expertise, and reputation to match their capacities to deliver material assistance.

Sutherns views the need for the new division of labour as arising from a commitment to local empowerment: '[w]hatever division of labour is considered optimal will be grounded in our fundamental values and beliefs about development ... A commitment to local empowerment will lead us to organize ourselves in such a way as to affirm that the burden of responsibility for development in the South lies with indigenous NGOs', adding the punch-line '... no matter how poorly managed or ill-experienced they may currently be. Strengthening the competencies of Southern NGOs means Northern NGOs moving away from a directly operational approach.'

The decision of Northern NGOs to relinquish the directly operational role to their Southern counterparts may be strategic, but it certainly is not altogether voluntary. Southern NGOs have for years been calling for it. They have been highly critical of Northern NGOs for being operational, and have long pushed to be given the funds and left to do the job.

Underlying this separation of roles seems to be the assumption that Southern NGOs more effectively hear and represent the authentic voices of the poor, while Northern NGOs are better able to articulate — in sufficiently sophisticated language — their concerns to Northern governments, multinational corporations, and global institutions. The law of comparative advantage is thus employed.

# Southern NGOs: the authentic voice of the poor?

Southern NGOs have made many positive local-level advocacy-type contributions. As one respondent to the draft of this article wrote:

> we have ... to acknowledge the great efforts and the remarkable accomplishments of (S) NGOs, as part of civil society, over the last decade, especially when we have to consider the political and cultural constraints they had to struggle with. The role they are playing, contributing to the democratization process in Africa, the recent changes of family and customary laws (marriage, inheritance, child custody) in many countries; and their contribution to the reshaping of state vis-à-vis society relations on the continent is worth pointing out. (personal communication)

However, uncritically to equate Southern NGOs with the voice of the poor could be somewhat misleading. Another respondent — a senior staff member of an international NGO — put it thus:

> There is the danger of assuming that Southern NGOs necessarily speak for the poor and the marginal. This is a matter which is sometimes avoided out of politeness or fear of offending (S)NGO colleagues. Listening to those on the margins requires a stretch for anyone who has become part of the 'development set'. It is harder when based in the North, but even when working for an NGO in the South, there are many filters, barriers and distractions. How to genuinely listen and represent (as opposed to speaking for) different poor communities is a significant challenge for all NGOs. (personal communication)

Even for Southern NGOs, poorer people are, for a start, hard to reach. Chambers (1993, p.28) argues that:

> they are typically unorganized, inarticulate, often sick, seasonally hungry, and quite frequently dependent on local patrons. They are less educated, less in contact with communications, less likely to use government services, and less likely to visit outside their home area ... They are relatively invisible, especially the women and children ... Visitors could easily spend a week in a village without either seeing or speaking to the poorer of its inhabitants; and without ever entering one of the colonies where many of the poorest live, visitors tend to see, meet, and interact with, only the more influential and better off rural people.

We can quote the example of some villages in Kabale in south-western Uganda which the author recently visited. There, NGOs are little known. In fact, only one — World Vision, which runs the Rukiga Area Development Project — is resident and operational. NGOs are not evenly or systematically distributed in geographical terms. Rather, there are pockets of concentration and competition in some areas, but in many others NGOs are virtually absent. There are, however, a number of community-based organisations (CBOs) in Kabale as elsewhere, stretcher (*engozi*) groups, *Biika-Oguze* (savings and credit) groups, and digging groups. CBOs are working throughout Uganda (Nyamugasira, 1995) and are making substantial contributions in forging community solidarity, uplifting the human spirit, promoting togetherness, and helping to combat the feelings of helplessness that poverty can induce.

CBOs are, however, primarily a coping mechanism. They cannot encompass everybody, and often the poorest do not belong and do not voluntarily participate. CBOs are typically functional, addressing one specific need at a time. People are simply preoccupied by the struggle for survival and do not have time to think about longer-term objectives. In the area visited, there was little evidence of CBOs interacting to develop any semblance of a common advocacy strategy. Neither did the author find any systematic gathering of information for such purposes by the operational NGO. On the whole, CBOs are too small and localised to have an impact on poverty reduction, let alone on its elimination. They do not add value to what the poor already do, for example by encouraging the planting of high-value crops to maximise effort. Recent research into improved crops and better markets is simply inaccessible to them. And neither NGOs nor government bodies are effectively bringing these services to the people.

Even *in loco*, Southern NGOs can, at times, be a poor imitation of and often distort the voices of this 'silent' mass. All NGOs tend to be self-appointed, and neither consult nor give feedback to their constituencies. As Sutherns (op.cit., p.5) puts it, the people 'have no independent voice or authority over the NGOs in their midst'. In fact, NGOs rarely have constituencies which have mandated them as their advocates. Rather, NGOs have often created their own abstract constituencies; are socialised in the value systems and thought patterns of the global élite; and project their own construct of the issues purported to be those of the poor, while they consciously or unconsciously protect their own interests and those of their kind. It is not a question of Northern versus Southern NGOs, as is often portrayed: it is the poor versus both.

# The bottom line

With all due respect, many Southern NGOs do not qualify as 'indigenous', in that they are not born out of the situations in which the poor live. Rather, they are modelled on the Northern NGOs who founded and/or fund them, often with strings attached. Consequently, they feel accountable more to the North than to the local poor, whose values and aspirations it is hard to prove that they represent. Indeed, they seem to be more concerned with their own survival and advancement. In situations where poor people still walk bare-foot, for example, their purported NGO representatives will insist on the latest four-wheel drive vehicles and so are necessarily biased to roads and urban areas. Many are thoroughly foreign, with all the trappings of the aid industry, and can be accused of patronising the poor. They love status and are committed to maintaining the *status quo* so long as it works in the their favour. They have weak management structures, as well as problems of vision and accountability in relation to their local-level partners.

This situation will not get any better simply by Northern NGOs' delegating more development responsibility to their Southern counter-parts. It will be improved only through the genuine search for viable alternatives. The good news is that the NGO sector has become a growth industry. The bad news is that this growth has spawned a multitude of small, localised organisations which are often invisible and ineffectual and have little influence on local or national development processes. This truth must be faced. In our view, a relinquishing of operational roles by Northern NGOs risks being an abdication of their responsibilities to the poor.

The poor need effective organising, and need to be perhaps more aggressive in order to be competitive and more efficient. Southern NGOs have little track-record in high-level organising, constrained as they are by inherited shortcomings in this realm. The capacity to organise independently was destroyed during the long period of colonialism and neo-colonialism. The poor need access to capital, technologies, and markets. Indeed, the very term 'South' is almost synonymous with their absence, as if they were intrinsically incompatible. What the poor do not need is pity, exploitation, or patronising; they already endure more than their fair share of these. Their genuine partner is one who adds value to what they are already doing. NGOs should perhaps concentrate less on projecting their supposed altruism and work harder to develop more of the appropriately selfish interest that spurs and drives people's (including poor people's) entrepreneurship. Aid must be run on sound business principles of measurable efficiency and effectiveness, even in respect of qualitative parameters. For this, NGO philosophy has to change. A world is passing away, leaving a fine line between myth and reality in terms of what Southern NGOs can and cannot do. There is value and strength in being interdependent, if the terms of this interdependence are equitable — a view that is now beginning to emerge from the South.

## Northern NGOs: chasing an advocacy agenda

Northern NGOs also need to get their priorities right in defining their agendas. Agendas for advocacy should grow out of action and practical development experience, not from the minds of thinkers in the North, however brilliant these may be (Edwards op.cit., pp.168, 173). For when government policy-makers are challenged by advocates from the North, their line of attack tends to be to question these advocates' mandate to speak for the poor. There is a need to rise to such challenges, for the real strength of NGOs lies in their simultaneous access to grassroots experience in the South, and to the decision-makers in the North.

By the same token, Northern NGOs must be held accountable for the advocacy agenda they pursue. Otherwise, information flows between field and Northern headquarters may be weakened, because field-staff do not feel part of one system with common objectives, driven by and supportive of their own work. Without a constant supply of high-quality information, advocacy cannot be successful. But if the desire is to focus attention on the opinions of the traditionally voiceless, then their voice must be clearly heard before their message can be clearly articulated. This voice is constantly changing. However, if Northern NGOs are still relatively weak in advocacy, then Southern NGOs are even more so, while the linkage between them and the local or grassroots organisations who are in direct touch with the people on whose behalf they purport to speak is weaker still. NGOs need to stop being preoccupied with their own narrowly interpreted bureaucratic mandates and get down to the business of seeking out and listening to the poor in order to secure a mandate to speak clearly and with conviction on their behalf. The poor live in the so-called culture of silence from which they must be liberated. The first step is, then, to meet them at their own level before they will speak.

Doing so must mean seeking out all the sections of society, in particular women and children. Gender-awareness campaigns have shown us that there is a marked difference in the perspectives of women and men, arising from women's lack of social, economic, and political power. What is not yet emphasised enough is the perspective of children.

For example, as a result of genocide in Rwanda in 1994, a new phenomenon called 'child-headed households' has appeared, with families being headed by children as young as 10 years of age, of whom 75 per cent are girls. Prior to the genocide, the child in Rwandese society occupied a central and key position. Although children-headed households are a reality, it is one still not acknowledged by most Rwandese in their thinking and planning. The children say that they are not involved in making the important decisions affecting the nation or even their own well-being. Now, according to a qualitative needs-assessment study conducted by World Vision and supported and publicised by UNICEF, these children feel detached from the community, to which they desperately want to return. But they are becoming resigned to their situation. For example, when children are asked to draw pictures to show how they feel, they sometimes draw pictures of people with no mouths, signifying that they no longer want to speak, because they feel that no-one is listening. Yet they also argue that they have something to say that no-one can say for them. These children have latent abilities which can bring benefit to those communities who choose to listen to them.

There are other examples of children in need of a voice: those abducted by the Lord's Resistance Army in northern Uganda, those taken into prostitution in many countries of Asia and Latin America, and more recently in Europe and Africa, AIDS orphans in East and Central Africa, and many other examples. All this implies that there are different and sometimes even conflicting needs and perspectives among the poor, even when they are united in their poverty. Various groups and sub-groups have very different stakes in the *status quo*, as they do in engendering change. Priorities for advocacy and other appropriate forms of support can emerge only if we listen, so that we gain enough trust to enable the different groups to 'articulate' their needs. While the issues are urgent, nevertheless we must hasten slowly, ensuring that we have not left behind those very sectors for whom we purport to speak.

## Redefining partnership

Rather than 'specialise' in different roles, NGOs North and South would do better to revisit the concept of true partnership. A first element must be making space for each other within their traditional domains. If advocacy must grow out of, and be informed by, grassroots experience, Northern NGOs can ill afford to abandon the operational arena. It may be their only way to retain an 'authentic' voice, and hence there continues to be plenty of room for them to co-exist in partnership with their Southern counterparts. To hear and join in with these 'authentic' voices, however, they also need to go beyond their partners and counterparts to the people to whom these voices belong. Relying on second-hand information is inadequate, especially as this is filtered and necessarily distorted. For too long, the sources of information have been the small select group of intermediaries who largely share the Northern NGOs' basic philosophy and objectives. But these do not necessarily represent the poor in any significant sense (Edwards, op.cit.). The need to go to the people themselves may call for a greater rather than a diminished presence, albeit one of a different kind. There is a call for a new generation of partnership, or 'joint ventures', to use the language of modern commerce.

Allowing Northern NGOs to have greater access to the authentic grassroots experiences must, however, be reciprocated; Northern NGOs should not seek to monopolise access to Northern-based institutions. Representatives from the South must also be afforded unrestricted access into these enclaves of power so that they can engage with the relevant actors directly. Ultimately, the people must represent themselves, and all NGOs — Northern or Southern — need to internalise this way of thinking. After all, most of the global institutions do not belong exclusively to the North. They are universal, and are only housed in New York, Washington, London, Geneva, or Paris. Conceptually, we need to view them as belonging to all of us, which is how they too must learn to see themselves. They do not represent just a Northern NGO constituency; NGOs and people from the South need no 'permission' to engage constructively with these institutions, but simply require certain barriers, such as language, to be removed.

In short, we should aspire to a joint venture of effective engagement with the political and economic powers that control and allocate the world's resources, and not get excessively concerned about interfering in each other's supposed constituencies. A free unhindered flow of, interaction with, and access to authentic opinions and experience in the South and to policy institutions in the North and the South is what one could call genuine partnership. We believe that this is the alternative to the current division of labour in which Southern NGOs literally do development 'hardware' in the South and Northern NGOs do development 'software' in the North. The ultimate objective against which success must be measured is that the people's voice increases, while that of NGOs themselves declines. The litmus test is that this withdrawal becomes voluntary on the part of the NGOs. For the goal is not to build up NGO empires but to integrate the poor into the global mainstream in a manner that maximises their benefits and minimises their exploitation.

## In search of 'linguistics'

Whether from North or South, advocates must obtain the people's mandate and regularly return to have it renewed. At best they must have twin citizenship, or be what Chambers (1993) calls 'new professionals', and Bourdieu refers to as the 'new middle class'. This is not the monopoly or preserve of people from one hemisphere. An advocate from the North should not be written off just because of geographical origins. S/he could, with some effort, be as effective, even 'authentic', as someone from the South, especially if s/he spends quality time with and has the right attitude towards those who are poor. The poor are universal. (A better criterion for carrying out genuine advocacy might be that the 'advocate' goes to the poor and immerses herself or himself in their lives, value systems, and thought patterns and regularly returns, so as to be sure that s/he keeps in touch.)

We believe that the poor, in spite of the supposed proliferation of Southern NGOs, do still lack 'linguistics', a term used in West Africa which here would describe a capacity to interpret the reality of the poor, and translate it into conceptual frameworks and policies that are intelligible to the outside world but retain the original meaning. Exploiters have never been limited by language barriers, so why should do-gooders be so limited?

## Interim representation

Interim representation, the duration of which is jointly defined, is another approach to genuine advocacy. Ultimately, the poor must be the ones to make their voices heard at the highest levels possible, and they have the potential to do so. 'The ability to analyze life situations, structures of society and development processes is not the preserve of intellectuals or development professionals. Individuals and communities possess these abilities in varying degrees ... A transformed people need no outside representation' (Muchina, 1995, p.4). This is the ultimate in capacity-building: a matter of emancipation, working oneself out of one's job.

Part of capacity-building is to enable advocates to acquire the ability to disempower themselves in order to empower others: self-disempowerment. Muchina suggests that beyond ten years, expatriates (who see themselves as interim representatives) cease to enhance others and start to perpetuate themselves. Muchina is brave in assigning a timeframe to a process, but she speaks for many who feel that open-ended timeframes are unacceptable.

'Linguists' in this sense need not lose their identity completely. Rather than attempt to identify with their target group by adopting a similar and literal external social style (where they are obvious misfits), external advocates need to realise that they can instead adopt the attitude of 'accompaniers', for which all they require is respect for their partners. They can act as sounding boards, asking the kinds of question that enable people to identify the real issues and in turn formulate their questions to those in power. The accompaniers can be there as people discuss these questions with the policy-makers. They can also be there to help them evaluate their achievements and set higher objectives. They can use their contacts to gain access for them and give them confidence when walking in the corridors of power, which can indeed be daunting to the uninitiated. But they must never lose sight of the fact that they themselves are not the actors. They only accompany and act as temporary brokers.

## Looking to the future: alternative approaches to capacity-building

Critically analysed, capacity-building as we now know and interpret it often results in further alienating the advocates from the grassroots by coaching them to speak the 'language' of the advocacy target while ignoring that of the grassroots. Genuine capacity-building must incorporate an aspect of 'reversal' if, as Edwards (op.cit., p.174) argues, we need better ways of linking local-level action and analysis with international advocacy. To achieve this, we need the 'linguists' and accompaniers who can enter into the reality of the poor and interpret or translate it into the sophisticated conceptual frameworks and detailed policies intelligible to the relevant policy-makers, without compromising the authenticity of the original views.

'Linguistics' must acquire the capacity to cross social class boundaries for the '[v]alue systems of those with access to power and those far removed from such access cannot be the same. The viewpoint of the privileged is unlike that of the underprivileged. In the matter of power and privilege, the difference between the "haves" and "have-nots" is not merely quantitative, for it has far-reaching psychological and ideological implications' (*Development in Practice* Editorial, 6/4, p.291). As we have already argued, the problem goes deeper than North versus South: '[C]ultural differences play an important part ... However, in the process of communication, intracultural differences are more difficult to bridge than intercultural differences ... it would be rather naive to assume that because they [local elite], work in their own country, (they) will communicate as equals with "target groups"' (Vink, 1993, p.25). We need 'linguistics' from both the North and South, learning together to listen and correctly interpret the voices at both ends. Presently, good 'linguistics' are few and far between.

Clement, commenting on a draft of this article, argued that churches may be well placed to play a 'linguistics'-grooming role, since they are, through their missionaries and priests, close to the poor and to some extent living almost like them. This is exemplified by the fact that there are numerous examples of leaders in Africa and elsewhere who were identified as potential leaders by the church and groomed accordingly. An 'incarnational' development approach is highly commended, especially if ultimately people can then rise beyond their current limitations. Unfortunately, in the case of Rwanda, for example, the church divided itself along ethnic lines and, instead of advocating for the poor, identified with those in power and now finds itself too divided and compromised to play a meaningful role in social reintegration, mutuality, and cohesion. Even now, when children speak of support they receive from family members, neighbours, churches, local associations, and local authorities as well as international NGOs, the churches fare poorly, rated only a shade better than local associations. (According to the children, the greatest assistance is received from international NGOs and neighbours, while the least comes from family members.) This type of behaviour is consistent with the kind of misrepresentation of the South by the South, of the serious gap between rhetoric and reality that is rarely exposed. It is reminiscent of tribal and religious wars elsewhere, where elephants fight and the grass gets trampled. The churches' grooming of future African leaders has, nevertheless, much to recommend it.

There is room for NGOs today to carry out a similar role, and equip and facilitate good 'pro-people' candidates to enter strategic representative forums, such as parliament. Although they may risk being accused of exceeding their mandates, unless good people are encouraged and supported to enter politics, 'other interests' will continue to dominate and misrepresent those of ordinary people.

World Vision Uganda developed a programme which is currently being successfully replicated in Tanzania, and serves as a good example of what can be achieved. Well-qualified university graduates are offered an opportunity to live in remote villages, and to research and initiate simple activities as a way to get to know the community well. After a short orientation, they are abandoned there with no 'basic' facilities as they knew them. World Vision enters a contract with the community to 'facilitate' these volunteers. In some cases, the houses provided are open shells with no doors and windows. Often there is no latrine in the compound. Beyond a little pocket money, these Technical Associates (TAs) have no regular salary. For the first few days, they are scared and want to run away, back to urban 'civilisation'. A few actually do so, but many stay and become part of the community.

The TA Programme has proven to be an effective process of dialogue, of mutual discovery. Volunteers acquire 'community degrees' in addition to their formal university degrees. Many are surprised at how their cherished university degrees pale into insignificance next to the experience gained by living in the villages. TAs also add value to communities which, through admiration for their new 'son' or 'daughter', are inspired to set higher horizons for their own children.

The TA Programme also builds capacity for future leadership. The process needs to be made more clearly focused as a way of grooming leadership and engaging in authentic advocacy. If there is a critical mass of such people, the voice of the poor will begin to be heard. If a good proportion keep the contract, in ten years they will be the policy-makers in their respective countries. NGOs which invest in this kind of process are building invaluable policy capital.

## Conclusion: learning from liberalisation and globalisation

Generally speaking, Africa as a whole is not part of the global agenda-setting mechanism. It does not in any significant way bring values or systems to the global table. It takes what is given: it has no authentic advocates. Africa is disenfranchised. In fact, one respondent during the research for this article commented that 'sadly, Africa's voice is absent in most global discussions. I would imagine that little interest was given to African perspectives at the recent meeting of the World Trade Organisation. Similarly, when I was at the Annual Meeting of the World Bank and IMF, although there were many African representatives present, there were no real alternative voices from Africa' (Commins, personal communication). There is no distinct African voice in global forums. 'Representatives' for Africa either sing the tune of the global élite or simply occupy space at the table. There is an urgent need for

NGOs, governments, and global institutions to change the way in which they present and represent Africa. This is a real challenge in a world that is seemingly indifferent to the continent's future.

This is not a time for 'business as usual'. The lack of distinct African voices is neither the creation nor the fault of NGOs; but one wonders whether NGOs have fared any better than governments. Have they sufficiently challenged the *status quo*? As the burden may fall on NGOs to push for this, change must necessarily begin at home. It is ironic that NGOs — the proponents of 'speaking truth to power' — are often unable to speak the truth to themselves. By obstructing such essential feedback, NGOs prove how big is the gap between rhetoric and reality. It is difficult to strengthen the competencies of NGOs if they take offence at the truth. Related to this, another respondent raised the issue of NGO ownership:

> [O]ne of the major issues in this discussion is who owns the NGOs. Who makes the final decision as to the leadership of the NGOs, especially in Africa. Also who pays for the NGO's existence. Often staff who hold radical views or 'revolutionary' ideas never reach the top. They are perceived to be difficult to work with, a threat. They are an embarrassment to the donors. Obviously the voice of such an NGO is muffled. It is a poor imitation of the people's voice. Gagging the voice of upcoming leaders, often the brightest and the best, failure to tolerate dissent, can certainly have far-reaching adverse effects. (Pappetta, personal communication)

Unfortunately, such influence, whether by remote or direct control, is disempowering. With their own houses in order, however, NGOs that survive can take leadership in giving Africa a voice.

Secondly, NGOs should take a cue from the paradigm of global economic liberalisation which challenges us to adopt new ways of thinking, new ways of doing business. It represents aggressiveness, competition, dynamism, and other survival strategies. Southern NGOs cannot be immune from this, and cannot develop a capacity to represent the poor through holding on to the 'protectionism' of the past; old forms of propping up NGOs in the South need to be re-examined and transformed. They should not settle for being handed responsibility for development in the South merely because they are Southern. They must be open to competition and be aggressive but business-like, proving that they can deliver. They must find out from the people they claim to represent how well they are doing. They must seek and accept feedback, including constructive criticism, if they are to continue to be relevant.

Maybe some must also accept death or at least retrenchment in order to rise again in a better and more effective form.

Finally, we must seek to empower the poor to act as their own advocates, so that when speaking for them we avoid giving the impression that someone somewhere owes them a living, and that this someone is most probably the government, primarily their own, but also governments of rich industrialised countries. It is this tendency that seeks answers from out there, not from within the people themselves. We in the NGO sector have not promoted, by our own example, the entrepreneurial spirit, creativity, and initiative inherent in people who are poor. (The children in Rwanda accuse us similarly.) We have demanded more and more aid, which in general has been badly administered and is now dwindling or being withheld. The new paradigm insists that the poor are primarily responsible for finding ways out of their immediate problems, though we are well aware that the perpetual struggle to survive is immensely tiring. But it is dead fish that swim downstream. Needs are not necessarily rights, in the sense that someone else has the obligation to provide for them. The poor need to demand accountability from their leaders who take loans on their behalf. They must be vigilant against corruption, a form of mis-allocation of national resources. But they must also create wealth and safeguard it. Ideally, inter-dependency in advocacy will mean that poor communities who 'pull themselves up by their own bootstraps' do not get repressed for doing so. Instead, there should be sufficient solidarity to fight even powerful adversaries.

To enable the poor to engage in their own advocacy, we should encourage global institutions to release resources to be used to finance wealth-creation by the poor themselves. We must form partnerships with, among others, the business community, and, where feasible, commit resources to attract its investment to areas where poor people live. We must engage the business community to pay decent prices for labour and primary products, but also facilitate the poor to produce high-quality products. The poor must find a niche in global trade, but must also appreciate the need to save in order to invest, to forgo consumption today in order to accumulate, grow, and so afford more tomorrow. In short, the challenge is to make trade liberalisation work for the poor (even though it is now seen to be 'anti-poor', notwithstanding some small gains made by a temporary opening up of more job prospects for women — albeit often in insecure, part-time, low-paid, and low-status work). We need to exploit the revolution in communication, opening up the world of the poor.

For example, through radio programmes in their own languages, poor people can know the world market prices for their products. They can then organise to get the highest prices. It is in such activities that NGOs should be investing to make the poor more dynamic, aggressive, and competitive; so that they bring themselves into the economic and political mainstream and so widen their overall opportunities. This is what will make it possible to break the vicious cycle of poverty. We must believe it and make the poor believe in themselves. In supporting them, economic advocacy perhaps has to take precedence over political advocacy on the NGO agenda. Otherwise the poor, and perhaps NGOs along with them, will continue to be marginalised in the emerging dynamic of the global economy.

## References

Caldwell, L.K. (1990) *International Environment Policy*, Duke University Press.

Chambers, R. (1993) *Challenging the Professions: Frontiers for Rural Development*, London: Intermediate Technology.

Clark, J. (1992) 'Policy influence, lobbying and advocacy' in M. Edwards and D. Hulme (eds) *Making a Difference: NGOs and Development in a Changing World*, London: Earthscan.

Eade, D. (1996) Editorial, *Development in Practice*, 6/4, pp. 291–2.

Edwards, M. (1993) 'Does the doormat influence the boot? Critical thoughts on UK NGOs and international advocacy', *Development in Practice*, 3/3: 163–75.

Muchina, O. (1995) 'Qualitative indicators of transformational development', *Together*, October–December 1995: 3–5

Nyamugasira, W. (1995) 'Vulnerable Groups and their Coping Strategies', unpublished paper.

Sutherns, R. (1996) 'Advocacy: A Call for Renewed NGO Commitment', unpublished paper.

Vink, N. (1993) 'Communication between inequals: development workers and the poor', *Bulletins of the Royal Tropical Institute: Culture and Communication*: Number 329.

World Vision (1998) 'Qualitative Needs Assessment of Child-Headed Households in Rwanda', internal report.

*This paper was first published in* Development in Practice *(8/3: 297–308) in 1998.*

# The international anti-debt campaign: a Southern activist view for activists in 'the North' ... and 'the South'

## Dot Keet

---

### The anti-debt campaign goes public

It is an enormous relief to anti-debt groups in the 'global South' that the crisis of external indebtedness has at last moved centre-stage in global public awareness. Whether based on the Christian principle of 'jubilee' renewal – the liberation of the bonded poor and debt-enslaved at the start of the new millennium – or on similar principles espoused by other religions, or on the basis of secular ethics against the exploitation and subordination of the poor and weak by the rich and strong, millions of people are joining the international campaign for a definitive solution to the scandalous extraction of the resources of the world's poor into the overflowing coffers of the rich.

Of course it was – as always – only after influential churches and other religious groups, development agencies, and NGOs in the North took up 'the Third World Debt' that it became 'an issue', something that causes wry observations among researchers and activists in the countries directly concerned, who have been working on debt issues for almost two decades.[1] Nonetheless, this growing recognition is welcome, and the research and information campaigns, political lobbying, and media interventions by anti-debt coalitions in Europe, North America, and Japan must be commended. They have made significant gains in terms of media coverage of the scale and effects of the debt, if not the complex causes. Some anti-debt groups have achieved advances in their respective governments' positions on payments owed to them by countries in the South. The campaign has even compelled the IMF and the World Bank to modify their implacable opposition to debt cancellation (above all, the cancellation of debts owed to themselves). It is mainly in an attempt to deflate growing public criticism, and deflect the full potential thrust of the campaign, that these institutions, in conjunction with the G7 countries, belatedly offered some 'debt relief' for the most Heavily Indebted Poor Countries (HIPCs).

All this is evidence of the impact of the international campaign against the growing 'Third World' debt.[2] The paradox is that, as public information expands, and the campaign makes ever greater gains, the options and issues are actually becoming more complex. As the number and range of participating organisations and countries grow, the discussions of objectives and tactics become more complicated. These debates relate not only to the methods and purposes of engaging with creditor governments, nor only to the aims and implications of, and appropriate responses to, the HIPC strategy. Within and among the anti-debt groups – particularly between some in the North and others in the South – there is a deepening debate on many of the common concepts and implicit assumptions, the tactics and strategies, and the fundamental aims and purposes of the campaign.

## Deepening debate on key issues

The IMF/WB offer of debt *relief* (or partial debt 'forgiveness', as the US and other governments refer to it) has been supported multilaterally by government creditors, but accompanied also by certain unilateral decisions on selective debt *reduction* by governments such as Canada, Norway, and Denmark. Meanwhile, non-government anti-debt groups in Europe and North America called for the *cancellation* of the 'unpayable' debts of the 'poorest' countries by the year 2000. However, there are some worrying ambiguities in their position. For, while public campaigns call for a 'halt' to the debt crisis, and for the debt to be 'dropped now', when grappling with their governments and with the IMF/WB, anti-debt groups repeatedly slip into the language of debt 'relief' or 'reduction', and resort to compromised calls for 'more substantial' debt cancellation[3] – that is 'wider, deeper and faster'.[4] The danger is that such arguments could become an implicit acceptance that debt cancellation need not be immediate or total. Yet debt cancellation is what radical activists in the debtor countries seek, and is the vision that is attracting millions of people to the campaign.

One problem is that the terms debt 'relief', 'reduction', and 'cancellation' are used interchangeably by different actors. 'Relief' can refer to relieving the burden-carriers of their burden, but may also mean alleviating rather than terminating the problem. 'Reduction' implies only partial removal of debt repayments. And, unless explicitly defined as 'partial', 'cancellation' should mean the definitive ending of all debt. There needs to be greater clarity and consistency on the part of debt analysts and campaigners in their use of these terms, and the same must be demanded of official spokespeople, in order to prevent unintended ambiguities and misunderstandings, or indeed the deliberate 'fudging' of what is on the table.

More problematic is the interpretation of what is 'unpayable'. The IMF/WB argue that debt is 'sustainable' as long as debt payments are being kept up without default. Some Jubilee 2000 (J2000) groups also base their proposals on 'sustainability' criteria.[5] Others point out that such payments are sustained only at the expense of essential social spending and to the heavy cost of the populations of debtor countries.[6] They argue for an approach based on 'development criteria', meaning that governments have the right to spend on essential primary education and health needs before repaying debts. This begs the question: what is 'essential'? Where are the limits to be drawn when essential social needs are also developmental necessities? Surely, there can be no *a priori* expenditure levels set on what are, and have to be, open-ended and ever-expanding resource requirements for full (not token) education for all, and fully effective (not minimal) health care. These are both a key measure and fundamental means towards self-sustaining development. Nor does the 'basic needs' or minimalist approach take on board the many other social needs – which are also human rights – such as housing, clean water, decent sanitation, accessible and safe transport systems, social and physical security, as well as the right to life-sustaining employment. So, at what level, or when, does Third World debt become 'payable'?

## Don't owe! Won't pay!

To anti-debt groups in the South, the very suggestion that their countries' debts are 'payable' is outrageous. And this is the moral position of many of their supporters in the North. In fact, the debts that these governments incurred, by whatever means and for whatever purposes, have in real terms already been repaid – in some cases, many times over. They have also been paid in the incalculable terms of social and environmental damage, political unrest, conflict and wars, and profound human insecurity and suffering. In January 1999, Latin American and Caribbean anti-debt campaigners declared in Tegucigalpa that not only do their countries not 'owe' anything, but that there is a moral, political, social, and environmental debt owed *to* them. The African non-government debt declaration, made in Accra in April 1998, similarly denounced any further debt repayments, citing reparations due to Africa for the damages inflicted by the slave trade, colonial, and neo-colonial exploitation. The myth of vast external 'aid' flows into Africa is exploded by the fact that US$1.41 in debt payments left the continent for every dollar received in grants in 1998. This is quite apart from the vast sums that have long flowed out of many countries in the South, in the form of super-profits on foreign direct investments,[7] dividends on foreign-owned equity, and unequal terms of trade.[8]

From such perspectives, any requirements for any further debt repayments are immoral and illegitimate. Not one cent more should be added to the prolonged outflows of precious resources from South to North: the indebted countries of the South 'don't owe, and won't pay'. For this to become the position of their governments is the challenge to anti-debt campaigners within these countries. However, it also has to be accepted and energetically pursued by Northern anti-debt campaigners in order to bring pressure to bear on their own governments.[9] Minimally, Northern groups must recognise the position of their counterparts in the South and so not contradict it, either explicitly or implicitly. For instance, it is deeply problematic when prominent J2000 spokespeople warn creditor agencies that they must act promptly or 'poor countries will take matters into their own hands'.[10] Rather than trying to pre-empt such possibilities, campaigners should be actively helping to make debt renunciation a central component of international discourse. Influential anti-debt campaigners in the rich countries should be using their skills and contacts to prepare international public opinion — and through this the governments of both North *and* South – for this legitimate resolution of the debt crisis.

## Different approaches

Other differences within the international anti-debt campaign also need to be admitted. Many development NGOs,[11] although supporting the debt campaign, have been trying to 'improve' the HIPC initiative to embrace more than the current half-dozen qualifying countries, and to be implemented more rapidly than originally planned. However, intensive research by UK Jubilee 2000 revealed[12] that, even if applied to all 41 designated HIPCs, the IMF/WB terms would largely provide 'relief' only on debt that is already not being paid, and which the international finance institutions know will never be paid. In fact, some HIPCs would be paying out more than they are already; and there would actually be an overall gain for creditors from this 'debt relief' exercise. However, the more fundamental objection is that the IMF structural adjustment conditionalities driving the HIPC programme have been a major factor in the deepening economic and social crises in the South, and a powerful reinforcement and aggravation of their external financial dependence and subjection to external controls. HIPC *and* its conditionalities are unacceptable, both in their aims and effects and in principle. Anti-debt groups that do not assimilate this are failing to understand some of the basic causes of the debt crisis, and they may in fact be helping to sustain the debt-bondage of the very countries and peoples they want to assist.

In entering into 'debates' with the IMF/WB and in engaging with their own governments to advocate more advanced policy positions, Northern anti-debt groups are also in danger of accommodating themselves to the creditors' selective and divisive approaches towards debtor countries. This is creating discrepancies, not only within the positions of such groups but between them and their Southern counterparts. The International J2000 Coalition explicitly focuses on 'the poorest countries', identifying 52, with a combined population of almost one billion, in urgent need of debt cancellation. In practice, however, many J2000 groups and development NGOs are drawn into the focus of the IMF/WB and their own governments on the most heavily indebted Least Developed Countries (LDCs). This is not necessarily wrong in itself, but it begs the question as to where the 'qualifying' line – other than simplistic quantitative GDP measures – should be drawn. Does a country such as Brazil, which is not an LDC but has the worst income disparities in the world, and dire social and environmental crises, not qualify for debt cancellation? At what real cost will Brazil 'sustain' debt repayments? Similarly, does South Africa, supposedly a 'middle-income developing country', but with income disparities and social problems as acute as those of Brazil, not need debt cancellation in order to apply all possible resources to dealing with the legacy of apartheid? And what of the dozens of other deeply indebted, socially and environmentally stressed, countries?

## More countries, more than 'poverty alleviation'

Anti-debt groups in the South need to take a wider and more strategic approach to the country coverage and adopt broader arguments for the debt cancellation campaign. They are aware of the divisive and potentially weakening effects of selective and exclusionary debt-relief proposals and so must maintain a united front among themselves. This does not mean that all national anti-debt campaigns will be identical. There are clear differences in the scale and the structures of specific country debts, and these have to be carefully researched, the targets identified, constituencies mobilised, and diverse tactics employed. However, debt campaigners do need to agree on a set of common principles and maintain the broadest unity and strongest joint positions and common actions possible. Indebted countries cannot allow themselves to be played off against one another. Nor should there be any acceptance of arguments that debt cancellation for some countries can only be done at the expense of others that are more urgent or 'deserving'. Such issues were at the heart of the November 1999 South–South debt summit in South Africa. Already, the official position of the African non-government anti-debt campaign is that its call for total debt cancellation applies to all African countries, irrespective of the size or structures of their debts or their official economic categorisations by the IMF/WB or other international bodies.

Campaigners in the South must also prevail upon their Northern counterparts to take on broader arguments for debt cancellation than 'poverty reduction' alone. Even if employed tactically in arguments to expose the contradictions between the official 'poverty reduction' and 'debt reduction' policies of the rich countries in the OECD,[13] the mere use of such notions can give additional prominence, and legitimacy, to the very limited proposals on offer in the dominant discourse on world poverty. This is counterproductive to the broader need to challenge the OECD's approach, which is to call for a 50 per cent reduction in the numbers living in absolute poverty, by the year 2015. It needs to be absolutely clear in any engagement with the OECD that poverty 'reduction' is a totally inadequate aim, and that debt 'reduction' will simply perpetuate the outward flow of 'poverty reducing' resources. Otherwise, such notions can – unintentionally and imperceptibly – displace the South's call for poverty *eradication* and debt *cancellation*. The alternative is to legitimise the 'half a loaf is better than none' approach, which leaves both the half-fed and the unfed in ongoing hunger and misery. And, once again, it begs the question of where the line will be drawn between those to be alleviated of their misery and the remainder, who must continue in 'absolute poverty' – for how long? Fifteen years? A generation? A century?

## Wider arguments and perspectives

There are other strong justifications for debt cancellation. Most of these were endorsed in the International J2000 Declaration in Rome in November 1998, but have been inadequately projected in practice.

Anti-debt groups need to promote, for example, the proposal to cancel debts incurred through ill-conceived, poorly implemented 'development projects', mainly World Bank-supported, that entailed onerous repayment undertakings without generating appropriate financial returns, or without confirming the availability of other financial resources to meet those obligations. Countries struggling with post-conflict reconstruction and rehabilitation require the same sympathetic and enlightened consideration as was accorded European countries, victors or vanquished, after the Second World War.[14] In fact, such countries in the South require even more generous understanding, since they are labouring under more adverse circumstances, with far poorer human and technical resources.

Southern groups are also insisting on the illegitimacy of debts incurred by military dictatorships and other repressive regimes, which are left for successor governments, and the victims of the former regimes, to pay off. The illegality of loans wittingly made to illegitimate régimes – like those in Argentina, Chile, and Brazil, or Mobutu in Zaïre, Marcos in the Philippines, and a host of others – is enshrined in the Doctrine of Odious Debt, already part of international law and precedent. The creditors of such regimes – whether governmental, commercial, or institutional – have to be confronted with the legal, as well as legitimate, right of subsequent governments to renounce responsibility for such debts. The illegality as well as the illegitimacy of the debt inherited by democratic South Africa from the apartheid régime falls squarely into this category.

These arguments constitute a more comprehensive and just approach, although a politically more challenging one. Some argue that bringing up all these other dimensions will simply cloud the main issue and confuse the majority of supporters. This is debatable. The more real danger is that anti-debt campaigners – North and South – might allow themselves to be drawn into the questionable proposition that the respective country debts have to be broken down so that such 'illegitimate' debts can be clearly identified and dealt with.

## Political illegitimacy and illegality

It would be an extremely complex exercise to isolate 'illegitimate' debts, and would hardly be possible without the fullest co-operation of all the parties involved. Further, the guilty banks and governments could deliberately prolong the process. More significantly, such an approach could be falling into the trap of implicitly accepting that the other, or remaining, parts of the debts are somehow 'legitimate'. The main point about the different aspects or components of national debt is that they apply in different combinations in the respective countries, and precisely because these different dimensions and sources of indebtedness are extremely difficult to unravel, these considerations should not become the basis of 'technical' investigations and legal processes. They would have more effective impact if they were marshalled as part of the argument for straight debt cancellation *tout court*.

A further set of problems relates to the use of international law and judicial bodies to pronounce on the 'illegality' of specific cases of odious debt. There are undoubted uses to be made of this concept, and of selected cases, to highlight a significant source of indebtedness in many countries. But there are also questions about using odious debt as a legal weapon *per se*. There are manifest problems within most countries in pursuing such processes through biased and discredited judicial systems. However, even within somewhat more reliable international judicial bodies and processes, experience has shown that in cases between rich and poor, strong and weak, an essential precondition for equity and justice is that disadvantaged complainants are provided with all the financial, legal, technical, and other backing required to pursue such processes. Such considerations would have to be an integral part of any legal strategies by national or international campaigns in this direction, and would still not guarantee full success.

There is an argument which holds that achieving success in even one such case would be a powerful deterrent against further and future irresponsible and illegal lending practices.[15] This assumes, somewhat naïvely, that, under the threat of possible legal action against them if they are uncovered, banks will desist from their traditional *modus operandi* and refrain from using their vast financial and legal resources to continue evading the law as long and as far as they can. This is made all the more likely with the proliferation of dubious banks around the world. Skilful evasions of legal actions are even more feasible with the extensive deregulation of the global financial system, and the uncontrolled, weakly supervised, and poorly monitored practices of banking organisations in the global economy. In fact, campaigners should not rely on the voluntary compliance of banks with national or international legal pronouncements. Nor should they be trying to encourage better 'self-regulation' by banks. The grossly irresponsible behaviour of banks exposed by the Third World debt crisis, and the success of any 'odious debt' legal process, should rather be used –

in combination with much broader global campaigns – to call for the international public re-regulation of all financial institutions. This requires closer supervision of banks and related financial organisations, and their subjection to full national and international public scrutiny, social and environmental responsibility, and democratic accountability.

## Roles and responsibilities

Clearly, the above considerations raise challenging questions and pose broader tactical and strategic possibilities for the international anti-debt campaigns. Unfortunately, not all of them have yet been taken up with conviction by Northern anti-debt groups, let alone by the general public. Most of these activists are still mainly motivated by the traditional desire among people in rich countries to alleviate the suffering of the 'helpless poor' elsewhere. This may be sincere, but it will not end the suffering of the poor as long as it does not tackle the multiplicity of causes of that suffering, which include the roles of their own governments, banks, and other lenders, as part of the *sources*, and not only the 'solvers', of the crisis.

This failure of understanding is evident in the tendency of some influential development organisations in the North[16] to focus mainly, like their home governments, on the responsibility of Southern governments for the indebtedness of their countries. And they see the improvement of such governments, or 'governance', as the priority condition for debt cancellation. There are certainly sound arguments for improving the technical reliability and the political accountability of government, and these go way beyond the requirements of debt (re)payment. However, even within the framework of debt cancellation, this is not a simple matter. None know better than the long-suffering peoples of the South the self-serving abuses of power, irresponsibility, indifference, incompetence, and gross corruption that characterised most of their governments most of the time. However, not all governments are totally or equally guilty of such abuses. It is a sweeping generalisation, and shows a superficial understanding of the real process, simply to hold debtor governments responsible, let alone solely responsible, for the predicament of their countries. It is ironic that many Southern campaigners, strongly critical of their own governments, find themselves having to point out to NGOs as well as official agencies in the North that many such governments were both victims *and* culprits in the process. In most cases, the debts escalated due to factors beyond their control, such as dramatic rises in international interest rates that were caused by economic processes and self-serving decisions in the richest countries, particularly the USA. At the same time, countries of the South were handicapped by declining incomes, due to the deteriorating prices for their commodity exports: the harder their people worked, and the more they exported, the lower prices fell. Some governments tried to diversify their national economies to reduce such commodity dependence and vulnerability, but that often entailed further external borrowing. Many indebted governments tried in vain to appeal to their creditors to lessen the burden. Others did not even attempt that. Most often, cash-strapped governments feared the reaction of their populations more than they resented their own dependency upon their creditors, and thus they kept returning, year after year, for their next financial fix, just to keep going. And each year they would be rewarded with another 'debt-rescheduling', and another tranche of 'aid' in the form of loans and grants – but only if they had dutifully followed the right policy prescriptions. Whatever their approach, all were inextricably tied down by their creditors' payment demands and heavy macro-economic conditionalities. And these were upheld and secured by the mutually reinforcing 'cross-conditionalities' between the bilateral (governmental) and multilateral (institutional) lending agencies.

What needs to be underscored is that there are many causes for the deepening of debt, and responsibility rests on many 'culprits' on all sides. Some argue that much of the problem of developing countries can be attributed to the 'objective workings of the market'. But active agencies include not only commodity brokers, stock-market speculators, and currency dealers, but also legal and illegal (odious) commercial lenders, together with their clients, and industrialised-country governments, along with the multilateral financial institutions that they control. Thus, if anti-debt groups in the North support their governments' demands, as many do, for proof of 'good governance' by erring debtors, as a political condition for debt relief or reduction, they should also call for equally demanding conditions to be placed on the whole range of self-serving, unprincipled, and irresponsible financial agencies, whether governmental, inter governmental, or commercial.

## Conditions and counter-conditions

To be consistent, effective, and fully legitimate in the South, anti-debt campaigners in the North should demand that conditions be placed also upon their own governments, the banks they support, and the institutions they control. A major factor in the creation of the debt crises and democratic deficits in the South derives from the geopolitical, as well as financial, motivations of Cold War governments in bank-rolling highly dubious (but useful) governments in Africa, Asia, and Latin America. Criticisms can also be made of many of the creditor governments which supplied 'tied' grants and loans to promote the interests of their own producers; and which provided (and continue to provide) guarantees to their own exporters, and protections to avaricious and irresponsible banks. And yet these same governments now self-righteously demand that debtors prove their probity. If such Northern 'democratic' governments now eschew responsibility for the bad practices of their predecessors, they must allow the same latitude to today's governments in the South, who bear little responsibility for the acts of their predecessors in creating their countries' debts.

The leverage that is being incorporated in proposals for debt 'relief' is a blunt instrument to deal with the complex combination of domestic and international factors underpinning governmental abuses and failures in many countries of the South. The domestic factors are many and varied, and arise both from objective factors and subjective failings. The latter include inadequate self-organisation and self-assertion by independent civil-society forces and information media, to challenge and correct the harmful practices of their political, bureaucratic, managerial, and business élites; or to counter their own suppression by them. But, most often, these ruling élites were able to behave as they did by courtesy of the indifference or the conniving *Realpolitik* of the dominant international forces, governmental and entrepreneurial. As the Accra Declaration states, accountability, transparency, and democracy must be established in all government institutions in Africa, but also in the structures and operations of international lending agencies. This includes both public and private, governmental, commercial, and institutional actors. Without such international regulations and institutional controls, attempts to stop debt crises re-emerging just by disciplining current debtor governments will simply not suffice. Conditions and controls do have to be set, but they must be effectively designed, internationally agreed, transparent in operation, closely monitored – and applied to *all* involved.

In this respect, a further guarantee is in the effective role and rights of popular civil-society organisations (CSOs) in the indebted countries to monitor and help to determine the social uses to which the financial resources released by debt cancellation will be applied. This is supported by anti-debt groups in both North and South, although a particular responsibility rests on Northern groups to give all the support they can to the strengthening of popular organisations in the debtor countries. Without this, the role of civil society in the South could be largely tokenistic, and the task will, in effect, be carried out mainly by well-positioned, powerful (and sometimes self-promoting) NGOs in the North 'on behalf of' the South. A case in point is the proposal by some Swiss development groups that the 'savings' made by Swiss-government debt relief in Africa be channelled through 'debt swaps' to the projects of Swiss NGO groups working there. This would in effect divert to themselves resources that should be within the purview of independent local groups and national governments. In this way, well-meaning – but frequently paternalistic and self-serving – Northern development agencies effectively displace local people from determining how their own resources recovered from external debt drainages should be used.

The real empowerment and effective role of local groups and social movements in the South is even more difficult with respect to proposals for the inclusion of 'all stakeholders' in a future international debt summit under the auspices of the UN. The same applies to the role and 'right of local organisations' to be heard in the proposed Debt Review Bodies,[17] or in relation to other debtor–creditor arbitration panels, as proposed by UNCTAD. Given existing patterns in many such international processes, the role and rights of 'civil society' will largely be enjoyed by the better resourced and strongly organised Northern CSOs 'on behalf of' all global social forces, whose needs and aspirations they do not necessarily understand or represent.

## Resources and reimbursements

Much of this debate revolves around ensuring that the resources released by debt cancellation will be turned to good social use and not mis- applied or squandered by incompetent governments, or stolen by the corrupt, as has so often happened in the past with monies received from abroad.Campaigners in the South note this new-found concern about such abuses with some irony. It would have helped to control irresponsible external borrowing if the lending agencies – governmental or commercial – had been more scrupulous in their choice of those upon whom they bestowed their loans in the first place. However, the more crucial point now is that the financial resources being 'released' are from the resources of the debtor countries, their own export earnings, which would then be available for essential external expenditures requiring foreign exchange (such as medicines) and other needs within their own economies. *In other words, debt cancellation amounts to 'allowing' these countries to keep and use their own hard-earned money!*

The second point relates to the argument constantly posed by creditor governments, and implicitly or explicitly taken up by many non-government groups, that debt cancellation will somehow carry 'costs' and even require 'new resources'. There may well be costs to creditor governments, and some will undoubtedly have to forgo some income. The alternative is to argue that government coffers in the rich countries should continue to receive such inflows – which, though minuscule within their overall revenues, are huge within the revenues of debtor governments. More importantly, many of the so-called costs or losses will actually be incurred by commercial banks. This would be income forgone rather than real losses, since most have already been fully reimbursed for the loans they provided. However, even if some have not totally recouped their outlays, loan defaults are part of the calculated risks that creditors have to take and plan for. In fact, most such banks have long ago written off many of the 'bad debts' owed them in the Third World, although, in order to maintain the myth of the 'inviolability' of banking principles and the inescapable 'obligations' of creditors, they do not publicise this. Any talk by Northern governments about 'new resources' needed to compensate banks for their losses is a matter between them and their banks and other financial bodies. Alternatively, if the public assumption of responsibility for private debts is unacceptable to Northern tax-payers, then it is a domestic issue between citizens' campaign groups in these countries and their governments. This is not the responsibility, nor the concern, of the victims of these processes in the South, and it should not form part of the international negotiations on debt cancellation.

The 'losses' that will be incurred by the multilateral financial institutions entail two other considerations. The first is the formal issue that the statutes of the IMF, World Bank, and related financial bodies prohibit them from writing off debts, as private banks do all the time. This is a question to be resolved between them and their main financial under-writers and decision-makers, the G7, and other rich countries. The same applies to the regional banks, such as the African Development Bank and its counterparts in Asia and Latin America. All these multi-lateral financial institutions have to be made to take responsibility for their wrong decisions in the past, their poor project assessments, and, above all, their bad policy impositions. If not, they will continue with the practices and the policies that have contributed to creating economic decline and debt crises in their client countries.

The more immediate issue for countries in the South, above all in Africa, is the proposal[18] that the losses incurred by the international finance institutions should be off-set by the sale of some of the IMF's gold reserves. On the one hand, this may merely be used by the IMF to ensure that its Enhanced Structural Adjustment Facility (ESAF) receives the necessary financial resources to become self-sufficient and self-perpetuating.[19] On the other hand, such massive gold sales will affect yet another area of the commodity-export earnings of a whole range of countries – from relatively 'rich' South Africa to poverty-stricken Burkina Faso. Of course, such dependence upon commodity exports and vulnerability to international commodity-market price fluctuations is a fundamental problem in itself. However, what this (well-meaning but ill-conceived) proposal means is that, once again, what is purportedly (but not actually) being 'given' to the countries of the South with the right hand is taken away with the left.

## Unilateral, bilateral, and multilateral approaches

There are various proposals for multilateral debt-negotiation forums, processes involving the UN, or the creation of international arbitration bodies. There are also innovative proposals for the establishment of international and national legal instruments enshrining the right of effectively bankrupt countries to have recourse, like struggling companies, to insolvency procedures and protections from their creditors. This is part of the legal approach to the debt problem, which could also include the use of Bisque Clauses that entitle debtors unilaterally to suspend or defer debt payments. These are not 'revolutionary' proposals, but core principles and well-established procedures within the capitalist economic system. They are designed to encourage the entrepreneurial endeavours that are supposedly at the very core of the market dynamics that drive capitalism; and to do so by underpinning risk-taking business ventures with guarantees and protections in the event of operational difficulties or business failures.

Some argue that these proposals – and the recourse to the Doctrine of Odious Debt – are overly legalistic, compromising, and constricting. They hold that governments should simply go into unilateral *de facto* default, as some have done even in the recent past (although this is not widely publicised by their creditors, in order not to encourage others to do the same). But, unless a number of countries happen to do so simultaneously, debt default could expose weaker economies to financial, trade, and other reprisals. The more radical and definitive solution would be for all Third World debtor countries explicitly and collectively to renounce or repudiate their debts – but they would also have to be prepared to stand united against counter-actions by the world's financial and political forces. This strategy would require both political will on the part of such governments, and informed popular support and preparedness for the probable short- to medium-term economic consequences. It would also require extensive prior preparation and mobilisation of international public opinion. Thus, recourse to the collective repudiation of their debts by the countries of the South, as a legitimate, definitive, and last-resort resolution of the debt crisis, needs to become part of international discourse and campaigning activities. Getting there will have to be an incremental political process, although culminating as joint public action. The political ground must be laid to encourage ever-wider – if unpublicised – commitment by increasing numbers of governments to a joint public declaration.

Another collective approach is to make debt cancellation an integral part of international economic negotiations in multilateral institutions, such as the World Trade Organisation (WTO). Already there are tentative proposals that developing countries should insert the 'trade-related' aspects of indebtedness, along with 'trade-related' commodity-price instabilities and other issues of concern to them, into their negotiating packages in the multilateral processes. In this view, such demands could be used as possible trade-offs in the multi-sectoral 'Millennial Round' of WTO negotiations that was to have been proposed by the developed countries at the WTO meeting in Seattle in December 1999. The problem is that this approach proposes trading off the essential needs of developing countries and relatively limited concessions to the weaker economies, in exchange for major gains in the restructuring of the world economy in the interest of the strongest economies and 'their' global corporations. Hence the increasing demand by many developing-country governments, and a growing international campaign by non-government forces, against the proposed 'Millennial Round' altogether.

Needless to say, virtually all debtor governments are still counting on continued bilateral agreements, or multilateral negotiations, between themselves and their creditors in the Paris Club to alleviate their burdens. Even the 'collective' position of the Organisation of African Unity (OAU) does not go beyond appealing for 'better' HIPC terms and more 'under-standing' of Africa's problems by the creditor governments and institutions.

# Varied tactics and targets

Radically different as these approaches are, they need not all be mutually exclusive, but nor are they equally useful. Many, such as the moderate appeals for further debt relief and re-schedulings, have long proven ineffective. Other approaches can be utilised simultaneously, or at different phases, by differently situated actors for different targets or specified purposes. However, these multiple or parallel tactics are not without their dangers. For example, skilled researchers who can analyse and expose the fallacies in the arguments of the international financial institutions can certainly make an important contribution. Anti-debt campaigners situated in influential development organisations and social/religious bodies in the North should indeed use their influence with their national media and lobby their governments. But individual researchers or lobbyists, however effective, cannot substitute for organised public opinion. And organised public opinion in the North cannot substitute for organised popular mobilisation in the South.

Although all useful to differing degrees, such varied players, tactics, and targets are not of the same order of significance. Organised popular forces in the North can help to create a propitious climate within and through which governments can be persuaded or pushed towards the required positions. Intellectual efforts and information should be aimed primarily at informing and activating increasing numbers of people. The cogency of technical arguments and the weight of the data amassed are simply not enough, in and of themselves, to impel governments towards making real policy changes. Similarly, popular mobilisation in the South is of a qualitatively different order from that in the North. Northern groups are important in influencing the media, general 'public opinion', and their own governments; and thereby even influencing the governments of the debtor countries to adopt more assertive positions. It is an unfortunate fact, and testimony to their level of political and psychological dependence, that many governments in the South take more notice of such developments taking place in the North than within their own countries. But the empowerment of the people of the South is both a crucial means and has to be the ultimate end of such a campaign. This is essential, if they are to be truly 'liberated' from their bondage and poverty with and through the process, and if their countries are to break out of, and move beyond, economic and political subordination.

As we have already seen, however, there are other real problems when individuals or groups mainly focus on directly 'influencing' government or media figures, or institutions. Although projected as mere differences of tactic, or as a neutral 'division of labour' between different forces in a campaign, the gradualist 'tactical engagement' approach has dangers in itself, and can pre-empt its more far-reaching aims and potential.

The focus on government structures, or even specific official or 'entertainment' figures, can achieve some gains. But these efforts can also distract attention, energies, and resources from the broader public information and mobilisation that is the most fundamental way to bring 'influence' to bear upon governments, both in the North and the South. Among the tried and tested tactical responses by governments to growing popular campaigns, partial concessions – used skilfully by government 'spin doctors' and institutional PR operators – are presented as being much more than they actually are, in order to placate and effectively demobilise campaigners, and to undermine the campaign's potential and fundamental aims. Such 'engagement' tactics invariably entail conscious moves by campaign strategists towards the positions of governments and related institutions, so they can operate within their frameworks and use language that is 'acceptable' to them.[20] The aim may be to draw their adversaries towards the intended objective; but this approach generally has the contrary effect of imperceptibly drawing leading campaign figures into their adversaries' 'logic', rather than the other way round. Similarly, anticipating where adversaries will draw the final line, and preparing in advance for accommodations or compromise positions, are measures that invariably assume a dynamic of their own. 'Fall-back' stances rapidly become 'front-line' positions, or are drawn to the fore by perceptive adversaries on the basis of how they assess the susceptibilities of leading negotiators or spokes-people on the other side.

The alternative to accepting piecemeal 'gains' through 'engagement' tactics is for campaigners to adopt advanced bargaining positions, using creative initiatives and energetic pro-active strategies to draw or impel governments forward. This is integral to the planning and organisational debates among campaigners everywhere and represents the perennial dilemmas and tactical options that face trade unionists confronting employers, NGOs dealing with governments or their own funders, or even governments negotiating with other governments or institutions. Tactical choices reflect assessments of the nature of the adversary; the mood, potential force, and direction of action of supporters; the real and perceived balances of power; and so on. But such choices are also a function and reflection of the underlying strategic aims and objectives – that is, whether these aims are minimal and reformist, or radical and transformational. In the anti-debt campaign, many of the *tactical* choices being made reflect differing conceptualisations of the overall *strategic* aims and objectives.

## Strategic aims and objectives

At one end is the view that (some sort of) debt cancellation is an important – and achievable – end in itself, as long as the campaign remains suitably focused as a 'single issue' campaign, with simple or straightforward demands. In this view, the general public in the developed countries who have taken the debt question to heart would be confused by more complex analyses of all the contributing factors, or would be put off by attempts to add legal, political, and economic dimensions to what they see as a clear moral or 'justice' issue.

At the other end is the view that even if the total debt were to be cancelled immediately, this would not solve the profound socio-economic and environmental problems of the debtor countries, and failure to take this into account could be fundamentally counter-productive. It would be seriously disillusioning and demobilising if inadequately informed debt-campaign supporters in the North were to see their efforts, even their success in getting the debt fully cancelled, fail to solve the poverty problems in the South. And it is the people of these poverty-stricken countries who would bear the brunt of the ensuing general defeatism, or specific 'Afro-pessimism', or 'poverty fatigue', or 'donor fatigue' in the North.

Focusing only on debt is addressing a symptom, rather than the underlying causes of financial dependence and economic subordination. Tackling the debt problem is necessary but totally insufficient as a response to the long-standing structural features of these economies and the nature of their role and location in the global economy. The underlying causes of dependence certainly reside, in part, in economic factors internal to these economies – limited technical and management resources, structural distortions, and sectoral disarticulations, with heavy orientations to external markets and extreme vulnerabilities to external shocks. But these, in turn, are produced and aggravated by factors and forces in the international system. Industrialised-country governments and international companies constantly act to reinforce such external dependence, and their own trade and investment access to, control over, and exploitation of the countries of the South. More recently, the international financial institutions have been marshalled to place pressure on these economies to 'open up' to global investors, exporters, TNCs, and service companies. And it is in this context that the indebtedness of countries is important not merely, or even mainly, for the financial returns produced – although these are substantial. More critically, indebtedness is an effective way to exert political controls or 'policy leverage' (as expressed by the World Bank) which it secures for creditor governments and financial institutions over other governments and economies throughout the world.

The strategic approach lying somewhere between or linking the differing approaches would argue that the issue of debt *is* important in itself. But, because of its very clarity, debt provides an excellent prism through which to expose to wider public view the full spectrum of international financial relations, particularly North–South relations, the functioning of global financial institutions, and the global economic system. If perceived in this way, the anti-debt campaign could carry many millions of indignant and already mobilised people towards these broader issues and to a deeper and fuller understanding of the nature and sources of the poverty and injustice that so move them. They would be activated not only by the plight and needs of millions of poor people in the world, but by the underlying inequitable and exploitative nature of relations between the rich North and the poor South. Millions of people would see more clearly the nature of the relations, or collusion, between rich governments, banks, and other financial agencies, the driving forces behind the increasingly liberalised global economic system. And the exploitative, damaging, and polarising essence of the global free-market system dominating all peoples and countries would become the active concern of many more millions, North and South.

## Related issues and campaigns, alliances, and coalition building

The corollary to this is that anti-debt campaigners have to include such arguments in their campaigns, and must link up with other related inter-national campaigns, such as that against MAI (the Multilateral Agreement on Investment), and for the international imposition of the Tobin Tax and other instruments for re-regulation and controls on global financial forces. The problem of indebtedness and the demand for debt cancellation must be inserted into the debates, decisions, and demands of these campaigns; and these constituencies must be drawn into supporting the debt campaign. And *vice versa*. This can be done without necessarily reducing their main focus on debt *per se*, while wider alliances will certainly help to strengthen their efforts. It is through such multi-faceted, mutually supporting coalitions that the range, combination, and weight of inter-national popular forces will become commensurate with the challenges posed by the unaccountable power of gargantuan TNCs, the vast resources of international banks, and the global institutions they use in shaping the 'global economy'.

Building such global coalitions demands political skill and strategic vision on all sides, as is clear from the challenges of building North–South cooperation and mutual support even within the international anti-debt campaign. Engagement in the same campaign, and even fundamentally shared concerns, do not automatically translate into mutual understanding and unity. This paper has highlighted some of the differences between some groups located in the North and others in the South, although, it must be stressed, these divergences and convergences of tactic and strategy also cut across the North–South divide. However, a basic difference that must be recognised is that anti-debt groups in the North can opt out whenever they feel that they have done what they can (and some J2000 groups indeed plan to 'close shop' in December 2000, whether total debt cancellation has been achieved or not), whereas their counterparts in the South will still have to live with, and continue to struggle against, the causes and consequences of economic exploitation and subordination, of which indebtedness is just one symptom.

This is what gives anti-debt campaigners in the South such an important political role. It is their unequal burdens and respective roles and responsibilities that require groups in the North to give full weight to proposals and demands emanating from the South. (It is interesting to note here that there are significant differences between many Northern development agencies acting somewhat paternalistically on behalf of the South, and political solidarity groups in the North that tend to be somewhat more sensitive to the nature of such relationships, and rather more realistic about their role and 'rights'[21].)

However, 'moral authority' and 'political principle' are insufficient bases upon which anti-debt groups in the South should expect their Northern counterparts to take their lead. This role and these relationships have to be securely underpinned by their own research and analyses, mobilisation of their own peoples, and actions within their own countries. Groups in the North cannot expect their counterparts in the South to do this rapidly or easily. They often operate under extremely difficult economic and political circumstances, and require all the support they can get. Certainly, groups in the South should not have to contend with divisive interventions into their

## Jubilee South

*Extract from South–South Summit Declaration, 'Towards a Debt-Free Millennium', Johannesburg, 18-21 November 1999. (Full text available at www.aidc.org)*

The External Debt of countries of the South is illegitimate and immoral. It has been paid many times over. A careful examination of the origins, development, effects, and consequences of this debt can lead us to no other conclusion. We thus reject the continued plunder of the South by way of debt payments.

Peoples and countries of the South are in fact creditors of an enormous historical, social, and ecological debt. This debt must be repaid in order to make possible a 'New Beginning'. In the spirit of Jubilee, we demand restitution of what has been taken unjustly from us, and reparations for the damage wrought.

We forcefully denounce the growing concentration of wealth, power, and resources in the world economy as the essential cause of the increase in violence, impoverishment, and 'indebtedness' of the South. The elimination of extreme poverty cannot take place without the elimination of extreme wealth. We thus demand the eradication of extreme wealth and the vicious system that generates such inequalities. In this context, we reject the perpetuation of external debt collection and debt payments which are Life or Death matters for the millions of persons who are exploited and excluded in our societies.

The External Debt is an ethical, political, social, historical, and ecological problem. It entails responsibilities at different levels and demands imperative and comprehensive action so as to resolve in a permanent and definitive manner. There can be no piecemeal solution to the 'Debt problem'. We thus welcome the momentum that Jubilee 2000 initiatives around the world have generated on this issue and we call on them to broaden and deepen their understanding, educational efforts, and mobilisation beyond the year 2000, in order to achieve our overall aim of a Debt-free Millennium, including the repayment of the debt owed by the North to the South.

Debt is essentially an ideological and political instrument for the exploitation and control of our peoples, resources, and countries by those corporations, countries, and institutions that concentrate wealth and power in the global capitalist system. The accumulation of Foreign Debt in countries of the South is a product of the crisis of that very system and it is used to perpetuate the plunder and domination of our nations often with the acquiescence, if not active collaboration, of local élites.

The neo-liberal global economic system is destructive and genocidal in its workings and effects. Women suffer disproportionately its consequences, as do children, the elderly, and the environment. The same institutions and system responsible for its creation cannot bring about a lasting solution to the 'Debt problem'. That system must be changed and can be changed.

In the process of addressing the 'Debt problem' and changing the neo-liberal global economic system, we must continue to develop an ever closer understanding of the linkages between debt and other related aspects including trade, finance, investment, consumption patterns, food security, environmental depredation, and diverse forms of military and anti-democratic, neo-colonialist intervention and repression.

Many working-class and impoverished and excluded peoples' groups and movements in both the South and the North are engaged in different ways to challenge and transform this system of domination and we must join with them. As Jubilee South we will add our voice and support for the strengthening and creation of alliances and coalitions deeply rooted in historical struggles against all forms of oppression within the long-standing anti-imperialist framework and tradition.

Resistance to debt-related domination unites us as social movements and organisations throughout the South and provides us with an historic opportunity to organise ourselves as part of a broader movement. As Jubilee South, we are born and rooted in Africa, Asia, the Pacific, Latin America, and the Caribbean, but we reach out to all who are part of this historical, political, and ethical South.

Respectful of our different identities and traditions, as well as our varying forms of struggle, we must be united in a common determination to achieve Justice for all: a New Beginning in the New Millennium. In this way South–South and South–North solidarity can be strengthened, as we exercise our collective human right to determine our own future and engage in the struggle to build and defend inclusive and comprehensive alternatives to the present global system that are:

- from the bottom-up

- reflective of different sectoral needs

- respectful of cultural and biological diversity, and

- conducive to new modes of democracy and development that are respectful of human rights, justice, and wellbeing for all.

initiatives by their counterparts in the North, some even using the familiar 'neo-colonialist' method of promoting and using their own 'client' groups. While there clearly are differences of method and objectives between anti-debt groups in and of the South, there are also intense debates going on among them and an emerging consensus on strategic objectives and common principles (see the box on the previous pages). It would be seriously divisive for groups in the North to pick off specific groups in the South – particularly any that choose to stand outside the nascent South–South consensus. Nor should groups and coalitions in, and of, the South have to contend with defensiveness and possessive-ness over the global campaign by longer-established and relatively well-endowed groups in the North that, consciously or unconsciously, resent their 'leadership' being encroached upon.

The North cannot act without the South, even if it is argued that the industrialised countries have a particular responsibility because the chief culprits are 'their' governments, corporations, and banks, and the global institutions controlled by them. This understanding is to be welcomed, but such groups in the North must also recognise that 'their' governments, banks, and international institutions are also 'ours', and indeed 'everyone's' in today's highly integrated global system. We have to find ways to oppose these dominant forces together. Northern groups cannot substitute for and certainly cannot continue to act paternalistically 'on behalf' of the South, particularly as the South becomes more organised and enters more fully into international campaigns. However, while campaigners in the South need to develop a strategic vision based upon their own experiences, understanding, and unity, they must also acknowledge the vital role that supporters and counterpart forces in the North can and must play. Popular movements in the South need allies in the North, because of the strategic positioning of the latter nearer the centres of global power, their accumulated experiences, considerable skills, and greater resources. These are invaluable in supporting organisational development and campaigning endeavours in the South.

In the final analysis, however, what must unite all such movements are not mere tactical considerations or pragmatic calculations about the mutual or respective gains to be made. The quintessential basis of North–South people's solidarity and united action has to be the strategic understanding of the vital importance of people's global coalitions and unity, on the basis of our common humanity and in the interests of our common planetary home.

# Acknowledgement

An earlier version of this paper was produced by the Alternative Information and Development Centre (AIDC) in South Africa. It was published in *Development in Practice* (10/3&4:461–77) in 2000.

# Notes

1 With some pioneering writers in the North such as Susan George.

2 This paper assumes that readers are familiar with the statistics of Third World debt. Further information : www.jubileeplus.org

3 'Crumbs of Comfort', UK J2000 Coalition, June 1999.

4 World Development Movement, 'Stop Sapping the Poor', June 1999.

5 Jürgen Kaiser, J2000 group, Germany – email 5 June 1999.

6 UK J2000, Christian Aid, and others.

7 UNCTAD's 1995 study of foreign direct investment (FDI) in Africa points to very favourable rates of return to foreign investors – up to 25 per cent. This is much higher than their profit ratios in both developed and developing countries for most years from 1980 to 1993. This pattern was borne out by the 1999 UNCTAD analysis, which revealed rates of FDI profit in Africa of 29 per cent; compared with six per cent even in most of the Asian 'emerging' economies.

8 The terms of trade for Africa declined every year during the 1980s, with losses of US$19 billion in export earnings in 1985–86 alone. It is estimated that sub-Saharan Africa lost potential exports earnings of some US$278 billion between 1980 and 1994, according to UNCTAD and the African Development Bank.

9 Such as the UK J2000 'Don't Collect! Won't Collect' call to the British government.

10 Anne Pettifor, Director of UK J2000.

11 The most notable, in this respect, being Oxfam GB.

12 Joe Hanlon, 'What will it cost to cancel unpayable debt?', UK J2000 Coalition, March 1998.

13 Ibid.

14 Joe Hanlon ' We've been here before: debt default and relief in the past – and how we are demanding that the poor pay more this time', UK J2000, April 1998.

15 Patricia Adams, *Odious Debts: Loose Lending, Corruption, and the Third World's Environmental Legacy*, London: Probe International.

16 Such as Oxfam GB, Bread for the World-USA, and others.

17 Anne Pettifor in the *New Internationalist*, No. 312, May 1999.

18 Originally formulated and promoted by development agencies such as Oxfam GB and Christian Aid.

19 This would free the IMF from having repeatedly to go back to its financial under-writers and 'would equip the IMF with a permanent ESAF that will keep it forever involved in the poorest countries and their economic policies', according to Carol Welch, writing in *Economic Justice News*, Vol. 2, May 1999.

20 This has been explicitly stated to this writer by a leading J2000 researcher.

21 Although in this respect there is often a tension over whether they 'take their lead' from counterpart CSOs or from the governments of the countries with which they are in solidarity.

# Human rights and religious backlash: the experience of a Bangladeshi NGO

## Mohammad Rafi and A. M. R. Chowdhury

The individuals who belong to social organisations may also form part of a broader group. Social organisations do not always coexist in harmony. When the tensions are so great that one organisation does not want the other to achieve its aims, it may even take violent measures to prevent its 'opponent' from functioning.

An organisation which faces such resistance may or may not react against it. If it is prevented from working but fails to react, its objectives will be frustrated. In contrast, if the organisation reacts to and overcomes this resistance, it will be able to meet its objectives, albeit at the cost of extra resources, energy, and time. Thus, for an organisation to be successful and cost-effective in its work, it must frame its objectives and activities in such a way that it does not encourage resistance from any other social organisation. Where resistance cannot be avoided, it is important to establish the reasons for it and take remedial measures.

Two important organisations in the social fabric of Bangladesh are the religious organisations and the Bangladesh Rural Advancement Committee (BRAC). The mosques and *madrasa* (Islamic theology schools) are here taken together to constitute the religious organisation.[1] For centuries, since mass conversion to Islam, this organisation has been in charge of Muslim religious expression in Bangladesh (Khan 1996). Its prime functions are to ensure that the Islamic faith is believed in and properly practised. Any idea that is considered not to be in accordance with the tenets of Islam and any practice considered contradictory to its dictates are opposed by this organisation. BRAC, by contrast, is a recent introduction to Bangladesh. It has been developed to promote welfare and development of the poor through a range of programmes to alleviate poverty and empower poor people. Its activities mainly involve training, providing resources such as loans, and facilitating occupational changes to create opportunities for people to employ the training and make use of the resources provided. By the end of 1996, BRAC was working in 57 per cent of the villages in Bangladesh (Freeman 1996, Agricultural Census 1996).

An overwhelming proportion of the rural poor in Bangladesh are unaware of their legal rights. This not only prevents them from defending these rights but also allows others to exploit them. This is particularly true for women. BRAC thus decided to take measures to redress this problem and in 1989 launched the Human Rights and Legal Education (HRLE) programme, which aimed to empower the members of Village Organisations (VOs) formed by BRAC through educating them about human rights and some essential laws of Bangladesh (BRAC 1996a; BRAC 1997).[2]

The rights and laws addressed in the programme concern four areas:

- Citizen's Right Protection Law
- Muslim Family Law
- Muslim Inheritance Law
- Land Law

The training of VO members is the pivot around which the whole programme revolves. By 1996, 560,066 VO members had been trained, and BRAC intends to reach one million members by 2001 (BRAC 1996b; BRAC 1997).

BRAC's assumption was that raising legal awareness among the VO members would help them to protect themselves from illegal, unfair, or discriminatory practices (BRAC 1996a). But the rights of VO members were sometimes infringed by individuals who were themselves not aware of the laws or of people's rights. In addition, VO members were sometimes compelled to violate certain laws, again by people who were not aware of these laws. BRAC therefore concluded that the rights of VO members would be better protected if non-VO members were also more aware of the relevant laws. This is what BRAC set out to do, as described below.

Local community leaders' workshops were organised for the elite[3] within each catchment area and participants; the workshops sought to advise participants about the laws covered in the HRLE curriculum; to inform them that these laws do not contradict religious laws (*Shariah*); and to facilitate their co-operation in the implementation of HRLE training in the village.

BRAC developed a set of seven posters, representing some of the contents of the HRLE training curriculum. These were fixed in VO meeting spots, BRAC schools and field offices, government offices, health centres, and in the bazaars located in administrative towns (*unions* and *thanas*). Short descriptions and translations of the statements shown on the posters are presented in Box 1. Some 700,000 posters were put up in early July 1997. The poster displays immediately provoked a good number of unwelcome reactions. These included verbal condemnation of the posters, tearing the posters down, and organising demonstrations against the posters and BRAC. In addition, BRAC staff were taunted, rebuked, and physically assaulted for putting up the posters. Poster campaigns are widely used to convey information and encourage attitudinal change at a community level. Although they had been effective in achieving these objectives earlier (Musaiger 1998; Lyttleton 1994), which is what encouraged BRAC to go ahead this time, they sometimes fell short of the objectives or had an undesirable impact (Wienrawee 1995).

This paper investigates the nature and the cause of the backlash against the posters, and outlines strategies which would allow development organisations to pursue their objectives without provoking such hostile reactions.

A qualitative study was conducted in August 1997 in the catchments of BRAC field offices in Kachikata, Sharail, and Kuliarchar. The areas were selected to cover various forms of backlash. A checklist was administered in group interviews in order to collect data, with between four and eight interviewees per group. These were deliberately selected in order to obtain sufficient information about the poster programme and the backlash against it within each group. The interviewees represented a range of social sectors: BRAC field staff, VO members and their husbands attending monthly VO meetings,[4] people working/living near to where the posters were put up, clerics,[5] and the elite. Four to eight interviews were conducted for each of these groups. Information provided by individuals was corroborated through cross-checks.

## Reaction to the posters

After the posters were put up, people from different social sectors gathered around them. The BRAC logos indicated who was responsible for them. Some onlookers refrained from passing any opinion, but others did not. A schoolteacher remarked that the posters pointed out the real problems of society, and that BRAC had done a good job by displaying these problems in the posters. On the 'verbal divorce' poster,

## Box 1. The human-rights and legal-education posters

| Title | Description | Statement |
|---|---|---|
| 1. Contribution to development | Shows both men and women together participating in the development work, i.e. cutting earth to build a road. | We have built this world and this civilisation; men and women contributed equally to it. |
| 2. Child marriage | Points out a series of undesirable consequences of child marriage: child-birth at an early age leading to ill-health, because of which she fails to carry out family responsibilities; this failure leads to bad relations between her and other members of the family which eventually can result in divorce. | Many brides are crying because of child marriage; nobody pays attention to the flood of their tears. |
| 3. Violation of multiple-marriage policy | Indicates that it is essential for a husband to have the approval of his existing wife before remarrying. Without this, he may have to face jail and/or pay a fine. | Facing jail and a fine for re-marrying without the consent of present wife or for ignoring her disapproval of such marriage. |
| 4. Abuse of women | Abuse of women is a criminal offence; one can be sent to the lock-up for such an offence. | Those who torture women, send them to the lock-up |
| 5. Registration of marriage | Indicates that it is important to register marriage, as women are often left helpless after divorce. | Husband divorced, what am I to do? Married by reciting *kalema*[6] but without registration. |
| 6. Bride money | Indicates that in case of divorce, the husband must refund the bride money in all circumstances. | Have to pay the bride money whether dead or alive. |
| 7. Verbal divorce | Indicates that a marriage cannot be cancelled by verbally pronouncing divorce three times. | Divorce is not legal if given verbally. |

some remarked that the statement in it was correct and the poster was the most important in the set. However, some reacted negatively. For example, it was said about this same poster that the statement was against Islam and that BRAC was harming society. Within a short while, the verbal condemnation gathered into a storm and turned into organised group reaction against the posters. The backlash took place mostly in small towns. Three instances are discussed below.

## Case 1

A day after the posters were fixed in Kachikata bazaar, the one on verbal divorce was ripped down after sunset when nobody was around. For about a week after the posters had gone up, debate on them continued in tea stalls among the regular customers who usually spent their evenings at the stall, and the local clerics who, unlike the others, were not regulars. They discussed each of the posters and placed their arguments both for and against. In general, the clergy strongly criticised the posters from an Islamic perspective.

A workshop for local community leaders was scheduled in the local BRAC office a week after the posters were fixed. Discussion on the posters was an agenda item. In the workshop, BRAC clarified the objectives of the posters and argued that the messages depicted did not contradict Islam. The local *union parishad* chairman praised BRAC for the poster campaign and asked all present in the workshop to support BRAC's initiative. After this, the posters were no longer publicly criticised in the bazaar, and no adverse reactions were noticed.

## Case 2

An hour after the posters were fixed in Sharail bazaar, supporters and opponents of the posters started debating the contents. Discussion became heated and at one point turned into a fight. The shopkeepers calmed down the two groups and ripped off the posters, fearing that, if they remained in place, there would be further trouble. The same evening, when BRAC staff were walking through the bazaar, they observed that a group (including clerics) was vehemently criticising the posters. Seeing the BRAC staff, they taunted them. Some of them even came up and asked where they had got the idea that divorce could not be given verbally. The BRAC staff avoided them and did not respond to the taunt. Later in the evening, a group of clerics visited the house of a member of BRAC's staff and rebuked him for fixing the posters.

The next day, a number of *imams* and *madrasa* teachers met in a mosque after late evening prayer (*Esha*) to decide what action to take against the posters. Accordingly, a group of *madrasa* students went early next morning and ripped off the posters on 'verbal divorce' from all the locations in the town. A set of posters in the lobby of the BRAC office, however, remained intact. In reaction to this, some clerics decided to take action against the office staff. To pre-empt such an attack, the BRAC manager proposed to meet the religious leaders and explain the posters to them. This offer was turned down.

On July 15 1997, a nationwide lockout was held to protest against the defaming of Prophet Muhammad in Israel.[7] That day a group of 40 to 60 *madrasa* students came to the same BRAC office to check whether it was observing the protest call by remaining closed. The office manager stopped the group at the outer gate of the office. But half a dozen of them forced an entry into the building. After seeing the posters in the lobby, they remarked that these were against Islam, and objected to their being displayed. One of them ripped off the poster on 'verbal divorce'. When this was going on inside, the students standing in front of the gate threw stones at the office. Seeing this, the shop-keepers and college students hanging around in the nearby bazaar came forward and drove the *madrasa* students away.

## Case 3

A day after the posters were fixed in Kuliarchar, the Principal of a local *madrasa* met with two members of the town's elite (actively affiliated with two major political parties) in a mosque to discuss the posters. A number of devotees were also present and asked the Principal for the teaching of the Holy Koran on divorce. When responding to the question, the Principal remarked that BRAC had committed a grave sin and offended Muslims by displaying the posters. He convinced the group that they should stand against any misinterpretation of the Holy Koran and *Hadith*. As a first step, they decided to hold a protest rally against the posters in the town next day and take it to the BRAC office.

The rally was later abandoned, but the teachers from the *madrasa* instead filed a 'first information report' against the posters in the police station. Afterwards, the police officer-in-charge and one of the elite with whom the Principal had spoken the day before visited the BRAC office. The community leader rudely attacked the conduct of the office staff and BRAC's policies. The staff remained calm by not retorting. At one point, the officer politely requested the leader to leave the office, because he was capable of handling the situation alone. The leader complied. The police officer told BRAC staff that they had hurt the religious sentiments of the townspeople. He advised them to take down the posters around the town and to pacify the clergy and influential local people by talking through the issues with them. He also warned that if they did not take his advice, the Police Department would be unable to protect them from any undesirable eventuality against them.

The BRAC manager, realising the gravity of the problem, asked for guidance from her superior, who instructed her to follow the advice. Accordingly, the BRAC staff went out to take down all the posters, but none was found intact. Not only that, but some of the walls where posters had been fixed were covered with mud and cow-dung. In fact, when the police officer was in the BRAC office, some *madrasa* students had gone around the town ripping off all the posters. Their actions were not resisted by any witnesses. That evening, a group of BRAC staff met with the clerics. The staff managed to pacify them by saying that it had been a mistake to put up the posters, conceding to a request in future to seek the clergy's permission before fixing any posters in the town.

## Opponents and supporters of the poster policy

It is apparent that the clergy were against BRAC's point of view. They were supported by a small group of devout Muslims with only a shallow knowledge of Islam, along with some misconceptions, and little or no schooling. They were in close contact with the clerics, who stirred up their religious sentiments against the posters. A number of ex-VO members who bore a grudge against BRAC also opposed the poster campaign.[8]

The group who supported the rights education policy included BRAC's field staff, the VO members and their families, and educated sectors of the community who had attended secular school and were below 45 years of age. It was also observed that non-VO members whose socio-economic status was similar to that of the VO members also came out openly in support of the poster campaign. These groups together constituted the overwhelming majority of the population of the rural areas and small towns in Bangladesh.

## Reasons for opposing or supporting the campaign

The supporters as well as the opponents of the campaign rationalised their respective positions through their analysis of the posters (below). These rationalisations were not always based on correct interpretations of the Holy Koran, and respondents did not comment on the 'violation of multiple-marriage policy' poster.

### Poster 1: Contribution to development

Opponents mentioned that Islam recognised equal rights for both males and females but bestowed different responsibilities on each of them. By showing both sexes doing similar work, the poster contradicted Islam. Besides, the women in the poster were considered to have been drawn obscenely. For these reasons they opposed the poster.

Supporters believed that the poster encouraged women to participate in productive activities which would lead to more income for the family.

### Poster 2: Child marriage

In justifying the opposition to this poster, it was mentioned that Islam allowed child marriage in special situations — a father not able to support his daughter can marry her to an able-bodied husband. For example, one of the wives of the Prophet Muhammad was only six years old at marriage. The poster was thus considered to have contradicted the dictates of Islam.

Supporters argued that child marriage brings unhappiness in the family. They emphasised that every parent should know the minimum age of marriage. The poster was important because it told people what that age was.

### Poster 4: Abuse of women

There was no opposition to this poster as such, and the message was considered significant by all interviewees. The problem lay with the way the abused woman was depicted. The clerics strongly objected to the abused woman being shown without her body being sufficiently covered. They therefore considered the poster to be obscene and that it should not have been displayed.

The VO members agreed that the woman was a little under-dressed but did not object to this. Some, however, remarked that women who were abused seldom had enough saris and blouses to wear, so the picture reflected the context and there was nothing wrong in displaying the poster.

### Poster 5: Registration of marriage

The group opposing the poster said that, according to Islam, marriage was conducted by proposing marriage, acceptance of the proposal, and recitation of *kalema*. Registering marriage is not a requirement. They thought that the statement in the poster had been so framed that it gave more importance to registration than to *kalema*. By making *kalema* insignificant or subordinate to registration, the poster made mockery of it. It was also felt that if registration became an integral part of marriage, that would mean that all the marriages that took place without registration since the revelation of Islam had been conducted incorrectly. Consequently, the group opposed the poster.[9]

In contrast, supporters considered the registration of marriage to be significant as it made divorce difficult and so would save lot of marriage break-ups.

## Poster 6: Bride money

Two arguments were voiced against this poster. Some believed that according to Islam there were circumstances when the wife needed to repay bride money to her husband after a divorce. By dealing only with the bride money for the husband, the poster failed to provide complete information on the issue as stipulated in Islam. Others, however, argued that Islam did not say anything about repaying bride money after divorce, and so rejected the poster on the grounds that it was not based on the dictates of the *Holy Koran* or *Hadith*.

The other group considered that bride money could provide real economic assistance for divorced women. They considered it important for rural women to know the laws on bride money and so felt this poster was useful in providing such information.

## Poster 7: Verbal divorce

Those who opposed the poster identified two technical problems in denying the right to verbal divorce. First, according to the *Holy Koran*, divorce could only be conducted verbally, so to deny this right would leave the marriage with no scope for conducting divorce. Denying the concept of verbal divorce would also mean denying marriages that had been conducted verbally. In other words, to establish a marital relationship verbally would be illegal. Denying verbal divorce would also mean that all divorces conducted verbally since the introduction of Islam were illegal.

Second, since verbal divorce was acceptable according to Islam, any marital relationship after such a divorce would be tantamount to adultery, and children born of such relationship would be illegitimate. It was felt by the opponents to it that the poster stating that divorce could not be given verbally was, in fact, encouraging marital relationships after such a divorce.

The group supporting the posters felt that abolishing verbal divorce would make divorce difficult and less frequent. This would have the effect of saving a lot of families from breaking up and from the consequences of such a separation, in particular the economic hardship faced by the divorced wife and her children, as such women were often left without an earner in the family.

## BRAC's reaction to the backlash

The poster policy brought both VO members and others in the community within the scope of the HRLE programme. Since the posters were intended to empower ordinary people by giving them some knowledge of the law, it was likely that there would be some social sectors who would not appreciate this policy and would oppose it.

BRAC's reactions were pragmatic and depended upon the nature of the backlash. BRAC staff did not make any effort to prevent the posters being ripped down, as it was assumed that to do so would have heightened the intensity of the opposition and put BRAC in the firing-line. Staff attempted to meet with those opposing the posters to explain the objectives and meanings of the posters. Where such meetings could be held, they produced the desired result. But there were also cases where meetings were not possible, because the opponents of the posters did not wish to co-operate. Where severe opposition was encountered, staff compromised by surrendering to the apparent interests of the opponents of the poster campaign. This decision was taken to avoid immediate harm being done to BRAC's activities and to ensure the success of the policy in the long run.

## Causes of the backlash against the posters

There appeared to be three interlinked reasons which led the clerics to react against the posters.

### *Different perspectives*

Past experience, self-interest, and the objectives of the organisations to which they were affiliated all influenced people's response to the posters. Since supporters and opponents differed on these fundamental issues, it was likely that they would take different stands on the posters.

BRAC initiated the poster campaign with a view to bringing about a positive change in society by ending a number of unjust practices or social problems. It believed that an end to such practices would not in any way contradict the dictates of Islam. The group supporting the policy emphasised the practical implication of the posters. They judged the posters according to their relevance to day-to-day problems and their solutions. They were also concerned with whether the laws of

Bangladesh were properly reflected, not so much with whether the posters contradicted the dictates of Islam. Essentially, they analysed the content of the posters from a secular perspective, irrespective of their religious beliefs.

The clerics made a literal reading of the statements in the posters and then analysed whether those contradicted the dictates of the *Holy Koran* and Islamic practices past and present. After such scrutiny, they concluded that some of the posters were incompatible with Islamic teachings and were a real threat to existing Islamic practices in Bangladesh. The clerics, whose training and profession are involved with religion, want to see that society functions according to the dictates of Islam. The introduction of any new idea or practice that was not considered to be in accordance with Islam or which posed a threat to existing Islamic practices was likely to be resisted. As one cleric commented in the group discussion: '*It is our moral obligation to preserve Islamic values in society. The posters attacked the iman (belief) of those having these values, thus we had to stand against them.*'

## Encroachment on professional territory

The clerics were well aware that they were the only ones with formal Islamic training. They were therefore of the impression that they were the only group competent to deal with the issues related to Islam. Psychologically, then, they developed a territory for their professional activities. This is not unusual, as all social groups have the tendency to possess, acquire, or preserve territory and territorial rights (Andrey 1967). Thus, it is quite likely that the groups who represent particular organisations may experience internal conflicts concerning the scope of the organisation's activities.

A number of issues dealt with by the posters, such as marriage or divorce, had religious connotations. Hence, the clerics considered that the issue fell within their exclusive professional domain: *Marriage and divorce are decided according to Islam; thus it is only we who have the right to say anything on these issues.* When BRAC dealt with these issues, the clerics therefore considered it an intrusion into their territory. Thus, they reacted against the posters to protect their territorial right and professional domain.

## Upholding socio-economic interests

There were also socio-economic reasons which prompted clerics to oppose the posters. The respondents noticed that after a verbal divorce, the husband usually became repentant and intended to reunite with his former wife, who might also be willing for such a reunion. For this reunion it is customary to conduct *hilla-nikah*.[10] To make the reunion socially acceptable without going through *hilla-nikah*, the separated couple needs the help of the clerics. After receiving money, the cleric makes a public statement (usually in a village court) that when the husband pronounced verbal divorce he was not of sound mind, so therefore the divorce was not valid and their reunion without *hilla-nikah* would not violate any Islamic code. After the announcement, the couple reunites. The VO members believed that the poster on verbal divorce would gradually stop this practice, in which case the clerics would be deprived of an income.

Besides, the abolition of verbal divorce would mean that the role of clerics in relation to a marital problem (i.e. verbal divorce) would become obsolete. Consequently there would be a decline in their functional importance in society. Grasping that this was a possibility, and because of their interest in maintaining the *status quo*, they opposed the poster. It is likely, after all, that the group which stands to lose if change takes place will resist the change agent stubbornly (Allen 1971).

BRAC seeks to empower the poor, which in turn affects the existing power structure (Chen 1991). The clerics are often part of this power structure in villages and small towns. In empowering the poor, the poster programme would disempower the clerics in socio-economic terms and so destabilise their position in the existing power structure. BRAC's catalytic role in promoting such change prompted religious organisations to react against it.

## How to avoid negative conflict

It appeared that the Police Department was under the influence of the local power structures and did not respect BRAC's legitimate and justified development efforts. The shopkeepers and college students in Sharail (Case 2) supported BRAC when *madrasa* students attacked the office, as most of its staff were personally known to them. Because they thought well of BRAC, they wanted no harm done to it. But this support was not unconditional: some of these shopkeepers ripped off the posters to avoid further trouble in their area.

Although there were more villagers in support of the posters than there were opponents of them, the ripping off of the posters was not resisted, even when it was done in broad daylight in a public place (Case 3). Besides, the indifference of the Police Department to development efforts, and the reservations even among those who supported the poster campaign, indicated that it was not difficult for an organised few to foil this development initiative. To ensure the smooth functioning of development organisations, a number of strategies may be recommended in the light of this study.

The resistance that resulted from attitudes and conclusions based on different premises can be resolved or minimised by establishing effective communication between development organisations and those which resist their efforts. Development organisations might choose to explain their objectives and mode of action to other social organisations ahead of time, in order to clarify their position. Through dialogue, it might be possible to modify any false impressions concerning the development organisation which might lead to opposition. Although a little late in the day, BRAC correctly sought to establish a dialogue with the clerics, and this may have prevented the intensification of the backlash in some areas, such as Kachikata (Case 1). (However, a similar effort in Sharail (Case 2) was in vain.)

Any programme that takes a holistic approach to development is likely to cut across the territorial boundaries of other social organisations. But one can enter another's territory only by being invited, as nobody likes to see their 'patch' getting crowded (Andrey 1967). The opposition resulting from the infringement of an organisational boundary may be minimised by incorporating the opposing organisations fully or partially into the process of formulating and/or implementing the development programme. It is important to take care that such a course of action does not dilute the objectives of the development organisation. A positive relationship is only likely to develop among groups that are working for common goal (Sherif *et al.* 1961). BRAC's decision to contact the clerics and the elite before finalising and fixing posters in future in Kuliarchar (Case 3) was a process of including the opposing group into the activities of HRLE programme.

As an alternative or in addition to the above strategies, the development organisation may convince and mobilise the support of influential members of the community to its cause. For example, in Kachikata (Case 1) when the chairman of the *union parishod* urged the participants in the LCLW to co-operate with BRAC, the policy did not face any opposition in the area.

In those cases where threats to one group's socio-economic interests underlie the resistance, it is likely that this group will oppose the development organisation for as long as the threat exists. In such a situation, measures should be taken to stop the group in question having a pretext for mobilising resistance against the development organisation. Development organisations, for their part, need to analyse the social organisations from which resistance may be expected, and to think about the likely nature of that resistance. This should help the development organisation to fine-tune its objectives, but without diluting them. For example, the statement 'divorce is not legal if given verbally' could have been formulated as 'according to Bangladesh law, divorce is not legal if given verbally'. Had that been done, the poster could not have been turned into a protest issue through being linked to Islam, but would still have achieved its objective.

Development organisations may also form an alliance with similar-minded groups. It was observed, for instance, that the clerics were not homogeneous in their beliefs and actions, for there were some who considered verbal divorce incorrect (Rafi *et al.* 1997). Certain clerics and certain members of the elite could thus have been included in a pro-development alliance. Any major alliance is likely to discourage opponents from taking any action against the development effort, and may even put up a joint counter-resistance to such opposition.

Development organisations will often face resistance by others in society. It is likely that there will be sectors which will not appreciate endeavours to bring about social change. The resistance that development organisations face in working for the welfare of the poor should not be underestimated. To be effective, they should work out strategies to avoid or minimise any such resistance in the process of formulating their development programmes.

## Notes

1 The mosque and *madrasa* are traditionally considered to be two separate organisations, as they function with distinctly different objectives. For convenience of expression, the organisations have been referred to as one in this paper.

2 A Voluntary Organisation is an organisation of the poor, supported by BRAC. Female villagers whose families own less than half an acre of land and whose members sell manual labour are eligible to join. A VO is formed with 45 members.

3 That is, elected local government officials, chairmen and members of the administrative units (*union parishad*), preachers of the mosque (*imam*), marriage registrars (*kazi*), primary school teachers, and other influential people.

4 The policy is for the husbands of VO members to remain present in the monthly meetings held in VOs.

5 'Clerics' has been used here as a generic term to refer to religious

officials (*imam, moazzine*) authorised to conduct services in the mosques, instructors in Islamic theology, and students at religious schools (*madrasa*).

6   Verses from the *Holy Koran* that are recited in conducting a marriage.

7   Posters of a pig with 'Muhammad' written on it were fixed on the walls of Jerusalem.

8   These ex-VO members defaulted in repaying BRAC loans, and BRAC therefore cancelled their VO membership – something they resented.

9   Although the group recognised the advantage of documenting marriage, they did not use the word 'registration'.

10  A matrimonial dictate on the reunion of the divorced couple. The wife needs to marry another person, live together with him for a minimum of four months, get divorced, and then remarry the previous husband with whom the reunion is intended.

# References

Agricultural Census (1996) *Bhorer Kagoj* (in Bangla, 1997), 28 August 1996.

Andrey, R. (1967) *The Territorial Imperative*, New York: Collins.

Allen, Francis R. (1971) *Socio-cultural Dynamics: An Introduction to Social Change*, New York: Macmillan.

BRAC (1996a) *RDP Phase III Report (1993–1995)*, Dhaka: BRAC.

BRAC (1996b) *RDP Phase IV*, Dhaka: BRAC.

BRAC (1997) *BRAC Annual Report: 1996*, Dhaka: BRAC.

Chen, Martha A. (1991) *A Quiet Revolution: Women in Transition in Rural Bangladesh*, Dhaka: BRAC Prokashana.

Freeman J. (1996) 'A huge grassroots organisation', *Earth Times* 10(18): 16–31.

Khan, Akbar Ali (1996) *Discovery of Bangladesh: Explorations into Dynamics of a Hidden Nation*, Dhaka: UPL.

Lyttleton C. (1994) 'Knowledge and meaning: the AIDS education campaign in rural northeast Thailand', *Social Science and Medicine* 38(1): 135–46.

Musaiger A. O. (1998) 'Evaluation of a nutrition education program in Oman: a case study', *International Quarterly of Community Health Education* 17(1): 57–64.

Rafi, Mohammad, David Hulme, Shah Asad Ahmed and Md. Nurul Amin (1997) *Impact Assessment of BRAC's Human Rights and Legal Education Training*, Dhaka: BRAC.

Sherif, M. *et al.* (1961) *Intergroup Conflict and Co-operation*, Oklahoma: University of Oklahoma Book Exchange.

Wienrawee, P. (1995) 'Capacity building and developing communication materials: one poster's story', *Aidscaptions* 2(2): 22–3.

*This paper was first published in* Development in Practice *(10/1: 19–30) in 2001.*

# Disaster without memory:
## Oxfam's drought programme in Zambia

## K. Pushpanath

*Disaster response has been described as the last resort of the amateur,*
*an unkind assessment but not without a grain of truth. Disaster*
*generates an emotional response and, with each new disaster, new*
*disaster organisations are born. And past lessons on disaster*
*management have to be learnt anew. (World Disasters Report 1993,*
International Federation of Red Cross and Red Crescent Societies)

Disaster in Southern Africa is not a new phenomenon. Indeed, the
region has suffered and continues to endure more than its share of
disasters — political and so-called natural. In Angola alone, the UN
currently estimates that at least 1,000 people die every day as a result of
war and its devastating consequences.

Even against this backdrop, the drought of February 1992 to
September 1993 was significant, because of the extent and scale of its
impact on an already vulnerable population, in the context of the limited
capacities of governments in the region. Indeed, most independent
observers and development workers feared that relief measures would
be neither effective nor sufficient to stave off a major tragedy.

In retrospect, however, the collective response to this impending
disaster demonstrates that, if there is political will and a commitment
to work with the people affected, real achievements are possible, in
terms of development as well as relief. For many Zambian NGOs, the
experience was one of remarkable co-operation and co-ordination,
including innovative relations with the government. Most commentators
and politicians agree that the experience of collaboration between the
Zambian government and the NGO community in Zambia was very
positive indeed, and quite unprecedented.

## Background: Oxfam in Zambia

Zambia's economy is overwhelmingly dependent on copper as its
major export commodity — a legacy which it inherited from its colonial

past. Its economic and social development has thus been intricately linked to the ups and downs of the international market for copper. During the boom years of the 1960s–70s, Zambia was able to adopt a benign, social-welfare model of development, pumping substantial resources into health, education, and urban infrastructure, and generous food subsidies to an already predominantly urban population.

Zambia showed spectacular achievements in education and health during this early period of post-independence. Some areas of the economy were nationalised, and a highly centralised state apparatus emerged. A new Zambian middle class developed, along with a tiny elite which controlled the economic and political reins of the country. Political changes, in the form of a one-party State, reflected an ideological alignment with the then Soviet bloc countries. However, fluctuations in the world copper market led President Kaunda's government to borrow heavily from the IMF and commercial banks to fuel the state-subsidised economy. Accumulated debt started weighing down on the economy, and the quality of life of most Zambians began to suffer. In the largely neglected rural areas, women-maintained households had already become the norm, because of extensive male migration to the urban centres.

Access to land is not necessarily a problem for these rural households, but the lack of appropriate and effective commitment, in terms of either policy or resources, has been a severe constraint on their capacity to break out of the poverty to which their subsistence economy confines them. Food insecurity has become severe in the rural sector, as confirmed through indices of malnutrition and mortality. Economic liberalisation has made these problems even worse.

Oxfam's pre-drought programme in the rural sector kept these factors in view, aiming to enhance and strengthen people's productive capacity through the sustainable use of available natural resources. Oxfam's programme in Zambia is thus characterised by support for local-level groups — such as women's associations, youth groups, organisations of disabled people, cooperatives, and so on — who are engaged in a range of productive and economic activities, as well as support for skills development and small enterprises. Training is also encouraged, through workshops and meetings. A small proportion of Oxfam's support is channelled through intermediary NGOs.

It was the combination of this micro-level experience in Zambia, together with the opportunity to draw on the previous experience of the Country Representative in development and relief programmes in

India, which enabled Oxfam to embark on a large-scale drought-relief and rehabilitation programme in the Eastern Province of Zambia. The programme enhanced existing capacity and confidence within Oxfam's team in Zambia, while also laying the foundations for a recovery programme which aimed to secure rural livelihoods. Oxfam's experience in Zambia has also attracted the attention of other international NGOs and official aid agencies for its innovative approach to disaster relief.

Oxfam's approach was based on two assumptions:

- it is possible to approach relief within the framework of development;
- it is feasible to facilitate, motivate, mobilise, and train local people to take charge of the relief effort.

In other words, Oxfam wanted to resist the temptation to administer relief through high-profile operational programmes, which are so beloved of the international media and (consequently) of the people who donate money to aid agencies. For instance, the international media constantly criticised the Indian government for being 'too rigid' to invite foreign aid-workers to assist after the 1993 earthquake — even though well-informed observers were pointing out that the government could rely on the enormous reserves of in-country ability to deal with such disasters. Without denying that there were problems, gaps, and considerable political posturing in the provision of post-earthquake aid, this serves as a good example of the collective mind-set of agencies and media alike in relation to disaster response.

This article suggests that operational aid programmes are not the best way to approach relief work, and that often these are not only expensive, but unsustainable and disempowering. The approach adopted by Oxfam in Zambia aimed not only to empower the immediate constituency — the people affected by the drought — but also those who worked alongside them, and ultimately the donors themselves, who became involved in the struggles of ordinary people in an active and dynamic way.

## Oxfam's drought programme

The mandate of field staff employed by Oxfam (UK and Ireland) stipulates that 'it is a priority ... to investigate a disaster and to assist with appropriate relief'. In the context of Zambia, this was interpreted as aiming to:

- support the capacity of Zambian groups and NGOs to prepare for and respond to emergencies, thus reducing the temptation for

Oxfam to go operational during disaster situations;

- make its own independent assessment, while training its counterpart organisations to become involved in the assessment process;
- ensure that responses are informed by an analysis of the respective roles of men and women, and by attention to issues of sustainability;
- design relief interventions to address causes as well as effects, so that relief and recovery are seen as the two sides of the same coin;
- communicate the underlying causes and future implications of the disaster for vulnerable people to policy-makers, donors, and others, through all possible channels;
- share and build on Oxfam's in-country and international experience;
- promote co-ordinated and integrated approaches among and within NGOs;
- encourage and give voice to local perceptions of problems, and to community-based participation, especially of the most vulnerable categories of people.

The first assessment was undertaken by Oxfam staff, through which a number of civil servants who had had some previous contact with Oxfam were encouraged to act as link people, informing and mobilising other volunteers. Over the following two months, 'information gatherers' were asked to use a standard questionnaire to identify two geographical areas in each of the seven districts in the province to show (a) households that were completely without food; (b) households that might soon run out of food; and (c) households that might run out of food before the next crop. They were also advised to look for other significant factors, such as water shortages, which would intensify the impact of drought. These 'information gatherers' received some token assistance for travel, but otherwise worked mainly as volunteers.

Running parallel to this, a more comprehensive drought profile was being built up by Oxfam across the country, using organisations and individuals who had been trained in the 1991 Development Communication Workshop in Lusaka.[1] This documentation was greatly valued by policy-makers and official aid agencies, and has continued to be used extensively.

It is important to note that most of the 'information gatherers' had no specialist or formal training, but were backed up by Oxfam's staff through means such as telexes and telegrams to remote areas of Zambia. The fact that their feedback came back in time to compile the drought file is a testimony to the commitment and motivation of these individuals, as well as a demonstration of their good grasp of the issues.

# Community mobilisation

From May 1992, over a period of 40 days, Oxfam staff held 14 community workshops in all the seven districts of Eastern Province in Zambia — mass meetings under the sky. These open meetings (using public-address systems) were attended by between 1,000 and 5,000 people each, women and men, old and young — an unprecedented event in the history of NGOs in Zambia. Critical to their success was the participation of women in not only sharing their particular problems, but taking leadership of the various committees that were elected during the meetings.[2]

These mass meetings achieved the following:

- A clear perception and recognition of problems faced by the people, as articulated by them.
- Ways and means to address these problems by enlisting support from within the community, and thus strengthening its capacity.
- Identification and election of new community leaders.
- The development of a new relationship between government district officials and local communities.
- An enabling climate for the open and confident participation in relief interventions of those people directly affected by the drought.
- The transformation of despair and dejection into an opportunity for people to take control and embark on many new collective activities.

The process also led to setting up village-level and chieftain-level committees to oversee working parties charged with receiving, distributing, monitoring, and accounting for food aid. At district level, it became possible to create disaster and development support groups, consisting mainly of civil servants who came forward as volunteers.

This process mobilised communities and motivated civil servants to work in a radically different way from what they were used to. In all, over 150 civil servants from different ministries came forward. More striking still was the democratisation process that got started at the village level. There were, of course, many problems in terms of party politics, as well as from within traditional areas of authority. The district groups did not always find it easy to work together in a people-focused and sensitive manner. But the fact remains that, in spite of the many hurdles, the programme gradually developed and started bearing results.

# Programme implementation: June 1992 — September 1993

The Eastern Province became a bee-hive of activities, which included a government-run Programme for Prevention of Malnutrition in which Oxfam played a major role. The sheer dimensions of the programme attest to the capabilities and capacities of the structures that were established. Over 35,000 tonnes of white and yellow maize had been delivered within 14 months of the programme's launch. An estimated 70,000 households (that is some 350,000 people, representing 33 per cent of the population of the province) were involved, of which about 70 per cent were maintained by women.

A number of Food For Work (FFW) programmes were also planned, monitored, and implemented by the community structures and the district groups. The figures for the year show a remarkable achievement: in a total of seven districts, 2,673 km of roads were constructed and 807 wells built or repaired, in addition to the construction of 82 bridges, 150 houses, 77 clinics and classrooms, 12 storage sheds, 947 pit latrines, and 22 earth dams.

In some areas, the choice of a particular activity was clearly made by the community, while in others it was strongly influenced by the district volunteers. Consequently, the sense of ownership over each FFW programme varied from one area to another, though in general a fair level of success rate was recorded.

There is no doubt that some activities took place because the community had only one option: to participate in the FFW programme in order to get food. But equally, there were cases where the activity started before the food arrived, and others where the activity was completed even when there was no assurance of food. This is an impressive reflection of the efficacy of a people-oriented approach, especially considering that most of the people involved (including Oxfam staff) did not have a great deal of previous experience. More impressive still is that communities were able to achieve all this.

Of course, there was a lot of learning on the job. We improvised and adjusted directions as the programme unfolded. For instance, a technical team, assembled within one month of starting the relief work, went around the province assisting other groups. Oxfam staff made repeated visits to monitor, advise, and resolve outstanding conflicts through the structures that were established. The process gave people an experience of grassroots democracy at work.

# Recovery: agricultural production

A crucial part of the relief response was to integrate Food For Work programmes within an agricultural production programme. Oxfam's experience in the Eastern Province before the drought enabled the staff to identify the main factors behind food insecurity at household level, particularly among the women-maintained households that comprised over two in three households in the area. It was established that these suffered mainly for want of adequate labour, proper and sufficient tools, and reliable fast-maturing seeds.

An outstanding feature of the agricultural production programme was the revival of a cultural practice of working together in groups, but within individual families. This helped labour-deficit women-maintained households to meet planting schedules, and slightly to expand the amount of land under food cultivation.

The same structures which were established for other FFW programmes undertook the distribution of 350 tonnes of maize seed, 10,000 x 30kg bags of groundnuts, and 34 tonnes of newly introduced sorghum seeds. The anticipated yield was 450,000 x 90kg bags of maize, 6,290 tonnes of groundnuts, and 7,150 tonnes of sorghum. In other words, almost 20 per cent of the maize output of the entire province was to be contributed by just 70,000 households!

Distribution and production were not uniformly successful, with occasional practical problems, such as the late delivery of seeds, unmet demand for seed in some areas, and excess supply in others. Overall, however, the intervention justified the assumptions that had been made, and proved that the programme has potential for replication. Perhaps for the first time in decades, many subsistence households produced considerably more than enough to cover their own food needs. A foundation was laid for development work to increase food security and establish sustainable livelihoods in the district, as a part of Oxfam's longer-term strategy in Zambia. Furthermore, the programme proved that relief work can take special account of women's needs — opening up new ways of thinking about the issue among women and men at village level as well as district level.

## Communications: advocacy and lobbying

As the relief measures were being implemented on the ground, we as Oxfam staff saw the critical need to communicate what we were witnessing and hearing, and what was being done about it. Every possible opportunity and channel was explored and used to communicate our findings, and people's responses to the drought-intervention programmes — from village level through to government officials, politicians, and international agency representatives.

For over a decade, Oxfam's programme in Zambia had tried to communicate its micro-level experience within the framework of macro-level policies. The pre-drought work on issues such as debt, poverty, and economic structural adjustment had a comparatively low profile, but nevertheless Oxfam initiated and led many small-scale research projects.[3] Interestingly, some of these campaigns had very good support from the government of Zambia.

In October 1991, after the multi-party elections, Zambia saw the emergence of independent mass media, lobby groups, and a more dynamic judiciary. Civil society started to become more vigorous, and non-partisan organisations were slowly showing more courage and determination. In other words, new political spaces were created, discovered, and revived.

The change in political climate meant that Oxfam was able to take a more public stand than before. Other factors also played a part, including:

- its reputation as a genuine grassroots support organisation;
- its effective and substantial response to the drought;
- the Zambian government's invitation to Oxfam, through the Minister of Agriculture, to activate the relief process, because of its own limited experience of drought-response work;
- the government of Zambia's openness and commitment to NGO-led relief activity and the de-politicisation of aid;
- Oxfam's direct and indirect support for communications work in the past;
- a positive attitude on the part of official donors towards NGOs;
- Oxfam's capacity to respond rapidly, through providing information and supporting local organisations to undertake campaigning and advocacy work, including through media channels;
- Oxfam's ability to seize the opportunity and mobilise the people affected by drought in such a way that they felt confident to articulate their concerns and aspirations.

The combination of these factors enabled Oxfam to take a more solid public stand in the context of the drought programme. The most strategic aspect of the communication work was through the mass media — radio, television, and newspapers. Many national journalists found that the Oxfam office was an important source of up-to-date and accurate information.

The staff were also able to co-ordinate with the broader campaigning efforts of Oxfam (UK/Ireland) and other European initiatives. Three successful media visits were made at the beginning, middle, and end of the drought programme: reporters from the BBC and *The Observer*, and other European and North American journalists, were helped to understand the drought, its impact, and various responses to it. In every case, a great effort was made to communicate the *context* of the drought, including the transitional nature of the Zambian economy and the country's new-found democratic process.

In conclusion, it was felt that communication is a vital component of relief work, and that our investment repaid positive dividends, not just to Oxfam as an institution, but also in helping people to gain greater control over the relief efforts. The voices of ordinary people were heard, loud and clear, placing those in power under pressure to respond quickly and sensitively to their demands.

Villagers and civil servants for the first time experienced the potential for using the media and other communication channels to influence events and bring about positive change for the benefit of disadvantaged and voiceless people. It was a significant departure for Zambian NGOs to see, appreciate, and make use of these opportunities. Similarly, Oxfam's constituency in the UK and Ireland was actively engaged. The team in Zambia facilitated a visit by a young journalist from a popular music programme on BBC Radio 2, and visits by Oxfam communications staff; their findings helped to inform Oxfam's fiftieth anniversary campaign messages. An outstanding piece of North–South collaboration was a letter-writing campaign, in which the team in Zambia encouraged 15,000 ordinary people, young and old, male and female, to write letters challenging the Structural Adjustment Programme, and describing the impact of debt repayments and government cut-backs on their lives. Oxfam staff in the UK organised the presentation of these letters to world finance ministers at an IMF/World Bank meeting in Washington in 1993 — an initiative which generated much interest in the press.

## Lessons from the drought

Oxfam's drought programme in Zambia represents a departure from the usual operational approach to emergency relief. The process was very much an intensive, people-oriented one. The operation faced innumerable hurdles: logistical problems, difficulties in social organisation, and problems of intrusive party politics. Some of the elected committee members distorted information, and abused the trust and confidence of the people. There were sporadic cases of the misuse of maize supplies and improper accounting for relief goods. However, all these problems pale into insignificance when they are put into context — a context in which there were very few people in Zambia with experience in drought-relief operations, particularly at the ground level; where (at the outset) there was no commitment to the level of funding required to respond to people's needs and expectations; where most of the civil servants opted to work as volunteers (though the government did offer some form of subsistence later); where there were extreme difficulties in transport, and communications systems were unreliable. It must also be noted that Oxfam staff were new to this type of work, and the scale of operation in financial terms was at least four times more than anything the office had handled before — indeed, for six months there were only three staff handling the whole operation, besides managing an on-going development programme in the rest of the country.

Irrespective of the programme's serious and admitted shortcomings, one of its major achievements was to incorporate its drought-relief work into a longer-term strategy for ensuring livelihood security — not only where Oxfam continues to be actively involved, but also in those districts where there are no plans for further follow-up.

The programme's main achievements can be summarised as follows:

- It has been shown in Zambia for the first time that ordinary people, given an enabling climate, can make enormous positive breakthroughs.
- A body of experience has been developed which will remain in Zambia as a basis for future work. This applies not just to Oxfam staff in Zambia, but to the civil servants and, most importantly, at the grassroots.
- The approach has laid solid foundations at the community level for other initiatives to find long-term solutions to problems such as insecure livelihoods and food insecurity; it opened up new approaches to drought mitigation and preparedness, and to communication, campaigning, and advocacy work.
- It has exposed many civil servants to a more people-sensitive approach to the issues and challenges of development, and reinforced this through practical experience.
- It released the creative energy of villagers and gave them a means of challenging authority, taking charge, and implementing programmes that were relevant and accessible to them.

The programme represents an experiment with new ways of thinking. It is an experience with real potential for replication. It challenges the conventional approach of disaster-relief agencies which prefer to embark on their own operational programmes because these seem to offer easier, more predictable, and more superficially attractive programmes — but which, in so doing, miss the opportunity to develop more sustainable, people-based approaches.

Often when development projects are assessed, there is a tendency to view sustainability only in terms of the material and physical inputs that are needed to run the programme. But the human and social dimensions are even more crucial. The drought crisis was confronted in many different ways, by different people. This is one form of empowerment: people developing the confidence to confront a situation, and daring to do something about it.

In the Zambian context, people's public behaviour had been largely conditioned by their experience of a one-party State. Anything not initiated by the Party was to be viewed with suspicion. It was important for Oxfam staff to demonstrate the importance of accountability in the context of the drought, and the relief goods that were arriving. It was a novel experience for many people to realise that they had a right to have a say in the process of implementing relief programmes. Similarly, it was new and exciting for people to learn that mistakes made by the elected leadership could — and, where possible, should — be rectified.

The way in which the district volunteers were dealt with by the village participants in a recent workshop, especially by women who stood their ground in wanting direct dealing with Oxfam, is a case in point. Their new-found self-confidence had come from actual experience of doing things, having access to information, confronting those in positions of superiority, removing those who obstructed the smooth running of the programme. All this does not mean that villagers have for ever overcome their powerlessness and silence, and will never revert to the obedience and meekness of the past. Rather, the experience has shown that there are alternatives, and has given them confidence to believe that these are possible. That is perhaps the most important lesson to learn from this experience.

This article opened with a quotation from the IFRC *World Disasters Report*, which suggests that every disaster means that we have to learn lessons anew. Must we really invent the wheel every time a disaster strikes, or can we usefully learn from what we have done so far?

Notwithstanding all the efforts of governments, donors, NGOs, missions, and charities, it was mainly the courage and remarkable determination of ordinary people that contained the disaster in Zambia. This is not to deny the value of all the aid programmes that were so effectively carried out, but rather to pay tribute to the people who were at the receiving end, and in particular to the peasant women of Zambia.

## Notes

1. The proceedings of this workshop are recorded in the 'Report of the Development Communication Workshop Jointly Organised by Oxfam and The Weekly Post and UNZA Great East Road Campus, 25th – 29th November 1991', compiled by Moses John Kwali. The workshop was organised in order to take advantage of the emergence of a more confident, independent national press in Zambia. It was attended by 25 people from both rural and urban areas of the country, to learn about information-gathering techniques.

2. The mass meetings were possible in part because of disaster-relief training run by Oxfam in 1989, which had been attended by senior civil servants and village activists. These contacts were critical in mobilising others to gather and communicate more information, and to identify areas of action. Oxfam's existing counterparts, especially the women's production groups and youth programmes, played a pivotal role in gathering and disseminating information, and mobilising others. The whole process took 40 days, and the running of the mass meetings improved with practice.

Each mass meeting was run like a training workshop, with Oxfam staff acting as facilitators. The logistics (food, material, money, public-address systems) were set up before each visit. The whole discussion was recorded for further use. Each district report was fully compiled within five days of returning from the tour. Oxfam staff mediated where conflicting opinions were emerging.

The participants were given general information about the drought, about Oxfam, and about existing govern-ment policies. Brain-storming sessions (each of about 2–4 hours) enabled people to come forward. Open elections were held to select representatives, of whom Oxfam stipulated that 50 per cent should be women. The volunteers from the districts who accompanied Oxfam staff at the village level were then asked to facilitate district meetings, in order to set up the district-level organisation.

3. For example, *Adjusting to Adjustment in Zambia: Women's and Young People's Responses to a Changing Economy,* a report commissioned by Oxfam from Gabriel Banda, and published in 1991 in the Oxfam Research Papers series.

*This article was first published in* Development in Practice *(4/2:81–91) in 1994.*

# Campaigning: a fashion or the best way to change the global agenda?

## Gerd Leipold

## Even bankers want to campaign

A new investment fund was recently launched in London. Climbers abseiled down the building of a financial institution, while unfurling a banner to advertise the new fund. A casual observer could have turned wearily away from what looked like another routine Greenpeace banner-hanging event.

Most NGOs these days want to do more campaigning.[1] Recent studies of the effectiveness of NGO campaigning to date (Chapman and Fisher 1999, 2000) identify the following reasons for this trend: the need of Northern NGOs to find new roles, as Southern NGOs take over project work; the recognition that projects will have limited effects without structural changes; an increasing call by Southern organisations for Northern NGOs to do more campaign and policy work; and the desire among NGOs for public profile. The latter has two distinct aspects: the belief that media coverage is crucial for policy change,[2] and the somewhat sounder assumption that it helps fundraising.

## Campaign organisations and organisations that also campaign

Campaigning is not a new phenomenon: it has been around for centuries. A characteristic of campaigns is that they spring up when legality and legitimacy find themselves at odds with each other, so that certain groups claim legitimacy for their cause and deny this legitimacy to the prevailing powers. Campaign organisations, whose very reason for existence is to campaign, have existed for a long time. Anti-Slavery International (formerly the Anti-Slavery Society) is one of the oldest such organisations, while Greenpeace and Amnesty International are probably the best-known modern ones.

The success of modern campaign organisations has stimulated organisations which had previously tended to limit themselves to project work to extend or create a campaigning arm. These organisations have quite distinct characteristics. A good campaign organisation is highly interactive, being able both to create an agenda and also to take advantage of existing agendas. It will spend a major proportion of its resources on communication, communication being its core business and not just a tool. Campaigning is a dialectical process, so campaign organisations tend to be confrontational and in turn attract confrontational people. Campaign organisations have to be opportunistic, not in terms of their beliefs and values, but in terms of reaching audiences. They derive their legitimacy from the popular support that they enjoy and from the quality of information that they provide. In a campaign – especially if it is directed at the general public – tactics are as important as strategy, a characteristic which campaigns share with politics.

Organisations that also campaign would obviously want to impose their existing organisational procedures on their campaigning activities. Their campaigning results will, therefore, be less than impressive. Alternatively, they will have to live with two different organisational cultures. Real conflicts of interests between campaigns and project work can arise where no compromise will do justice to both. Campaigns which are undertaken mainly for fundraising purposes may make it possible to avoid such conflicts, but generally at the price of a weak campaign.

## Three contemporary campaigns

Three examples will help to identify characteristics of campaigns and to address the difficult question of what campaigns can achieve.

### Brent Spar

Few campaigns in recent years achieved such a public resonance as Greenpeace's successful attempt to prevent the dumping at sea of the disused Brent Spar oil platform. Originally it was conceived as a medium-sized action to attract attention to a forthcoming meeting of the Oslo and Paris Convention. (Interestingly, the communication specialists of the organisation were opposed to the action, predicting that it would have little resonance.) It was not considered a campaign *per se*, only as a tactic within a long-standing lobbying strategy.

It rapidly took on a life of its own. Brent Spar gripped the attention of the European public. Individuals and organisations felt compelled to become active, and were soon followed by a number of governments. Organisations called for a boycott of Shell. Some individuals even firebombed a petrol station. European governments pressured their UK counterpart to reverse its position. Greenpeace occupied centre-stage in the media, but it certainly did not control what happened in the public and political arena. This loss of control – anathema to traditional management approaches – is typical of a successful public campaign. Truly activating people – probably the proudest achievement that a campaign could hope to claim – means that those people will decide largely on their own about the next steps.

The Brent Spar campaign effectively put an end to the dumping of decommissioned oil platforms. The environmental significance of this is low, if one looks simply at the amount of pollution entering the oceans through dumping. However, the symbolic importance is much higher. The oceans can no longer be considered as a convenient and cheap dumping ground far away from where the waste was created.[3]

After Shell abandoned its plan to dump the platform, Greenpeace experienced a severe setback when it admitted – on its own initiative – that it had overestimated the amount of oil left in the platform. For the central argument, this fact was of secondary importance. It was only brought up towards the end of the campaign, when people were already strongly supporting Greenpeace; and in some countries it was hardly mentioned. However, it tainted Greenpeace's success with the suspicion that the organisation had got its facts wrong: a serious problem for any campaign. Greenpeace's mistake and its ensuing apology were probably reported out of proportion to their real significance, but after the publicity it had received throughout its action, the organisation could hardly complain.

Brent Spar and – equally important – the execution of the activist Ken Sarowiwa in Nigeria were watersheds for Shell and other big oil companies. A large number of senior managers were replaced by a newer generation. The companies conceded that the legality of their action was not enough: they also needed public legitimacy. They committed themselves to listening more to the public. They withdrew from the Global Climate Commission – an industry group which denies the threat of global warming and has resisted all moves to reduce carbon dioxide emissions. Respect for human rights and a commitment to sustainable development were added to the companies' objectives. Investment in renewable energies multiplied. BP even conceded that the company would eventually have to move out of fossil fuels.

The oil companies reacted incredibly fast, more so than a government or for that matter a major NGO would have been able to do, and so demonstrated the degree to which campaigns can affect corporations. The deeper question of the extent to which these changes are more than a cosmetic make-over to reduce external criticism and restore reputation, however, is hard to answer. Even if the changes are for real, it is too early to judge what effect they will have on the global environment, on human rights, and on poverty. The impact of campaigns is generally extremely difficult and sometimes impossible to judge. One will usually have to wait a long time to tell, and then many other factors will also have had an influence.

## *Landmines*

Landmines appeared on the public agenda less than 15 years ago and the campaign to ban them became one of the most popular causes ever. Eventually, it was awarded a Nobel Peace Prize. The icon of the campaign was Diana, Princess of Wales. Had she been still been alive, she might have been honoured with the Nobel Prize herself. Her importance for the campaign is hard to gauge. Her involvement was as much the effect of the campaign itself as the cause of its success. Rarely do famous people get involved in an early stage of a campaign, with the exception of ageing rock stars who are bored with their own music and worried about their dwindling pulling power.

Once the landmines issue had reached a threshold of public interest, someone like Princess Diana almost naturally appeared on stage – and this is not to deny her seriousness or her importance. The popular media demand the personalisation of issues: they want figureheads and personalities, and they appoint their 'spokespeople', even if campaigning organisations do not nominate them. Popularisation should not be dismissed. On the contrary, it is an important aspect of campaigns, especially in their later stages. Not only does it create pressure: it also gives the cause a democratic legitimacy. Popularisation can be just as difficult as other aspects of campaigning. It requires different skills and also a new type of campaigner.

In the case of landmines, Robin Coupland from the International Committee of the Red Cross (ICRC), who provided the first comprehensive field data of mine injuries, and Ray McGrath, founder of the Mines Advisory Group (MAG), who worked in Afghanistan and pioneered mine clearance, probably most deserved to be honoured with the Nobel Prize. But in campaigning as elsewhere, those who sow the seeds rarely reap the harvest.

What was the harvest? Undoubtedly the landmines campaign created a huge awareness of anti-personnel devices and their effects. A sense of solidarity was created, and a call for action was the result. This awareness is not confined to rich countries. A recent study by ICRC (ICRC 1999: 65) in countries that have experienced war revealed a very high awareness of landmines, even in conflicts where they were not used.

The landmines campaign led directly to the Ottawa Treaty, which was negotiated, signed, and ratified unusually quickly. It bypassed the established institutions typically responsible for such a treaty, such as the UN Committee on Disarmament. What was, in the eyes of governments, a security issue best left to military specialists was transformed into a humanitarian issue, with ordinary people displacing the specialists.[4] NGOs exercised unprecedented influence in the negotiations. Mine clearance became accepted as a major task and is now a well-funded activity, and the medical treatment of mine victims has also much improved.

On the other hand, key countries such as the USA, Russia, and China have not signed the Ottawa Treaty. The number of landmines used has declined, but if one disregards Afghanistan, Angola, and Cambodia – where landmines were most heavily used, and which were the sites of Cold War-related conflicts – then there is probably not much change in practice. Some cynics have even claimed that the campaign provided the best propaganda for landmines. The campaign also failed to make it clear who carried responsibility: the weapon system was demonised, but its producers and users remained anonymous.

A by-product of the landmines campaign (not uncommon in campaigning) was the ban on blinding laser weapons. It happened almost overnight in 1995, inspired by a combination of three factors: an original report by Human Rights Watch, the concern of the US government about China and other countries developing such weapons, and public concern about inhumane weapons, created by the landmines campaign. Just a few months before the ban was agreed, no one, including the opponents of landmines, thought that such an outcome was possible. Campaign successes can happen overnight and can also produce completely unanticipated results.

All in all, the landmines campaign had tangible humanitarian benefits, but it failed to take the weapons out of use. Its real success lies in the awareness created and in the resulting shift in international politics. The secrecy of security and military issues was challenged, the process of negotiations 'civilianised', and the burden of proof shifted to the military side. Military need is no longer automatically regarded as more relevant than humanitarian necessity.

So: the campaign was a success, still more so in terms of its potential for the future rather than in terms of real change now. As Chapman and Fisher (1999: 15–16) point out, campaigns have limits. Real and lasting impact, implementation, and monitoring require tools other than national legislation or international conventions: education, involvement of the grassroots, or fundamental changes (addressing the causes of conflict), for example. If they don't happen, the legacy of the landmines campaign may just be another part of the Lady Di folklore.

## Debt and Jubilee 2000

The debt issue is more than 20 years old. Its was originally raised by Southern NGOs who observed the effects of spiralling debt on their countries' development. In the West, the argument about debt was highly politicised. The left was in favour of debt relief; the rest of the political spectrum saw the demand for relief as ideologically motivated, communist propaganda under a thin veneer of concern for the poor. The argument was mostly confined to circles of experts and hardly ever reached a broader public.

Somehow – and it is difficult to identify how and when the transformation happened – the debate about debt changed in the 1990s. The minority position that debt relief was essential became the mainstream view. Active politicians and ministers joined their retired colleagues and NGOs in calling for debt relief. A paradigm shift had taken place.

A number of factors caused that shift. A constant stream of reports on the effects of debt kept the issue alive. The quality of field research by NGOs improved (or, as likely, or even more likely, it conformed more to Western standards and adopted the language of economics), so it was harder to reject it out of hand. The end of the Cold War reduced the ideological content of the debate. Heavily committed banks had had time to reduce their exposure. The World Bank, under the assault of its critics, began to change its policy, while the IMF discredited itself through the patent failure of its own doctrines.

The argument for debt relief had probably already been won when Jubilee 2000 was formed. Jubilee 2000 had the task of further popularising the issue and forming and co-ordinating an international network to create pressure for substantial debt relief. To do so, it needed to demonstrate the widest possible support; so it rightly embarked on widespread coalition-building.[5]

Winning the argument, however, is a double-edged sword in campaigning. The new consensus that develops is typically less radical than the original campaign position. By adopting the new consensus, the mainstream also demands the authority to define it. Once finance ministers are in favour of debt relief, they will also assume the authority for defining the level and form that it should take. Those who campaigned over the years now find themselves easily sidelined, their arguments portrayed as the predictable response of special-interest groups which are never satisfied. Whether Jubilee 2000 managed to avoid this pitfall and achieve full success is probably a contentious matter, even within the campaign. The debt issue serves to illustrate that campaigns are an excellent, possibly even the best, tool to gain symbolic victories, but they cannot by themselves guarantee political and economic change.

## Challenges and opportunities for campaigning

The examples selected illustrate some general features of campaigns. Today's political environment poses additional and specific challenges and opportunities.

### Challenges

NGOs increasingly work as agents of governments and intergovernmental organisations and they seek co-operation with business. Even with the best possible will, such an approach reduces their independence. Campaigns are by their very nature mostly confrontational, and as such they are constrained if the campaigning organisation is too close to government or business.[6] Politics and politicians have a bad name the world over, though this reputation is probably unfair. NGOs, by contrast, are still mostly perceived as having integrity and compassion, albeit mixed with naïvety. As and when their influence increases, they could easily become engulfed in the crisis of the political system.[7]

As more and more NGOs want to campaign, the competition for public interest becomes stronger. For the campaign issues themselves, this competition is mostly beneficial. However, there is also an underlying (and often unacknowledged) competition among the organisations involved, which can weaken a campaign. In most international forums, NGOs appear united. But this unity is obviously a fractious one, given their highly diverse underlying interests. Once the globally operating NGOs fragment – or appear to do so – their collective claim to the moral high ground is damaged.

For most established NGOs, it is more cost-efficient to concentrate on 'upgrading' their members (that is, increasing the contribution per member) than on maximising the numbers of supporters. More members, however, give campaigns greater legitimacy. So an unfortunate choice has to be made between the two: the most cost-efficient fundraising method, on the one hand, and greater legitimacy on the other.

For a long time, campaigns were mostly for 'progressive' causes (which today may be more difficult to define). However, the instrument of campaigning is not necessarily restricted to progressive causes. Right-wing groups campaign against immigration, while inter-governmental organisations increasingly incorporate campaigns into their own agendas. Chris Rose[8] suggests that in the future campaigning might even become a commercial activity. Indeed, one could imagine a major coffee importer offering fair-trade coffee and at the same time campaigning for girls' education.

## *Opportunities*

The much-cited New Media (not to be equated with the Web) offer the possibility of a close and interactive relationship with members and supporters, and consequently the chance to mobilise people very quickly. The cost of communicating with members is also much lower, which removes the need to have to choose between efficient fundraising and broad-based support. Organised consumers can exert substantial pressure on companies and can produce quick results in a campaign. New technologies enable consumers to organise efficiently and effectively.

NGOs are used to forming coalitions based on shared objectives and values. Coalitions increase legitimacy, but they are slow and tend to create positions that reflect the need for internal compromise rather than relevance to the external world. The Jubilee and landmines campaigns could not, of course, match the speed of movement of the tightly co-ordinated Greenpeace organisation in the Brent Spar campaign. But then Greenpeace would not have succeeded without the wave of spontaneous and independent support from many quarters. It is certainly rare that such mobilisation happens, so there is a need deliberately to build wider constituencies in most campaigns.

It may be useful for NGOs to think more about strategic alliances based on shared interests. Shared interests have the advantage that they are more likely to lead to action. They reduce the need for co-ordination and allow for independent activities. They can help to push an issue to the centre of the stage (and increase the 'market' and thereby the profile of all involved). Strategic alliances are pragmatic, are intended to last for limited periods, and should ideally involve members from various areas (development, environment, and human rights).

For Southern NGOs, New Media offer the opportunity to find members and raise funds globally, reducing financial dependency, and so dramatically increasing their independence. Pilot tests show that this can be very successful, particularly if the Southern NGO is part of a global organisation.

## Can campaigns change the global agenda?

One of the most important objectives for development organisations is to achieve a fair global economic system.[9] Campaigns alone cannot achieve this objective, but they can make an important contribution. They can raise awareness and create symbols of the problem. They can activate millions of people and bring together organisations from around the world. They can raise and win the arguments about defining what is fair and what is patently unjust. They can develop a new narrative for development. As Maggie Black once remarked, NGOs are not good at making waves – indeed, they may even waste energy in trying to create waves – but they are good at riding them.[10] This is less a criticism of NGO campaigns than it is an acknowledgement of the limited political and economic might of NGOs.

We will see many organisations campaign for a new global economic system. The most dynamic and original of these campaigns will originate from small, radical, young groups. They will spring up where the problem is most urgent and visible. After all, riding waves is for young people. In the end, however, bigger organisations – and societies as a whole – will have to learn to make waves.

---

## Notes

1  This paper does not make a distinction between campaigning and advocacy, and for simplicity it consistently uses the term *campaigning*. Only campaigning by NGOs, mostly large organisations in the North, is studied. Commercial campaigns are left out, for obvious reasons, but also political election campaigning, as it is substantially different from the campaigning considered here. Key differences are the much shorter timespan, the clear demarcation of winners and losers, and the fixed stages in an election campaign.

2  'Public profile' is often used as a euphemism for media coverage. The importance of media coverage in campaigns is probably over-estimated. While important in later stages of a campaign, it is in all likelihood not essential before the popularising phase.

3  This was not just a symbolic result. Under the direct influence of Brent Spar, in line with long-standing campaigns on behalf of the oceans by Greenpeace and others, and following a trend among most European govern-ments, European

countries agreed strong restrictions on waste disposal at sea, coming close to a complete prohibition.

4 This was well expressed by Princess Diana's response to being criticised for meddling in political questions: 'I'm not a political figure, nor do I want to be one. But I come with my heart.'

5 Typically, coalitions in earlier stages of a campaign are less useful, sometimes even detrimental, because they reduce mobility and blunt the sharpness of the argument.

6 One should remember that neither governments nor business are monolithic. It is not impossible, therefore, to combine confrontation and co-operation.

7 NGOs would be ill-advised simply to join the blanket condemnation of politicians and politics. Politicians are probably less corrupt than business people, but are also under higher scrutiny. A weak political system will make it harder, not easier, for most campaigns to achieve real change.

8 Personal communication. Chris Rose is a campaign adviser to Greenpeace International.

9 Barry Coates, director of the World Development Movement, speaks of a 30-year campaign to regulate the global economy.

10 Maggie Black (1992) made this remark to the Oxfam Assembly.

# References

Black, Maggie (1992) *A Cause for Our Times: Oxfam – The First Fifty Years*, Oxford: Oxfam

Chapman, Jennifer and Thomas Fisher (1999) 'Effective NGO Campaigning', unpublished report, London: New Economics Foundation

Chapman, Jennifer and Thomas Fisher (2000) 'The effectiveness of NGO campaigning: lessons from practice' *Development in Practice* 10(2): 151–65

ICRC (1999) *ICRC Worldwide Consultation on the Rules of War*, Geneva: ICRC

*This article was first published in* Development in Practice *(10/3&4:453–60) in 2000.*

# Northern NGO advocacy:
## perceptions, reality, and the challenge

## Ian Anderson

## Perceptions

Northern NGO advocacy[1] has come a long way since the early 1970s campaigns, which John Clark describes as being 'poorly financed and run by highly committed but inexperienced volunteers but [which were] highly effective at capturing the public imagination' (in Edwards and Hulme 1992: 197–8). NGO advocacy has become more focused, more strategic, and has made more effective use of the media. NGOs have learned to gain access to and use the political processes, structures, and institutions of their home countries, as well as those of the multilateral agencies. This evolution of NGO advocacy has led to more effective interaction between NGOs and official agencies; to alliances between Northern and Southern NGOs, as those in the South have expanded their advocacy into the international arena; and to alliances between the broad-based development and relief NGOs and specialised campaigning groups and networks, including environmental organisations.

NGO policy-reform successes are widely acknowledged; Clark (1991), Salman and Eaves in Paul and Israel (1991), Edwards (1993), UNDP (1993), and Smillie (1995) all recognise that Northern and Southern NGOs, often acting together, have materially contributed to influencing policy changes by Northern and Southern governments. Clark (1991: 150), tracing NGO campaigning from its origins in the 1970s, notes the baby-milk marketing code, the drafting of an international essential drugs list, trade liberalisation for clothing manufactured in the South, an EEC emergency food reserve for the provision of famine relief, action on global warming and rainforest destruction, debt relief to African countries, and the imposition of sanctions to combat apartheid. To Clark's listing, Edwards (1993: 116) adds: influence on World Bank policies in relation to gender, participation, poverty, and the environment; cancellation of, or modification to, World Bank projects (notably dams and associated resettlement schemes), movement away from vertical interventions in health-sector investment (especially immunisation), improvements in food regimes for refugees and displaced persons, modification of IMF-imposed structural adjustment programmes to take greater account of their social consequences, and country-specific issues such as reconstruction aid for Cambodia and EU access for bananas produced in the Windward Islands. Smillie (1995: 229–30) notes NGO activity and influence at major UN environmental conferences, evidence given by NGOs to parliamentary studies and international inquiries, significant changes in African agricultural policy, and the improvements gained by Save the Children Fund (UK) in the standards of care required of organisations operating children's homes in Uganda. Salman and Eaves in Paul and Israel (1991), writing in a World Bank publication, cite examples of influence on a number of its projects. UNDP (1993: 84–99), in a chapter generally critical of NGOs, cites numerous beneficial advocacy initiatives by Southern NGOs, as well as gains by Northern NGOs. Amnesty International is singled out as having 'amply demonstrated the power of information to protect the rights of individuals and groups'. In referring to pressure from NGOs, which has brought about changes in the actions of multinational corporations, UNDP acknowledges that '[a]dvocacy clearly is – and probably will continue to be – the NGOs' greatest strength' (op.cit.:88 and 98).

More recently, NGO campaigning has been extended to representation at major UN conferences, starting with the 1992 Earth Summit held in Rio de Janeiro, where some 1500 NGOs were accredited to participate, through to the 1999 World Trade Organisation (WTO) meeting in Seattle, where, apart from the violent disruptions that attracted most media attention, NGOs concerned about the economic and social aspects of WTO policy and their impact on the environment, human rights, labour, and development were present and active. The recognition, through the award of the 1997 Nobel Peace Prize, of the achievements of the coalition of NGOs that formed the International Campaign to Ban Landmines, and the award of the 1999 prize to Médecins Sans Frontières for its highly visible public support to people in emergencies, and the present outcome of debt relief as a result of NGOs' work on the Highly Indebted Poor Countries (HIPC) initiative are further evidence of the growing effectiveness of NGO advocacy.

Notwithstanding these accepted gains, much of the literature is severely critical of NGOs and their advocacy. Principal among the criticisms of shortcomings of Northern NGOs are relationships with official donors (which NGOs are seen to be afraid to criticise, while being heavily reliant on their funding); the absence of a clear advocacy strategy; the limited allocation of resources to advocacy programmes, resulting from pressure to be seen to be applying resources to more tangible, marketable humanitarian relief and development projects; the failure of NGOs to demonstrate, through evaluation of their advocacy, its effectiveness and impact; the failure of NGOs to build the alliances needed to broaden and strengthen their advocacy voices; and the failure of NGOs to develop credible alternatives to neo-liberal growth-oriented economic orthodoxies which, critics suggest, requires more research by NGOs and a more conscious linkage of NGO field experience and the development models adopted by them. In addition, Northern NGOs' role as legitimate advocates for the Southern poor has been under scrutiny, as Northern NGO advocacy has evolved and Southern NGOs have themselves become increasingly involved in advocacy beyond their national borders. Northern NGOs are being challenged on issues that include the changing nature of relationships between Northern and Southern NGOs and demands for new forms of alliance between them; Southern expectations of their Northern counterparts; and tensions concerning who should determine the development agenda.

There is in the literature a broadly accepted recognition that structural macro-reforms are essential, if the fundamental causes of poverty are to be redressed. Watkins (1995: 216 and 217) summarises the need for reforms as 'requiring a transformation in attitudes, policies and institutions' and 'a fundamental redirection of policy on the part of other foci of power including the UN, international financial and trade organisations, corporations (TNCs), official aid donors and NGOs'.

This is the challenge facing Northern NGOs in their advocacy: how, by employing strategies which maximise their effectiveness and impact, they will be able to 'address the structural causes of poverty and related injustice' (Oxfam International 1999: 4).

## The reality

In the course of conducting doctoral research on the policy impact of the Washington Advocacy Office (WAO) of Oxfam International (OI), I surveyed larger Northern NGOs for the purposes of testing generalised criticisms of their advocacy. I obtained data covering the period 1981 to 1996, to provide benchmarks for detailed research into the WAO and its advocacy programme since its establishment in 1995; and to place the OI affiliates in the context of Northern NGOs, especially those with substantial international networks and affiliations.[2] For this purpose the survey sought data in respect of the allocation of income from government and private sources; the allocation of expenditure between development and relief programmes, advocacy, and other expenditures; advocacy strategy, policy objectives, staffing, and selection criteria for issues and alliances; the topics upon which NGOs had advocated; evaluation of advocacy; and, in the case of national Oxfams, the nature and extent of co-operation between affiliates, and with the WAO.

## The relationship between income from government sources and advocacy expenditures

By attempting to establish a correlation between official donor income and the resources allocated to advocacy, the survey sought to test the criticism that the increasing proportion and scale of NGO funding from official donors creates a dependency which constrains NGO advocacy. The survey sought to establish whether there is a correlation between official donor funding and advocacy resource allocation, without attempting to assess whether, as Edwards and Hulme (1995: 20) argue, NGOs' dependence on official funding 'emasculate[s] NGO attempts to serve as catalysts for the poor'.

No correlation between government funding and advocacy expenditures could be established, and in fact significant apparent contradictions were indicated. As might be expected, respondents whose institutions received the highest levels of government funding generally reported the lowest levels of advocacy expenditures. However, among the Oxfams, Intermón, the affiliate which over the survey period reported the highest rate of growth in government funding (80.4 per cent per year, from 52.3 per cent of total expenditures in 1996) also, over that period, increased its advocacy expenditures to the highest proportion of all the OI affiliates (11 per cent). Conversely, Oxfam America, which accepts no government funding, halved its advocacy expenditures as a prop-ortion of total expenditures over the survey period (from 10.4 per cent to 5.3 per cent in 1996), and on a non-inflation-adjusted basis barely increased advocacy expenditures over that period. Further support for the proposition that it is the NGO's policy orientation rather than dependence on official funding which influences the level of its advocacy activity is found in the case of the two Canadian OI affiliates: they are similarly reliant on government funding and may be expected to be subject to similar government influences, yet one has consistently spent more than 5 per cent of total expenditures on advocacy, while the other's advocacy expenditures declined from 2.3 per cent in 1984 to 1.2 per cent in 1996.

## Advocacy as a proportion of total NGO spending

It is Clark's hypothesis that, notwithstanding the broadly accepted view that advocacy is the strategy most likely to contribute to achieving significant reductions in poverty levels, NGOs have put few resources into it (Clark 1991:147). This proposition would seem to be supported by the levels of reported advocacy spending. By 1996, when NGO advocacy might be expected to have reached a level of maturity, reported expenditures (which exclude grant expenditures for Southern or partner advocacy) among OI affiliates and other respondents were overall 4.1 per cent of total expenditures, with the range varying from five respondents who reported zero or negligible advocacy expenditures, up to one reporting 12.5 per cent of total expenditures.

These levels of advocacy expenditures would support the view that NGOs themselves do not have sufficient belief in their advocacy to challenge the alleged constraints on their allocation of resources to advocacy. This allocation of resources to NGO advocacy may be compared, for example, with Greenpeace, which embraces an action-oriented strategy, which exists as a 'catalyst for change', and which has demonstrated the ability to mobilise large numbers of people in pursuit of specific achievable objectives (Greenpeace 1996: 1 and 3).[3] Greenpeace therefore employs a wholly advocacy-focused strategy, compared with development and humanitarian relief NGOs whose level of advocacy-resource allocation through to 1996, despite mission statements which include addressing the structural causes of poverty, at least appears to confirm Clark's view, expressed as follows:

> Advocacy may be seen as important but it is not urgent. Consequently it is easily squeezed out by the day-to-day dilemmas and crises arising from the project activities, from donor pressures and from media enquiries. (Clark 1991: 147)

## Advocacy strategy and staffing alliances: issues for advocacy

Much of the literature is critical of NGOs for being slow to adopt and clarify advocacy as a strategy. In particular, Edwards (1993: 165) identified a failure to combine 'different forms and levels of action in mutually supportive and reinforcing ways within a single strategy for change ... working simultaneously and in a co-ordinated fashion at local, national and international levels, both in detailed policy work and public campaigning, educational and media activity'.

Of the respondents providing data, 17 out of 23 claimed to have an advocacy policy. In addition to the 'yes/no' response in this respect, information was sought on the rationale, objectives, and policy for selecting topics for their advocacy. Predictably, the responses on advocacy objectives referred to influencing decision makers and public opinion to bring about change to the benefit of the poor. In selecting issues or subjects for advocacy, most respondents linked their advocacy to field experience, to their assessment of the prospects of successfully bringing about positive change, and to influencing opinion within their home-country constituencies. However, despite the linkage of advocacy with field experience, only two indicated that they consulted with Southern NGOs in selecting topics for their advocacy; a fact which would tend to support the questioning of Northern NGOs' legitimacy to claim to speak as advocates for the Southern poor, and criticisms of their failure to build effective partnerships with Southern NGOs.

Consistent with generally increased advocacy expenditures over the survey period, in every case where NGOs reported employing dedicated advocacy staff, total staff resources were greater in 1996 than in 1984, and generally the proportion of specialist advocacy staff at middle and senior management levels rose over the survey period.

Notable from the responses was the growth in the number of NGO advocacy topics over the survey period, and the very wide range of topics covered by their advocacy. In the period 1993–1996, several issues emerged around which Oxfams and other NGOs have coalesced: debt advocacy (in which almost all Oxfams reported active co-operation with the WAO since its establishment in 1995, and on which six non-Oxfams also reported advocacy), trade-related issues, and landmines.

Unsurprisingly, the survey responses in relation to advocacy alliances were overwhelmingly positive, with all respondents indicating some form (without being asked to comment on the depth and effectiveness) of co-operative advocacy relationships within their home country or region, and with Northern umbrella bodies or their own international network. The least-reported form of link was with Southern organisations, with which only 14 of the 23 respondents on this topic indicated an advocacy alliance.

In summary, the survey responses suggest that for the majority of participating NGOs advocacy has – through a combination of the allocation of human and financial resources, the recognition of advocacy as a strategy, and advocacy alliances – been integrated into the fabric of their organisations in pursuit of their missions to reduce poverty and offer humanitarian relief. While the survey findings therefore suggest that over time NGOs are to a progressively greater extent recognising, integrating, and providing resources for advocacy, they do not shed light on the effectiveness or impact of that advocacy.

### Evaluation

A recurrent theme in published criticisms of NGOs is the need for them to be more thorough, rigorous, and objective in evaluating their work, and the need to publish evaluation results as an essential component of NGO transparency. Among others, Clark (1991), Edwards and Hulme (1995), and Saxby in Sogge (1996) argue that this is necessary and, in Clark's view, to the advantage of NGOs. Edwards and Hulme (1995) and Smillie (1995) stress the need for greater attention to evaluating NGO advocacy as a prerequisite for NGOs being able more effectively to communicate their advocacy achievements. Without this, NGOs will be unable to win greater private and official donor support for the allocation of resources to advocacy.

In the survey, NGOs were asked to advise whether they consistently evaluate their advocacy (or at least claim to), the basis used for evaluation, and to which stakeholders the results are made available. The findings support the criticisms noted above. Only half (11 out of 23) of the NGOs which responded reported that their advocacy is formally evaluated, and of these only four stated that their advocacy was always evaluated. Survey responses indicate that release of evaluation results to stakeholders is much less of a priority to NGOs than commentators believe would be useful as a means of demonstrating effectiveness and transparency. Apart from funding agencies, to which six respondents reported that they made advocacy evaluations available, the survey responses indicate very little release of advocacy evaluations within NGOs' own networks, to donors, Southern partner organisations, researchers, or the media.

## Summary observations from the survey

Within its limitations, the survey has provided useful insights into Northern NGOs and their advocacy. The number of NGOs that recognise advocacy as a strategy to be employed in pursuit of their objectives, the increasing resources being allocated to advocacy, and the specialised and more senior staff being employed in advocacy all suggest that NGOs are heeding the calls for increased strategic priority to be given to advocacy.

The responses indicate that, although they clearly have some way to go, NGOs are increasingly addressing two[4] of the strategic weaknesses identified by Edwards (1993:168): the absence of a clear coherent advocacy strategy and the allocation of resources necessary effectively to implement that strategy; and the failure to build the alliances needed to broaden and strengthen their advocacy voices.

The third strategic weakness identified by Edwards, the 'emasculation' of advocacy for fear of reductions in official funding on which many are so dependent, was not substantiated by the survey. The lack of correlation between official funding and advocacy expenditures, and, indeed, the contradictions noted above suggest that it is the organisational culture and its priorities, rather than reliance on official funding, that determines the emphasis placed upon advocacy, and resources allocated to it. While the survey found no correlation between official funding and advocacy expenditures, it was beyond its scope to examine the nature of the advocacy and the extent to which the advocacy messages may be influenced by dependence on official donors. Thus, it is possible that the content of advocacy, rather than the decision to engage in and allocate resources to it, may be influenced by dependency on official donor funding (Minear 1987: 207).

The further major flaw in NGO advocacy that was identified in the literature is the failure of NGOs to demonstrate to themselves and their stakeholders, through evaluation, the effectiveness of their advocacy as justification for the financial and human resources dedicated to it. Evaluation, documentation, and publication of advocacy experience, in addition to helping to demonstrate both the effectiveness of NGOs' advocacy and their accountability, may help to 'facilitate scaling-up by others' (Edwards and Hulme 1994; Edwards and Hulme 1992: 224; Archer 1994: 232). Without the foundation provided by consistent, thorough evaluation of their advocacy, NGOs will be unable to assess its effectiveness, or address the criticisms made of it. Without being able to demonstrate their advocacy achievements through evaluation, NGOs are unable to fully commit the strategic priority and resources needed to realise the structural macro-reforms which are acknowledged to be essential if they are to have a substantial impact on world-wide poverty and related injustice. Until NGOs themselves have sufficient confidence in the effectiveness of their advocacy both to communicate and demonstrate their advocacy achievements, advocacy will surely remain a relatively minor component of NGO strategy, notwith-standing its potential contribution to their stated missions. If consistent, thorough evaluation of their advocacy is a prerequisite for such a level of informed confidence, the survey responses suggest a need for much greater priority to be given to advocacy evaluation by NGOs.[5]

# The challenge

This then is the challenge to NGOs' advocacy programmes: to evaluate the effectiveness of their campaigning, lobbying, and development education so that they are able confidently to demonstrate their advocacy achievements. By so doing, NGOs would be liberated from the constraints imposed by the beliefs of private and official donors that resources ought not be diverted away from tangible, currently more marketable, humanitarian relief and development projects. Having reached this level of demonstrable knowledge of their advocacy achievements, NGOs will be much better placed strategically to assess and determine the issues upon which they should be advocating, to set their advocacy goals, to plan desired outcomes, and to make more informed judgements about the people, organisations, and institutions that they should be seeking to influence, and the methods and forms of organisation and alliance that will be most effective. This increased level of confidence in their advocacy will enable NGOs to invest greater resources in advocacy programmes which contribute to the realisation of their poverty-reduction goals. Anything less will consign NGOs to being no more than bit players in the necessary transformation of the institutions, policies, and practices which sustain poverty and powerlessness.

## Notes

1 For these purposes, advocacy is assumed to incorporate campaigning, lobbying, and development education as the three principal streams of activity by which NGOs have sought to influence structures and policies and to bring about change in the interests of eradicating poverty and its underlying causes.

2 The survey was distributed to all 11 OI affiliates, plus 54 development NGOs listed in the 1992 Organisation for Economic Co-operation and Development Directory, whose entries referred to advocacy activity, and whose 1990 budgets were not less than that of Oxfam Canada, which in that year was the lowest of the OECD country-based Oxfams, and so indicative of a Northern NGO which encompassed the full range of development NGO activity. Further, because the OI affiliates include Oxfam Hong Kong as the only one not based in an OECD member country, two members of international NGO networks based in Newly Industrialised Economies were included in the survey, making a total of 56 NGOs not related to Oxfam. Fifty-two of the 67 (77 per cent) of the surveyed NGOs responded, although 29 of the NGOs not related to Oxfam did not provide data.

3 It may be argued that this comparison is unfair, because Greenpeace and other organisations such as Friends of the Earth and Amnesty Inter-

national have effecting change as their sole *raison d'être*, without the 'encumbrance' of development and humanitarian relief programmes, which were the purposes for which Northern NGOs were generally founded. Nevertheless, NGOs which claim to address the structural causes of poverty in the course of pursuing their mission and employ advocacy as the strategy for effecting change to improve the lives of people living in poverty have a duty to do so most effectively. Advocacy is not an optional extra for those NGOs, but is essential to bringing about the change in structures, policies, and practices which institutionalise poverty.

4 Of the four strategic weaknesses of NGO advocacy identified by Edwards, their failure to develop credible alternatives to neo-liberal economic growth-oriented orthodoxies was beyond the survey's scope.

5 Roche (1999), in a chapter devoted to impact assessment and advocacy, outlines current approaches to evaluating advocacy, by reference to a number of case studies. This work, which makes the case for assessing advocacy (applicable to both development programmes and emergencies), presents a number of qualitative, quantitative, and partici-patory approaches to evaluation. Through these case studies Roche therefore demonstrates that at least some NGOs are giving greater priority to advocacy evaluation than is indicated by the survey responses. Roche (p.193) recognises the need for NGOs to be able to demonstrate the effectiveness of their advocacy by stating: 'NGOs need to demonstrate that their advocacy work is not only effective but also cost-effective and has impact in the sense of making positive difference to people's lives. They must show that

lasting change in policy and practice actually results in improving the lives of men and women living in poverty and that this achievement is due, at least in part, to their research, capacity-building, and lobbying efforts. NGOs also need to know under what conditions they should advocate on behalf of others and when they should be strengthening others to speak for themselves. They have to demonstrate that they are going about this work in a professional and competent manner, and use the monitoring of this work to learn and to improve future performance.'

# References

Archer, D. (1994) 'The changing roles of non-governmental organisations in the field of education (in the context of changing relationships with the state)', *International Journal of Educational Development* 14(3)

Clark, John (1991) *Democratizing Development: The Role of Voluntary Organisations*, London: Earthscan

Edwards, Michael (1993) 'Does the doormat influence the boot? Critical thoughts on UK NGOs and international advocacy', *Development in Practice* 3(3): 163-75

Edwards, Michael and David Hulme (eds.) (1992) *Making a Difference: NGOs and Development in a Changing World*, London: Earthscan

Edwards, M. and David Hulme (eds.) (1995) *Non-Governmental Organizations – Performance and Accountability: Beyond the Magic Bullet*, London: Earthscan

Greenpeace International (1996) *25 years as a Catalyst for Change*, Amsterdam: Greenpeace International

Minear, Larry (1987) 'The other missions of NGOs: education and advocacy', *World Development* (Supplement) 15

Organisation for Economic Co-operation and Development (1992) *Directory of Non-Governmental Environment and Development Organi-sations In OECD Member Countries*, Paris: OECD

Oxfam International (1999) 'Strategic Plan 1999–2000', unpublished

Paul, S. and A. Israel (1991), *Non-governmental Organisations and the World Bank*, Washington DC: The World Bank

Roche, Chris (1999) *Impact Assessment for Development Agencies: Learning to Value Change*, Oxford: Oxfam

Smillie, Ian (1995) *The Alms Bazaar: Altruism Under Fire – Non-profit Organizations and International Development*, Ottawa: International Development Research Centre

Sogge, David (ed.) (1996) *Compassion and Calculation: The Business of Private Foreign Aid*, London: Pluto

United Nations Development Programme (1993) *Human Development Report 1993*, Oxford: Oxford University Press

Watkins, Kevin (1995) *The Oxfam Poverty Report*, Oxford: Oxfam

*This paper was first published in* Development in Practice *(10/3&4: 222–32) in 2000.*

# 'Does the doormat influence the boot?' Critical thoughts on UK NGOs and international advocacy

## Michael Edwards

Most UK development NGOs accept that significant improvements in the lives of poor people around the globe are unlikely to be achieved solely by funding 'projects' at grassroots level. This is because local initiatives can easily be blocked, undermined, or co-opted by more powerful forces, whether economic or political. Development work which fails to address these forces can expect to have an impact only on the short-term welfare of a small number of poor people. Those forces which emanate from the national or sub-national political economy must be addressed by indigenous institutions; others are international in character, and include the structure of the world trading system, financial and investment flows, energy consumption, technological innovation and intellectual property, and the policies of multilateral and bilateral donor agencies. The increasing internationalisation of decision-making in economic and political fields, and the limited accountability of global institutions, have increased the power of these interests.

Northern NGOs have tried to influence these international forces in order to create a more favourable climate for development in the South. They have largely failed to do so, and this article presents a personal view of some of the reasons which might underlie this failure. I have no wish to attack NGO attempts to exert greater influence at the international level. Rather, as a passionate believer in the importance of NGO advocacy, I am concerned by our collective failure to fulfil our potential in this field, and want to see how we can improve the effectiveness of our advocacy work. Although the article draws primarily on the experience of UK development NGOs (particularly Save the Children Fund (SCF)), the questions it raises apply to other Northern NGOs. The purpose of the article is to raise questions for discussion, not to provide the answers.

# A simple conceptual framework for NGO advocacy

The basic rationale for Northern NGO advocacy is identified as an attempt to alter the ways in which power, resources, and ideas are created, consumed, and distributed at global level, so that people and their organisations in the South have a more realistic chance of controlling their own development. It is useful to distinguish between two different forms of NGO advocacy:

a. *Attempts to influence global-level processes, structures, or ideologies:* for example, reform of the GATT and the world trading system, or attempts to overturn the 'neo-liberal orthodoxy' of market-led economic growth. These issues raise major questions for powerful interest groups and, in the absence of countervailing public pressure, mere dialogue is unlikely to induce significant change. Successful advocacy on such issues requires a mass base, so that sufficient pressure is exerted on Northern governments, and consequently on international institutions and multinational capital. Advocacy is likely to be confrontational, or at least publicly critical of existing orthodoxies. The stakes are high, not least because of the tendency, in the UK, of this kind of advocacy to fall foul of charity law. Logically, NGOs must call for lifestyle changes among their constituents. The aim is fundamental change.

b. *Attempts to influence specific policies, programmes, or projects:* for example, UNICEF health policy, or World Bank lending to resettlement schemes. These may be issues where the institution or government is under less pressure from interest groups and therefore accepts, or even welcomes, a dialogue with NGOs on alternative ways of operating – although on 'problem projects', such as the Narmada Dam in India, this is less true. Successful advocacy on such issues requires a high level of technical knowledge, information exchange, and practical experience. This kind of advocacy often takes place behind closed doors, and the NGO concerned will probably not broadcast any success it may have in inducing changes, lest avenues for future influence be closed off. Such advocacy is likely to be based on co-operation rather than confrontation. The aim is incremental reform.

Clearly, this model is an abstraction, and in reality the two forms of advocacy often merge into each other, so that NGO strategies contain elements of both. Some authors argue that UK NGOs will opt for piecemeal reform rather than a more fundamental challenge, because of the financial, legal, and other constraints that face them (Dolan 1992). In my view, these approaches to advocacy are complementary and mutually supportive. They share a common goal in the long term (system change), but adopt different strategies to reach it, because the short-term issues they address come from different levels in the system which they wish to change. Indeed, it can be argued that one kind of advocacy cannot succeed *unless* it is supported by the other. Hence, detailed policy work is unlikely to be generate significant change unless it is backed up by public and media pressure in the long run: NGOs can easily be co-opted, and the targets of their advocacy may adopt superficial reforms which fail to address more fundamental issues. For example, official donors or multi-lateral agencies may adopt the vocabulary of the NGOs ('empowerment', 'primary environmental care', and so on), while meaning and acting on a completely different understanding of what they imply. The title of this paper – 'Does the doormat influence the boot?' – is a quotation from an SCF Adviser working with government within the context of a World Bank loan for health and population programmes, who is rightly sceptical about the possibility of influencing Bank policy through co-operation in the field alone.

On the other hand, calls for global change are more likely to be heeded if they are backed up by a detailed, rigorous presentation of issues and a credible set of alternative options. It is not enough to present a critique of policy without also demonstrating what might have worked in its place. Rather than posing a dichotomy between 'gradual reform' and 'paradigm shifts', it may be more helpful to see the one slowly leading into the other, or to see the two approaches as complementary. For example, the extension of markets in health and education is a particular manifestation of a more general principle of the neo-liberal orthodoxy. By providing evidence of the impact of markets in particular situations, it may be possible to illumine, step-by-step, the weaknesses of the orthodoxy itself, and to do so more effectively than by mounting a full-frontal attack on the underlying ideology. Linking action and experience at the 'micro' (grassroots) and 'macro' (global) levels is perhaps the single most important element in successful advocacy, a theme to which I return later.

In spite of this, the distinction is relevant, because the two approaches to advocacy *do* have different implications for the NGO concerned, in terms of organisational structure and styles of work. One of the reasons underlying the relative weakness of NGO advocacy has been a failure to recognise this and make maximum use of the benefits which come from 'synergy' combining different forms and levels of action in mutually supportive and mutually reinforcing ways, within a single strategy for change. In this case, synergy means working simultaneously and in a co-ordinated fashion at local, national, and international levels, both in detailed policy work and in public campaigning, educational, and media activity.

There is in any case a wide spectrum of styles of advocacy, stretching between full-scale public campaigns and informal chats with civil servants in the corridor! It is no exaggeration to say that every staff member in an NGO is an advocate for the agency and its mandate, and plays some role in advocacy somewhere along this spectrum. Rather than seeing advocacy as a distinct activity separate from 'programme work', NGOs need to build all their activities into a single system in which each activity supports and draws from the others. To an extent this is a requirement in the UK in any case, because charity law demands that international advocacy is rooted in direct experience. But there is much more potential synergy here. 'Advocacy' is not the same as 'public campaigns', although campaigns may form one component of an advocacy strategy. Advocacy relates to all the activities of the NGO which aim to influence actors, systems, structures, and ideas – at many different levels and in many different ways. The failure of NGOs to grasp the implications of this constitutes a significant weakness, and is explored in more detail below.

Finally, the real strength of Northern NGOs lies in their simultaneous access to grassroots experience in the South, and to decision-makers in the North. This puts them in a unique position in terms of communicating what is actually happening to people in the South, to institutions in the North, and *vice versa*. This is not without its difficulties, not least in ensuring that the 'voice of the poor' is not distorted. But the potential for Northern NGOs to act in this way is clear. Providing an effective channel for real experience is more important than trying to compete with the World Bank and others in terms of theoretical research – although of course the two are not mutually exclusive. Experience has to be analysed and ordered if it is to have any wider significance. However, there will always be counter-arguments to NGO critiques; and with their hugely greater resources, agencies like the World Bank can develop these at a speed and a level of sophistication which no NGO can match. But what the Bank and others do not have (or are unwilling to develop) is access to accurate information on the consequences of their actions among real, living people. Neither do the official agencies have the same popular appeal, credibility, and access to the media which NGOs have developed over the last ten years. Potentially, this puts NGOs in a position of great power.

## What has international advocacy by UK NGOs achieved?

Most UK NGOs have increased their expenditure on international advocacy over the last five to ten years, although to varying levels and at different times. But what have we achieved? In his review of advocacy in the North, John Clark (1992:197) provides the following list of examples to illustrate some of the achievements of NGOs in this field:

- a code of conduct for the marketing of baby milks;
- the drafting of an essential drugs list;
- removing restrictions on the importation of certain clothing manufactured in the South (such as shirts from Bangladesh);
- establishing an emergency reserve so that EC food surpluses become more readily available for famine relief;
- concerted action on international environmental issues such as global warming and rainforest destruction;
- affording special debt relief to the poorest countries;
- the imposition of sanctions to combat apartheid.

To this rather mixed bag of 'successes' one might add:

- developments in World Bank policy in the areas of gender, participation, poverty, and the environment;
- reversal or modification of some 'problem projects' funded by the World Bank (mostly large dams and associated resettlement schemes);
- a move away from vertical interventions in health-sector investment, especially immunisation (although this year's World Development Report – *Investing in Health* – may reverse this trend);
- improvements in the food regime of refugees and displaced persons;
- modifications in 'structural adjustment' packages to take more account of social impact;

- country-specific initiatives such as reconstruction aid for Cambodia, or joint action (by Oxfam and Christian Aid) to promote access to EC markets for banana-producers in the Windward Islands.

According to Clark (1992:197), 'if it were possible to assess the value of all such reforms, they might be worth more than the financial contribution made by NGOs'. This might well be true, but also begs many questions. What have the achievements of NGOs really been worth? Can even these successes be attributed to NGO advocacy? And is this a cause for satisfaction or for circumspection? Perhaps it is unfair to seek answers to these, given the very long time-scales involved, the dimensions and complexity of the issues, the power of the targets of their advocacy, the relatively small resources devoted to advocacy, and the obvious point that UK NGOs cannot and do not expect to alter international policies or systems *by themselves*. NGOs expect their advocacy to work like a dripping tap, with policy changes coming about over the long term through the actions of many different agencies and individuals. Nevertheless, if we cannot begin to find some answers, strategic planning for advocacy becomes very difficult. Real success will always be hard to achieve when the issues are so broad. But there is always more chance of success when strategy is as strong as it can be. It seems to me that the following conclusions can be drawn from experience to date.

a. Most achievements have been at the level of detailed policy and/or on issues where NGOs have not come up against strong interest-group pressures (although the adoption of the international code on the marketing of breast-milk substitutes is a notable exception here). Least progress has been made at the level of ideology and global systems – trade, financial flows, and 'conditionality' (the growing insistence of Western donors on progress towards multi-party 'democracy' and respect for human rights). This may not be surprising; but it does reinforce the need to link the two forms of advocacy described above, so that the one supports the other.

b. Progress on more fundamental issues, such as the conservation of the environment and the impact of structural adjustment on the poor, appears less impressive the more one delves into the details. There have been superficial reforms, but basic ideology and structure remain intact. There has, for sure, been an increasing uptake in the official aid community of the traditional NGO agenda in areas like popular participation, sustainable development, poverty-focus, human rights, gender, and the 'learning process' approach to development work (Korten 1980). This year's *Human Development Report* from UNDP is a case in point. Even the IMF, in its *World Economic Outlook*, has moved to the use of 'Purchasing Power Parity' rather than GNP per capita, a measure long recommended by NGOs. However, these moves have yet to feed through into practice at the field level.

c. NGOs may over-estimate their own impact on certain issues (such as 'sanctions to combat apartheid' in Clark's list), where hindsight reveals other forces at work which were more influential. Structural adjustment is a case in point, with at least two other factors – pressure from other multilateral agencies (especially UNICEF), and the political unsustainability of the original package in countries being 'adjusted' – being crucial.

d. NGOs have failed to build an international movement for development, in contrast to the worldwide environmental or women's movements. While these are very different in character, genesis, and history, both have found successful ways of strategising across national boundaries and interest groups, in ways which have seem to have escaped development NGOs thus far.

Whether the UK NGOs' record on international advocacy is seen as disappointing depends on one's initial expectations, but we should at least register a concern that results have been modest. Is this inevitable, simply a reflection of doing advocacy work in a complex and hostile world, or are there steps which could improve our chances of success?

## Barriers to successful international advocacy by UK NGOs

Clearly, the scale and complexity of advocacy issues facing NGOs, and the relatively small resources devoted currently by NGOs to international advocacy, need to be borne in mind in the discussion which follows. It would be simplistic to assume that better results would be achieved solely by increasing the scale of resources devoted to international advocacy. However, I identify four strategic weaknesses in our current approach which require attention:

- an overall absence of clear strategy
- a failure to build strong alliances

- a failure to develop credible alternatives to current orthodoxies
- the dilemma of relations with donor agencies.

## Strategy

NGOs are increasingly concerned with strategic planning, evaluation, institutional learning, and 'distinctive competence'. But how have these concerns been applied to international advocacy work? Of course, evaluation is difficult where there are other forces at work, but it sometimes seems that the disciplines adopted in programme development are neglected in advocacy. The only indicator of success that seems to be used is the number of meetings attended as the same individuals jet frantically from one part of the globe to another! This is not helped by the tendency in some NGOs to separate 'advocacy' from 'programme management' and develop semi-independent advocacy units. Rather than seeing advocacy as an integral part of everyone's job at all levels, advocacy can become divorced from the concerns and priorities of people directly involved in development or relief work (whether staff or local counterparts). This produces a tendency to concentrate on general issues (systems and ideology) rather than on detailed policy lobbying tied to specific circumstances. Consequently themes for advocacy then tend to be determined by the international debate – even fashion – instead of by the work of the NGO and its local counterparts. This makes it more likely the NGO will either be co-opted into the concerns of the wider system, or retreat into ideology. Advocacy becomes *market-driven*, rather than *programme-driven*. Information flows between field and head office are weakened, because field staff do not feel part of one system with common objectives, driven by and supportive of their own work. Without a continuous supply of good-quality information, successful advocacy is impossible. NGOs need to develop a planning process which ensures that themes for international advocacy emerge from genuine priorities in the field. This does not mean that advocacy should be driven exclusively by field concerns, since there will always be trends and initiatives in the international environment which demand a response. However, there must be a clear link between an NGO's advocacy and its direct practical experience, so that influence can be exercised with some degree of authority, legitimacy, and credibility.

The rationale for separating 'advocacy' from other responsibilities seems to be two-fold. First, to be effective, advocacy requires special skills, access to decision-makers, and time. Second, senior managers may see international advocacy as a particularly attractive area of work because of its high-profile nature, and so attempt to control it. Neither argument stands up to scrutiny: special skills or access may be required for particular styles of advocacy, or for advocacy on particular issues, but there are many other aspects of advocacy where the skills and experience of people throughout the organisation (programme managers, researchers, fundraisers, and communicators) are decisive. Programme staff have the knowledge of local realities and access to decision-makers required to influence the details of policy, while fundraisers and other communicators have the ability and opportunity to enlist wider public support by conveying complex messages in a straightforward way. NGO directors and other senior managers can gain access to high-level bureaucrats and so help to expand the 'political space' within which more detailed work can be developed. The rationale for large and separate advocacy units is less convincing once an organisation sees advocacy as a corporate responsibility in which everyone plays a different but complementary role. This does not, of course, remove the need for overall co-ordination of these different efforts. A degree of centralisation is essential to achieve co-ordination, generate economies of scale (with regard to particular target agencies and themes), and develop a global overview; but, if centralisation is achieved at the cost of wider commitment throughout the organisation, advocacy can be undermined by the absence of a shared vision and understanding.

UK NGOs have generally failed to find the right balance between the two forms of advocacy described above – mass-based advocacy on global systems and ideology, and specialised or technical advocacy on specific policies and projects. Instead, individual NGOs tend to concentrate on one to the exclusion of the other. This might not be a problem if UK NGOs were to work more closely together, each contributing something distinctive to an overall advocacy strategy; but at present no such alliance exists. As a result, neither approach fulfils its potential. In SCF, for example, a huge amount of detailed work goes on to influence the policies of the official aid establishment, not only at the international level but also in the field (through joint missions with donors, staff exchanges, meetings with local aid representatives, information exchange, and so on). However, this is not yet backed by a similar attempt to enlist the support of SCF's huge UK constituency in a general movement for change. On the other hand, concentration on global systems alone is dangerous, partly because the issues at stake are well outside any possible influence that the NGO can hope to exert. A mass of general material on debt, trade, and environment is constantly being produced, but it is read only by the converted and makes little impact on its ultimate targets in the policy-making sphere because, quite literally, it is 'speaking another language'' A great deal of heat may be generated, but not much light.

UK NGOs face a real dilemma here: on the one hand, if they try to 'speak the same language' as the targets of their advocacy and go about their work quietly and constructively, they risk being co-opted or generating a superficial response, there being no wider pressures for more fundamental change. On the other hand, if NGOs opt for a more radical path, they risk being marginalised, because their recommendations are so far outside the intellectual and ideological framework of the prevailing orthodoxy that they are simply ignored. The logical conclusion is to combine the two approaches.

Finally, UK NGOs have failed to pay sufficient attention to building capacity in the South for advocacy work, either to strengthen the ability of local institutions to advocate for change at national level, or to assist them in playing a more active role in international advocacy. SCF has made some attempts to strengthen the capacity of Southern governments to negotiate more effectively in discussions with donors (Edwards 1991, 1993), while other UK NGOs, especially Oxfam, have tried to help Southern NGOs to develop their own advocacy work. A great deal of effective advocacy takes place within the countries of the South, both directly – such as with the national offices of donor agencies – or indirectly (i.e. strengthening the part played by Southern actors and institutions in a multi-layered strategy for international advocacy). It is in this area – developing alliances for advocacy between NGOs in the North and South – that some Southern NGOs have shown increasing disappointment with their Northern counterparts (Clark 1991). We cannot allow international advocacy to become a self-contained process among Northern institutions.

In summary, what is needed is a proper, multi-layered, and multi-faceted strategy for NGO advocacy which relates themes, targets, objectives, activities, roles, and responsibilities together in a coherent way; which is monitored carefully and evaluated at regular intervals; which integrates detailed policy work with public campaigning; which is rooted in real experience; and which embraces the whole organisation in pursuit of a common cause. Table 1 provides an illustration of how such a strategy might look in theory, in relation to one current theme: structural adjustment. The importance of advocacy cannot simply be assumed. Its structure must be planned and its impact evaluated in relation to other strategies to achieve impact. This requires much closer and more sophisticated monitoring, engagement, and follow-through, and the development of better indicators (or proxy indicators) of change in policies and attitudes.

## Alliances

Although individual NGOs can hope to exert influence on detailed policy issues in which they have a distinctive competence (for instance, SCF in health-systems development), more fundamental issues require a joint approach in order to achieve any impact. Are UK development NGOs prepared to form the kinds of alliance that will be necessary if international advocacy work is to be strengthened? Are they prepared to enter into a 'grander coalition' of development, environment, and other groups to work on the very broad but common issues of global systems and lifestyle changes? There are some NGO networks (such as the British Overseas Aid Group (BOAG), the Aid and Environment Group, Debt Crisis Network, EC–NGO Liaison Committee, and others), but until now their function has been to share information and/or organise joint events at donor meetings, rather than to co-ordinate inter-agency action on global campaigns over the longer term. However, there are some encouraging signs – for example, development and environmental groups worked with some success to shift the UK government's position on 'sustainable development' in the run-up to UNCED, and ran a powerful campaign against proposed cuts in the UK aid budget. Does this herald a new way of working, or is it the exception that proves the rule? The mood of UK NGOs and some international NGOs (and of churches, environmental groups, and even some political activists) may be changing towards a more positive stance on the value of co-operation, but this commitment is yet to be tested in practice.

There are some obvious reasons for the traditional reluctance of UK NGOs to work together: competition (for funds, but stretching into general agency profile), disagreements on ideology and policy, lack of a common vocabulary, differing priorities and so on – and some authors believe that these constraints are insurmountable (Dolan 1992). If this is true, the impact of NGO advocacy at the broader 'systemic' level is likely to be dissipated in a mass of individual approaches. It is a truism that 'the whole is greater than the sum of its

## Table 1: A model framework for international advocacy

*NB This framework is intended to give a 'flavour' of strategy; it is not intended to be comprehensive. It assumes that the organisation's aim is to replace existing approaches to adjustment with alternatives which generate equitable and sustainable development.*

**Objectives:** to increase understanding of the impact and weaknesses of current approaches; to develop credible alternative approaches; to have these approaches adopted by the World Bank and bilateral donor agencies.

| Levels of action | Types of action |
|---|---|
| Grassroots (programme staff and partners) | • building concrete alternatives<br>• action research to generate information<br>• capacity-building among local NGOs and government (research, information, advocacy) |
| National (country office) | • strengthen government capacity to negotiate with donors<br>• support to NGO federations/networks in developing policy critiques and alternatives<br>• join World Bank Missions in the field (take Bank staff into the field, work with them on individual loans)<br>• monitor implementation of agreed World Bank policy (e.g. Operational Directives) |
| Regional (regional office) | • lobby regional development banks (IDB, ADB, etc.)<br>• lobby regional offices of World Bank<br>• support for regional alliances<br>• Regional Co-operation |
| International (headquarters: Overseas Dept.) | • lobby task managers for specific loans and policy staff on general issues (maximise on-going information flows)<br>• work through World Bank/NGO Committee<br>• work through UK Executive Director and government officials in London<br>• participate in conferences and meetings (e.g. World Development Report)<br>• research/publications on macro-level alternatives (including in academic journals, and internal Bank publications) |

| Levels of action | Types of action |
| --- | --- |
| | • staff exchanges and secondments |
| | • contribute to World Bank evaluation methodologies, e.g. participatory poverty assessments |
| | • strengthen global NGO alliances |
| (communications and fundraising depts.) | • development education among supporters, schools, etc. |
| | • information to UK Parliament/MPs |
| | • increase links with other movements (e.g. environment) |

parts'; in addition, we need to recognise that alliances could help different NGOs to make more creative use of their different competencies and experience. For example, agencies like SCF have a much deeper involvement in the technical details of policy, because they have their own staff in the field and have tended to specialise in certain areas (such as health-systems development or humanitarian assistance) and in certain approaches (working within line ministries, for example) which give them access to considerable information and experience about what is actually happening as a result of particular donor policies (Edwards 1993). For example, SCF is currently engaged in a programme with FAO to develop a new and much more accurate early-warning system for predicting food crises, based on the integration of quantitative and qualitative data in the form of 'vulnerability maps', the potential benefits of which are immense.

On the other hand, other NGOs (or non-charitable trusts like the World Development Movement) may lack this sort of access, but be able to engage more effectively in public campaigns. If, for whatever reason, the two cannot be combined in the same agency, then at least different agencies can pool their expertise in pursuit of a common set of objectives. Rather than arriving at a consensus based on the lowest common denominator, a more creative approach to alliances would be to recognise and build on the differences which exist among the NGO 'community'. The aim should be *synergy* (working individually but in a mutually supportive way), not *standardisation* (all doing the same thing). UK development NGOs do not yet seem to have learned the lessons of the women's and environmental movements, which have succeeded to a far greater extent precisely because they are *movements* (not organisations funding projects), able to spread their influence through networks and coalitions of different groups sharing a broadly similar agenda.

## Alternatives

Among official donor agencies, a common criticism of NGOs is that, while strong on criticism, they are short on credible alternatives – or at least on alternatives which are credible to the donors. Advocacy is probably likely to be more effective if positive suggestions are included alongside NGO critiques. This is particularly true in the economic field, where we need to demonstrate that living standards among poor people in the South can be increased without the social and environmental costs associated with existing policies. In essence, this means developing alternatives to the current orthodoxy of global economic growth based on an ever-expanding trading system and 'free markets'. Because alternatives may involve choices about consumption in the North, the supporters of UK NGOs also need to be convinced of their validity. We do not seem to be making very much progress in this direction.

Of course, it is much easier to criticise the impact of policies which are clearly misconceived than it is to wrestle with the complexities of alternatives. There is no shortage of critiques of the existing system, but people faced with daily choices and decisions need much more than this if they are to make progress. The tendency of NGOs to focus on global-level issues may also reflect a reluctance to look critically at their own practice at the grassroots level. Yet NGOs need to consider very carefully whether they really do have any 'distinctive competence' in global-level research. They can certainly innovate and think creatively about alternatives, but real alternatives must grow from action and practical development experience, not from the minds of thinkers in the North. However, NGOs have failed to integrate the work they *have* undertaken on alternative development models at grassroots and global levels. There has been some work on 'Primary Environmental Care' (PEC) at local level, and some work on alternative trading systems and energy strategies at global level, but little that ties the two together in a convincing fashion. One of the major weaknesses of PEC is its localism and consequent failure to address issues of policy and power at other levels. Perhaps this is why PEC has been embraced so enthusiastically by the official aid community.

Strengthening links between global and grassroots activity is fundamental if NGOs wish to improve the effectiveness of their advocacy work, since only when these activities are mutually supportive can lasting change occur. NGO advocacy must grow out of and be informed by grassroots experience if it is to claim to speak on behalf of the poor. However, this is extremely difficult to do. I know of no NGO that has in place systems to collect, channel, analyse, synthesise, generalise, and disseminate information of this sort. In addition, UK NGOs usually base their advocacy work on what their 'partners' or 'counterparts' say, but of course these are a small group whom we select because they agree with us (and we with them) in terms of basic philosophy and objectives. They do not 'represent the poor' in any general sense – nor would they necessarily claim to do so. Northern NGOs must be careful not to use the groups with which they choose to work to legitimise a view of the world in which they believe, but which may not be shared by the broad mass of people in the South. Of course we should not be ashamed of voicing our own opinions (or even those of our partners), so long as we are explicit about 'who' it is that is speaking. However, genuine, credible, and sustainable alternatives must emerge from local debate and action in both North and South, even if the results are more complex and less comfortable than we expect. This is particularly true where the alternatives have a direct impact on people's living standards. In this respect, it is vital to promote the development of wider networks in the South which can be more truly representative of different shades of opinion than is possible if we listen only to 'our' (narrowly defined) partners. The same goes for the North – hence the importance of alliances and coalitions.

## Donors

While most UK NGOs see their relations with official donor agencies as involving a dialogue about policy, the donors by and large see NGOs as implementers of projects. There is certainly an increasing openness to working with or through NGOs, but to what end? Part of the neo-liberal orthodoxy is the privatisation of welfare functions previously provided by the state, but the impact of increasing NGOs' role in service-provision seems to be negative in terms of their advocacy. We cannot, after all, bite the hands that feed us and hope to find a meal waiting for more than a week or so! This is less of a problem for detailed influence on policy of the 'behind closed doors' variety, but 'a fundamental choice all NGOs will face is whether to scale-up along the lines that aid donors and host governments prefer, or whether to keep some distance and accept the reduced access to official funding that this will entail' (Edwards and Hulme 1992: 214). The likelihood is that UK NGOs will make different choices in this respect, something that hangs over the future of alliances between them. Increasing competition for funds may press NGOs into accepting ever more money from official donors, and so bring about a creeping compromise in their advocacy agendas.

## Some key issues for discussion

This brief survey of UK NGOs and international advocacy reveals four key issues.

a. We need to develop a clearer sense of strategy, to evaluate our efforts and learn from experience, so that advocacy work can be refined on a continuous basis. We need to exchange ideas on what seems to work best in different situations or with different targets and themes. We should evaluate how organisational structures and planning systems affect the impact of advocacy. We need to analyse the compromises and complementarities between detailed policy work and public campaigning, and explore how the potential synergy between the two can be maximised. We should embark on a systematic effort to learn from the experience of more successful international movements.

b. We need to find better ways of linking local-level action and analysis with international advocacy. How can the necessary information flows be developed in ways which do not compromise the legitimacy of grassroots views? How can the voices of real people best be combined with the sophisticated conceptual framework, detailed policy work, and wider public pressure required to induce significant change at the highest levels? The implications of moving into the 'information age', as Clark (1992) puts it, are significant, since NGOs will require people, systems, structures, and capacities to play an effective role in an emerging international movement, rather than a series of country programmes alone. How can we best contribute to the development of wider networks and a stronger capacity to enable institutions in the South to play more of a role in international advocacy, both directly and indirectly?

c. We need to devote resources to developing viable alternatives to accepted orthodoxies, particularly in the field of economics. This is a particularly good candidate for inter-agency work, because the issues are so complex, and no single NGO can claim a distinctive competence in all of them. The UK NGO group which is currently trying to harmonise research on structural adjustment might provide a basis for this sort of dialogue on wider alternatives. We certainly need in any case to develop stronger alliances among UK NGOs within this country, linking into broader international networks. Which other issues are suitable for developing such alliances? And how do we persuade UK NGOs to commit themselves to joint strategies?

d. We must bring our supporters with us as our international advocacy work develops and our agencies change to accommodate new styles of work. This is even more important if lifestyle changes are part of the strategy for change – otherwise our independent support base will gradually be eroded. The implications of UK charity law need to be considered carefully, as does the likely reaction of institutional donors. These factors may slow the pace of change in organisational development, since the choices involved are complex and require careful thought and analysis.

This is a formidable list, but not an insurmountable one. UK NGOs, as part of a wider movement for change, do have the ability and potential to 'make a difference', but not unless they adopt a much more critical, creative, and co-operative approach towards advocacy at the international level. Do we want to be the 'doormat' or the 'boot'? The choice is up to us.

## Note

This is a revised version of a paper originally presented to the NGO Study Group of the Development Studies Association (DSA). The author would like to thank the participants at that meeting for their comments, and also acknowledge the contributions of other colleagues in Save the Children, and of David Bryer, John Clark, and Paul Spray. The opinions expressed in the paper are, however, the author's own and do not necessarily reflect the views of any of the above, or of Save the Children.

## References

Clark, J. (1991) *Democratizing Development: The Role of Voluntary Organizations*, London: Earthscan.

Clark, J. (1992) 'Policy influence, lobbying and advocacy', in Edwards and Hulme (eds) 1992.

Dolan, C. (1992) 'British development NGOs and advocacy in the 1990s', in Edwards and Hulme (eds.) 1992.

Edwards, M. (1991) 'Strengthening Government Capacity for National Development and International Negotiation: the work of SCF in Mozambique', paper presented to the DSA annual conference, Swansea.

Edwards, M. (1993) 'International NGOs and Southern Governments in the New World Order: Lessons of Experience at the Programme Level', paper presented to the INTRAC Workshop on 'Governance, Democracy and Conditionality: What Role for NGOs?', Amersfoort, Netherlands.

Edwards, M. and D. Hulme (eds.) (1992) *Making a Difference: NGOs and Development in a Changing World*, London: Earthscan.

Korten, D. (1980) 'Community organization and rural development: a learning process approach', *Public Administration Review* 40, pp. 480–510.

Oxfam (UK and Ireland) (1992) 'Lobbying Methodology', Briefing Paper, Oxford: Oxfam (UK/I).

Spray, P. (1992) 'Advocacy in the North', mimeo, London: Christian Aid.

*This paper was first published in* Development in Practice *(3/3: 163–75) in 1993.*

# The effectiveness of NGO campaigning: lessons from practice

## Jennifer Chapman and Thomas Fisher

Development NGOs are devoting more and more time and energy to policy-influence work, yet there has been no corresponding increase in learning about effectiveness.

Until recently, lessons from even the best-known and longest-running campaigns have not been available. The increasing focus on campaigning and advocacy work applies not only to Northern NGOs, but also to those in the South. There are various reasons for this trend, not least changing South–North dynamics. There is, for example:

- growing recognition that, in many cases, Southern NGOs are better placed to carry out project work on the ground, leading operational Northern organisations to look for new roles;
- growing recognition among all NGOs that project work will have limited effects without changes in the structures that cause poverty;
- increasing links between ideas of development and human rights;
- on-going desire for public profile; and
- increasing calls by Southern organisations for Northern NGOs to do more campaign and policy work.

Concurrently, the arenas where NGOs are recognised as having an acceptable policy voice are increasing to encompass governments North and South, multilateral organisations, and the private sector. Frequently, issues are debated in all these different arenas at the same time, and by a growing diversity of actors. With both growing engagement in campaign and policy work, and increasingly complex policy arenas, many NGOs are concerned to gain a better understanding of policy processes and how to intervene in them effectively. They are asking questions about:

- *effectiveness*: how can NGOs effectively campaign in policy arenas?

- *impact*: what difference does such campaigning make, especially for those on whose behalf NGOs seek to campaign?
- *relevance*: is the campaigning relevant to the poor?
- *assessment*: how can NGOs assess whether this work is effective and making an impact?

The research project on which this paper is based set out to examine these issues through studying and comparing two case studies of long-running campaigns: the promotion of breastfeeding in Ghana and the campaign against the use of child labour in the carpet industry in India. The emphasis on looking at what international campaigns meant for people on the ground led to both case studies being based in the South. Both are campaigns that have met with considerable success, allowing the authors to analyse both their development from their early beginnings to significant change in practice, and the factors that contributed to their success. Both focus on corporate or industrial activity, since industry is an increasingly important target of NGO campaigns, and taken together cover influence on many different levels of the private sector: large transnational corporations, medium-size importers, nationally owned exporters, and the micro-scale, represented by individual loom-owners and market-women. These are all part of the chain of production and make the campaigning work indicative of a wide range of industrial activity. The case studies also showed the influence that NGOs may have in other arenas, for example on international bodies or on governments.

The research was undertaken during 1997–98 in collaboration with NGOs in India and Ghana. All research partners were intimately involved in one of the campaigns, which allowed access to files, activists, and beneficiaries. Semi-structured interviews were carried out with diverse stakeholders, including those directly affected, activists, industry, government, and international representatives. Interviews were supplemented by secondary sources such as newspaper clippings and documentary evidence. Workshops in both countries allowed opportunity for feedback and cross-checking or triangulation.

This paper introduces the two case studies, analyses them, and then presents the overall insights that arose from the research project.

## The promotion of breastfeeding in Ghana

The babymilk campaign is a long-established international campaign with significant direction given by Northern NGOs campaigning against large Northern corporations. Research in Ghana was carried out in collaboration with the Ghanaian Infant Nutrition Action Network (GINAN), a national organisation which is a member of both the Infant Baby Food Action Network (IBFAN) and the World Alliance on Breastfeeding Action (WABA).

Coordinated work on the issue of breastfeeding in Ghana began in 1987, after a Ghanaian doctor noticed the negative results of a donation of free samples of infant formula to health clinics. He formed GINAN and pressed the government to take action. Work on the control of marketing of breastmilk substitutes initially progressed fairly quickly, with a code committee functioning within a year and a Ghanaian code drafted by 1989 (although this is still waiting to become law, owing to bureaucratic delays). GINAN has also been monitoring the marketing of breastmilk substitutes in Ghana, using the international code as the benchmark.

The promotion of breastfeeding was given attention next: health workers were trained, and Ghana became involved in UNICEF's Baby Friendly Hospital Initiative, and in the celebration of World Breastfeeding Week started by WABA. More recently, work has gone into supporting nursing mothers through training women from the community as breastfeeding counsellors. These counsellors are then encouraged to support other women by setting up mother-to-mother support groups, or working through already active women's groups. GINAN have also trained a group of market-women, as they are the major distributors of infant formula in Ghana. Not only have many trained market-women stopped selling infant formula, they also advise women visiting the market on the benefits of breastfeeding.

The work on promoting and protecting breastfeeding continues to evolve and develop, with activists facing new challenges (Chapman 1999). Nevertheless, the campaign has achieved considerable impact at many different levels: the Ministry of Health and many health workers are now aware of the issue, and breastfeeding is included in the plan of action for health; a draft bill on the marketing of substitutes is awaiting passage through Parliament; current marketing practices are being monitored and violations reported internationally; and there are approximately 40 mother-to-mother support groups. These factors have led to exclusive breastfeeding rates increasing from 8 per cent at four months in 1996 to 18 per cent at six months in 1998.

Most importantly, although direct causal links are hard to establish, and many other factors have played a part, infant mortality has fallen from 82 deaths/1000 live births in 1978 to 66 deaths/1000 live births in 1993 (Government of Ghana 1993). Diarrhoea among children under two years of age has also dropped from 36 per cent in 1988 to 22 per cent in 1993 (*Daily Graphic*, 15 December 1997).

Despite the impressive achievements, there is still a long way to go. Many Ghanaian mothers still give their infants inappropriate foods, and the Ghanaian code is not yet law.

## The campaign against the use of child labour in the carpet industry in India

Research in India was carried out in collaboration with the South Asian Coalition on Child Servitude (SACCS) and the Centre for Rural Education and Development Action (CREDA).

The campaign against the use of child labour in the carpet industry in India (primarily in the State of Uttar Pradesh) was strongly influenced from the outset by Indian NGOs and was targeted at a local industry, although Northern NGOs, consumers, and importers played critical roles, because the industry is a major exporter.

The campaign within India had its roots in work on the issue of bonded labour, from which a focus on bonded carpet-children developed. This narrow focus was instrumental in getting international media attention. The campaign later widened out to include all children working illegally in the carpet industry, and then to a call for universal primary education.

The campaign used many different strategies. It started in 1983 with raids to free bonded children, which still continue. Around 1990, a consumer campaign, promoted by SACCS and German NGOs, was started in Germany, one of two main destinations for Indian carpets. This sought to educate consumers about the plight of children used in the production of hand-knotted carpets. At the same time, the Harkin Bill was pending in the USA, threatening to legislate against the import of goods made with child labour. These two pressures prompted talk of a labelling system. Initially this was discussed between the government-promoted Carpet Export Promotion Council (CEPC), NGOs, and the industry. However, the CEPC and industry representatives from the larger companies ultimately dropped out. The talks nevertheless led to the formation of the Rugmark labelling scheme in 1994, whereby looms are subject to surprise inspections, and a guarantee is given that a particular carpet is made without the use of illegal child labour. The Rugmark labelling scheme was followed soon after by various other (rival) labelling schemes.

Simultaneously, locally based NGOs which were working on social welfare and education in the carpet-weaving area also started to focus on the issue of child labour in the carpet industry. Work at the grass-roots included mobilising communities against child labour and empowering them to demand schools. One strategy used by CREDA is to train volunteers within villages who then serve three purposes:

- checking who replaces children removed from the looms;
- keeping a village-wide vigil to prevent children entering the labour market; and
- creating village-level Child Labour Vigilance Committees, 200 of which now take responsibility for primary-school enrolment, watching out for agents seeking to recruit child labour, and liaison with the district administration on the issue.

Since 1983, a great deal has been achieved. NGOs have worked with the judiciary and government officials to enforce existing laws; they have been able to threaten export markets sufficiently to bring about some changes in industry without actually implementing a boycott; they established the labelling scheme (Rugmark) as a constructive outcome for the consumer campaign; and they have also had a significant impact at the grassroots and on the emergence of civil society. Above all, there is some evidence of a reduction in child labour in the industries and areas targeted, although it is debatable whether there has been a reduction in the level of child labour overall. The work, however, is nowhere near finished. There has been a backlash from sections of the industry: many looms have been relocated away from mobilised villages or inspection; others have nominally become 'owned' by the weaver, allowing the family's children to work legally.

This campaign has helped to move forward the debate on child labour as a whole. It has fed into work on carpet-children in other countries and work on other industries in India, such as the production of firecrackers and footballs. It has also contributed to the Indian campaign for universal primary education.

## Analysis

### The nature of a campaign

The case studies demonstrate that the nature of campaigns is not straightforward. A campaign may have been running for many years and have unclear origins, having grown out of work on other issues, other campaigns, people's personal commitment and experience, or disasters and opportunities. It may evolve to focus on other issues, lead into new campaigns on related issues, alter its demands, grow, narrow, or widen at different times.

Campaigns can work at the international, national, and grassroots levels, within each of which they may be targeted at different actors. Work at different levels may be carried out by different organisations working independently of each other, whose approaches may sometimes clash, with gains at one level working against progress at others. In other campaigns, and at other times, work at different levels comes together to produce an effect greater than the sum of the parts.

Active groups may continually move into and out of the campaign. Some organisations will resonate with the Zeitgeist and take off and grow; later the same ones may decline or split, leading to a multiplicity of new actors, with different approaches and ideas. Institutions may retain the same name but change their nature or their approach, or they may lose key individuals who leave to establish new institutions, possibly working on related issues.

Most campaigns are based on an oral history which contains a range of multiple and conflicting perspectives. An effective campaign is based on stories and the extent to which these are accepted by different parties. Heroes or heroines are created, whose actions and exploits become mythologised, and so serve to motivate supporters.

Thus, an essential characteristic of campaigns is their fluidity, though this dynamism creates difficulties in assessing and managing them. Campaigns cannot be understood as a linear, mechanistic, or logical sequence. Neither can they be grasped at one time in their entirety. Nevertheless, insights can be gained by looking at campaigns from a variety of perspectives.

## What makes a campaign effective?

Reviewing the way in which the campaigns developed over time, and the different levels and arenas in which they were engaged, we can form a better understanding of the factors that have contributed to their effectiveness.

In campaigning against industry, NGOs can use the threat of disrupting markets as a powerful weapon. A consumer campaign featured in both case studies. The Indian carpet industry was particularly vulnerable to such action, being a prominent exporter of a luxury good with a limited main market and a small group of exporters and importers. The consumer campaign was coupled with the threat of a boycott and international legislation, which effectively persuaded segments of the carpet industry to enter into dialogue with the NGOs. In Ghana, the boycott was a feature of the international campaign, rather than being directly tied to the national one.

However, though both campaigns were selected because of their focus on corporate practices, mapping them showed that the focus had not always been on industry. In the Indian case, the campaign's focus shifted considerably over the years, yet fundamentally it remained the same campaign with mainly the same actors. At times, its focus narrowed to achieve a clear campaign message; at others it widened to reflect the real complexity of the issue. Similarly, the campaign on breastfeeding started with a narrow focus on the marketing of breast-milk substitutes, but later widened to include many issues related to infant feeding, the promotion of breastfeeding, and supporting mothers within the community. Thus, many of the lessons which emerged apply also to policy change and effectiveness on a wide range of issues.

Figure 1 shows how two organisations involved in the campaign against child labour in India changed their focus during its course. Here, the international campaign really took off when activists within India started to focus narrowly on bonded child labour in the carpet industry. However, this led to some inappropriate responses on the ground, such as schools reserved exclusively for ex-weavers (who are nearly all boys).

## The timeline

The effectiveness of NGOs in influencing policy is rarely dependent on a single event or campaign. Instead, there is a cumulative effect of campaigning over time which may lead to precipitative moments which have a major impact in terms of change in policy and practice.

As already described, campaigns are not linear and do not have defined beginnings and ends. Nevertheless, a linear model can be useful in drawing out the different stages of their evolution, though it is stressed that this is only a partial model. This can be conceptualised in the timeline shown in Figure 2. The line starts at the point where the issue is put on the agenda and reaches a plateau at the time of real change in practice. This is a process, so each stage is unlikely to be completed before the next begins. As a result, the role of NGOs adapts, with more possibilities and avenues opening up as the issue emerges, but few likely to be discarded. Likewise, while the diagram portrays progress towards the goal as a smooth, upward path, real life is not so

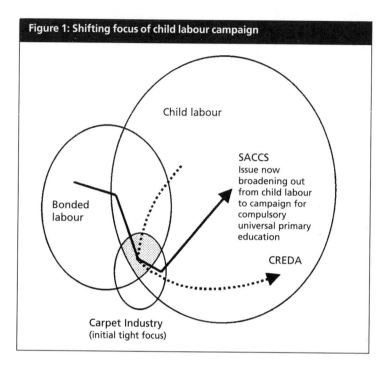

**Figure 1: Shifting focus of child labour campaign**

Child labour

SACCS
Issue now broadening out from child labour to campaign for compulsory universal primary education

CREDA

Bonded labour

Carpet Industry
(initial tight focus)

simple: progress will go faster at some times than at others, and may stall or even reverse. It is also likely that the campaign is at different stages of the timeline at different levels (for example, international and national) and in different locations.

This framework focuses attention on the long timescale needed to achieve real change. Understanding where the campaign is in terms of how the issue itself is developing can also help in planning which types of action are most useful when, and what sort of success is realistic in the short term.

### Concurrent work is needed at different levels and in different arenas

The case studies were selected as examples of campaigns against private-sector actors, in one case large corporations based in the North, in the other dispersed decentralised production in the South. What is clear from both is that it is not enough to target private-sector actors alone in order to bring about the change that the campaigns seek to achieve. Instead, work has to be conducted at many different levels and, within these, in different arenas in order to target other groups (UN bodies, officials, the judiciary, market-traders, health-workers, parents,

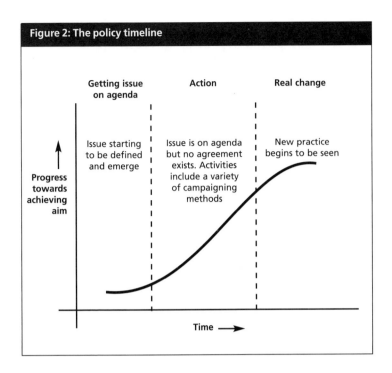

**Figure 2: The policy timeline**

Getting issue on agenda | Action | Real change

Progress towards achieving aim

Issue starting to be defined and emerge

Issue is on agenda but no agreement exists. Activities include a variety of campaigning methods

New practice begins to be seen

Time ⟶

villagers, etc.) This in turn may lead to a broadening of the campaign (for example, from child labour to education, from marketing of breastmilk substitutes to promotion of better health for babies).

The levels and the components that have proved most helpful in moving the campaigns forward are shown in Table 1. Working at all these levels is an immense challenge. In both case studies, the work started in only a few of the arenas, mainly at national or international level, expanding as the timeline progressed; it is not necessary to work in all of the arenas simultaneously. The challenge is to select the arenas which will be most effective in moving the timeline forward at different times, and to link up with appropriate organisations that can work effectively at other levels.

## Collaboration

It is clear that no one organisation can effectively campaign at all the different levels, which often require very different attitudes, strategies, and skills. To achieve this complex mix of work, different types of organisations are needed. In particular, a campaign may not exclusively resort to 'outsider' strategies, with NGOs campaigning against their targets, or 'insider' strategies, with NGOs working together with, for

| Table 1: What is helpful at different levels | | |
|---|---|---|
| **Level** | **Arenas** | **What is particularly helpful** |
| International | • international NGOs<br>• multilateral organisations<br>• national governments<br>• consuming public<br>• voting public<br>• industry | • existence of international codes, legislation, and conventions<br>• active international campaign<br>• consumer activism |
| National/ regional | • national government<br>• regional government<br>• judiciary<br>• public opinion<br>• national NGOs<br>• industry | • progressive legislation upholding rights<br>• legal pressure points (e.g. Supreme Court)<br>• history of social activism and NGO activity<br>• aware population<br>• labelling systems<br>• independent monitoring |
| Grassroots | • communities<br>• grassroots NGOs<br>• families<br>• individuals | • active civil-society organisations<br>• aware population<br>• active individuals |

example, government agencies to bring about change. Outsider or insider strategies may be more effective for moving the campaign forward when targeting different groups at different times. This makes it extremely difficult for individual NGOs to act effectively in all the different arenas at all times. NGOs in the two campaigns studied adopted a mix of outsider and insider strategies, although the overall strategy of each NGO remains characterised predominantly by one or the other.

Collaboration between different organisations can therefore help in moving the campaign forward. Even without formal collaboration, a variety of NGOs working with different strategies in different arenas is helpful. However, this can also lead to conflicts, and collaboration is particularly difficult among NGOs pursuing very different campaigning styles and strategies, something which can actually undermine the progress of the campaign. Likewise, as more players become involved, co-operation becomes more complex.

The study identified three structures for organising collaboration: the pyramid, the wheel, and the web. The pyramid has a co-ordinating secretariat with information flowing up and down to it; the wheel has one or more focal points with information flowing in and out, and also directly between members; in the web no focal points exist, and information flows to and from all organisations in roughly equal quantities. Table 2 shows the advantages and disadvantages of each.

## Legitimacy

All the actors in a campaign, both the NGOs and their targets, spend time and energy establishing and maintaining their legitimacy and contesting that of their opponents. This is often essential for the NGOs, in terms of campaigning successfully and raising adequate resources. For example, the three NGOs covered in the case studies have all derived significant benefits from being regarded as legitimate collaborators by some public bodies (for instance, government departments, the judiciary, professional associations) or international NGOs and donors, although not by others. At the same time, the pressure on organisations to show results can lead them to exaggerate their own importance. The desire of NGOs to establish their own legitimacy can thus create tensions in collaborating with other NGOs, especially if they are competing for funds.

Most NGOs draw on a variety of bases for legitimising their campaigning work. All are likely to be challenged by opponents of their position. The possible consequences of different bases are examined in Table 3.

## Individuals and mobilising the people

In both cases, individual champions played a key role in campaigning. Specific individuals were crucial to the process at both the national and grassroots levels. These were people with a flair for motivating others, who combined a social conscience with strategic vision on how to promote the issue. In both cases, they were particularly important at the national level in getting the issue on to the agenda and at the grassroots level in ensuring real change.

Thus, individual motivation is a key driving force, but the motives are varied. Some may make the issue their life's work or crusade out of strong moral conviction; others may be in it for a short period before moving on to another issue which appears more pressing.

| Table 2: | Advantages and disadvantages of different structures of collaboration | |
|---|---|---|
| Structure | Advantages | Disadvantages |
| Pyramid | • dynamic<br>• quick to act<br>• can speak with authority of many member organisations<br>• can mobilise a lot of people<br>• helps to get access to top level of policy | • members may feel loss of identity<br>• strengthening civil society at grassroots may not be given adequate attention<br>• danger of speaking 'for' clients rather than facilitating them to speak for themselves |
| Wheel | • more independence at the grassroots<br>• good for information exchange and sorting<br>• centres of specialisation in large networks can aid in information sorting | • can be harder to show a united front or common identity<br>• process of change is slow<br>• campaign may miss opportunities for sudden changes in practice |
| Web | • good for information exchange | • slow to take action<br>• possibly would need to change into a wheel or pyramid before effective campaigning action could be taken |

Campaigning organisations provide jobs and security for some, but rely also on much voluntary effort, and it can prove to be dangerous work. Many who are paid for their involvement could have greater financial reward elsewhere but can gain in other ways: there is an excitement in being part of a movement that is attacking the *status quo*, and there are opportunities for travel, profile, and status – and maybe a chance to make a real change. Some leaders become prominent national figures, gaining perhaps personal satisfaction, but also the opportunity for greater influence to achieve change for the better.

At later stages of the campaign, however, a few individuals alone are not sufficient. While in some cases a campaigning NGO itself may

## Table 3: Possible consequences of different bases for legitimacy

| Legitimisation | Possible consequences |
|---|---|
| **Practice to policy:** seeking to influence policy by pointing to practical experience on the ground. | • complex message, difficult communication tool<br>• less open to dispute<br>• works well for grassroots NGOs<br>• can be challenged if NGOs claim to speak for people whom they have not genuinely consulted |
| **Values-based:** where NGOs promote a particular value which is widely recognised within society and/or enshrined in international law. | • extremely powerful when combined with pictures and stories and when taps into innate values many people feel<br>• powerful when values are enshrined in international conventions etc.<br>• in countries where values are not universally held, can lead to accusations of selecting values to ensure funds from overseas, especially in professional rather than voluntary organisations<br>• can be challenged for just talking not doing<br>• can be accused of speaking 'for' beneficiaries rather than enabling them to express their own views |
| **Knowledge and research:** acting as an expert on a particular issue. | • works well when there is consensus on topic or you have credible allies<br>• particularly useful and relevant for more technically based policy issues<br>• can be open to challenge by views based on alternative research<br>• open to question of who funds/sponsors research or organisation |
| **Through grassroots and other civil-society organisations:** legitimise by adhering to and strengthening democratic principles and practice. | • works well at grassroots<br>• necessary for civil-society aims<br>• long-term engagement required<br>• may mean campaigning opportunities missed<br>• possibly weak impact at higher policy levels |
| **Alliances and networks:** legitimacy gained from other members of network who gain legitimacy from one of above. | • quickly spreads work to a wide audience<br>• gives strength of numbers<br>• disputes over who 'owns' work<br>• successful alliances often require significant management |

be an extension of its leader, providing him or her with the necessary organisational support, the need to mobilise people into a movement around the campaign issue is critical to achieving greater impact at the national and grassroots level. This was particularly apparent in India, which has a long tradition of social movements, where the NGOs have drawn together networks of hundreds of NGOs and activists, which also allows them to organise marches, mass meetings, and popular campaigns. A common value base has been essential for promoting such movements. The Ghanaian case has been less successful in this regard, partly because of the nature of the campaign issue, as well as a weaker tradition of social movements.

A key issue for such campaigning, given the long time-scale for achieving real change, is how to continue to mobilise people for that length of time. Giving them an active role, recognising their contributions, developing practical tools to allow concrete changes, and recognising successes along the way are all important for this.

### Narrow focus

There is growing concern that although NGOs are successfully addressing single issues, they find it harder to address wider ones. This study shows how a narrow focus can be extremely effective in getting an issue formulated and ensuring concrete progress. Such a focus need not hinder the issue widening out at a later stage, for example from marketing of breastmilk substitutes to promotion of better health for babies, when something more than campaigning and advocacy may be required. The question therefore becomes at what point on the campaign's timeline, and at what level, a narrow focus can be effectively used, and at what point the campaign needs to be broadened to tackle wider issues and causes (see Table 4).

### Role of government and judiciary

The case studies show the important role of the State, national law, and international conventions, and highlight the need for market regulations to protect the poor from exploitation. It is crucial that at some point government and the law are involved, in order to:

- get legal frameworks in place, often providing an essential lever for campaigners;
- ensure the law is implemented, although in practice it is often campaigning NGOs that pressurise the government and judiciary to implement the law, occasionally themselves

**Table 4: Advantages and disadvantages of focused approach**

| Advantages | Disadvantages |
|---|---|
| • moves national and international campaign forwards | • can oversimplify and distract from wider problem, or deeper causes |
| • works as communication tool | • can target response too narrowly |
| • makes people distant from situation feel they can do something | • can make involvement of grassroots harder |
| • helps to identify a target | • can undermine civil society in nascent democracies |

demonstrating that it is possible (for example, by conducting raids to free bonded labourers);

- carry out large programmes for which NGOs cannot raise the necessary resources;
- change practice and attitudes in government-run institutions;
- provide a level playing field for all companies; and
- give permanency: laws do not collapse in the way that industry codes of conduct sometimes do.

It is not necessary that every actor is an insider with the government, but some co-operation is needed if a government is to support the aims of the campaign. It is also helpful to recognise that some governments and corporations are actively seeking change; NGOs are only one set of players among many.

In Ghana, the NGOs played a vital catalytic role in introducing new legislation. In India, the NGOs did not have such a significant impact in introducing new laws (which already existed) or policies, although some such changes have occurred, but they have had a great impact in influencing the implementation and interpretation of such policies.

### International context

In both case studies, collaboration between Northern NGOs and Southern NGOs has been instrumental in moving the campaigns forward. Being a member of IBFAN and WABA has helped to legitimise the work of GINAN, as well as providing channels for sharing and disseminating the information needed. The work in Ghana has also benefited greatly from experience and knowledge gained in similar campaigns in other countries. In India, the national NGOs have benefited from international support, which has facilitated access to international platforms, helped to apply consumer pressure, and provided funds for projects to offer alternatives to the carpet-children.

International conventions have also been useful tools, both for national NGOs and UN agencies, to press for change within the countries. In Ghana, action got going quickly, due to the work that had already been conducted internationally; it was important not only that an international code existed, but also that other countries had already taken positive action on the issue. The international media can also play a big role, with national governments and industry sometimes paying more attention to international coverage than to reports in national newspapers.

However, both case studies also demonstrate the limited role that Northern NGOs can play in bringing about real change in Southern countries. In spite of extensive international campaigning on breast-milk substitutes, nothing happened in Ghana – a prominent African state – until a Ghanaian doctor, who knew nothing about the inter-national campaign, took up the issue of his own accord. Campaigning on child labour in India has been led by Indian NGOs, who persuaded (reluctant) German NGOs to launch a consumer campaign in Germany.

Though Northern NGOs have often provided critical support, they have not been able to engage in mobilising movements and promoting civil society at the grassroots. Particularly in controversial campaigns, such as child labour in the carpet industry, it has been critical to respect national sensitivities. For example, one international backer had to withdraw from a prominent role in the Rugmark labelling scheme when it came under fire for being internationally led.

### Campaigns in context

In the two case studies, policy change and advocacy on their own were not enough to bring about real change at the grassroots. For this, significant additional work was needed.

### Implementation and monitoring

Achieving policy change is not the end; organisations such as government or corporations can renege on or ignore policies. Both case studies show the importance of work to ensure that policies and laws are implemented. In Ghana, the international code needs to be constantly monitored, and violations publicised, to ensure that it is abided by. The Indian case study shows how NGOs can play an important role in pushing the judiciary to enforce existing laws and, where these are insufficient, to set up their own initiatives, such as the Rugmark labelling scheme, that build in a monitoring system.

## Tools

Campaigning on an issue is not enough if effective tools for making a change are not promoted as well. In the past, legislation or conventions were often seen as the ultimate aim of such work. Now, other tools are also being developed. These include codes of conduct, labelling, and social auditing. These are seen to be appropriate when either national legislation or international conventions do not exist, or are too weak, too broad, or unspecific, or when there is a problem with implementing them through the legal system or government.

However, each tool may also become a cause of conflict, with disagreements on which types should be used and how they should be administered. Opponents may try to use similar tools for their own ends, thus confusing the public. For example, in India there are now competing labelling schemes for carpets, and the labels do not have common standards.

## Work at the grassroots

A lot can be achieved in terms of policy change and awareness raising without grassroots involvement; however, such involvement is essential to ensure real and sustained change. In India, without work at the grassroots, the children would have been moved from the carpet industry into other work. In Ghana, without the grassroots work, mothers are likely to continue giving their babies other inappropriate foods, even if breastmilk substitutes were entirely unavailable.

The case studies thus highlight the essential links between policy and project work. International development NGOs first took up advocacy work which drew upon their practical experience on the ground ('practice-to-policy'). This developed into a trend of moving resources from development projects into advocacy, although recently this trend has partly gone into reverse, with NGOs increasingly identifying the need to inform macro-level policy proposals with concrete micro-experiences. The findings of this research close this loop, confirming not only the close links between advocacy and project work, but also the need for long-term work at the grassroots even after policy changes have been achieved; this could be termed policy-to-practice. Campaigning or advocacy work is very valuable, but its effect in isolation is limited.

The role of people at the grassroots is not straightforward; in some cases they are seen just as recipients. Both cases provide examples of where the grassroots have been included not to find out what they think, but to sell them a message. Thus, the flow of information to the grassroots is often one-way. Mothers are told the 'correct' way to feed their babies; information about the problems they encounter in carrying out the instructions may not be passed in the other direction. In India, villagers are encouraged to value education and to believe that children should not work. However, being a recipient of new ideas does not mean these cannot be valued; once they had assimilated the new ideas, many parents and children became activists in their own right.

The challenge comes when moving towards engagement and empowerment at the grassroots which will develop civil society in a way that also develops its potential influence on many other issues. Work at this level, to change attitudes and behaviour and to build capacity and skills, needs a lot of trust and requires non-hierarchical organisations with close personal contact. These cannot be built quickly. Conversely, change at the grassroots is speeded up and facilitated by work happening at the other levels.

Problems at the grassroots tend to be very complex, often with roots in poverty and isolation; they cannot be solved quickly or with a narrow focus, which can distract from the wider problem and target responses too narrowly (see Table 4). More seriously, a narrow focus can mean that grassroots voices are ignored in the campaign in the desire to move it forward. If the grassroots do not have a sense of ownership in the solutions advocated, they are less likely to co-operate and more likely, to take the India example, to move their child into another industry once one employment opportunity is shut off.

The limitations of the focused approach become particularly apparent when looking at the factors that influence how a child spends its time, or how a mother chooses to feed her baby. The factors that are susceptible to international pressure are only a very small part of the picture but, understandably, tend to be the ones that receive most attention by international NGOs. Many of the factors that influence the child's or the mother's behaviour are only susceptible to pressure or change at the community or grassroots level (Chapman 1999; Chapman and Fisher 1999). However, the case studies show that for changing other factors, national-level work can be quite effective without grassroots involvement at all.

# Conclusion

This paper has drawn out lessons about campaigns and about their limitations. It shows how effective campaigns happen at many different levels and may take a long time, showing a potential clash with the short-term campaign strategies of many Northern NGOs. It points out how no one organisation can be active at all the levels, which makes collaboration vital; yet, paradoxically, a few key individuals can make a real difference. It shows that concerns over the narrow focus of many campaigns are justified; yet such a narrow focus can be effective in getting an issue formulated and need not necessarily militate against the campaign widening out at a later stage. It recognises that in the two case studies considerable success has been achieved, but that this was not gained by campaigning alone. Changes in policy are not enough to ensure implementation and change at the grassroots; this requires additional activity such as monitoring, the use of appropriate tools, and also long-term project work.

---

## Acknowledgements

This paper is based on research carried out during 1997–98 for the New Economics Foundation, with funding from the UK Department for International Development. The views and opinions expressed are those of the authors alone.

The authors acknowledge the help and support of Subodh Boddisitwa, Shamshad Khan, Charles Sagoe-Moses, and Tina Wallace throughout the research which formed the basis for the paper.

## References

Chapman, Jennifer (1999) 'The Response of Civil Society in Ghana to the Globalisation of the Marketing of Breastmilk Substitutes', paper presented at the International Round-table on 'Responses to Globalisation: Rethinking Equity and Health' Geneva, Switzerland. Available at: http://www.sidint.org/new/globalization/papers/chapman.pdf/

Chapman, Jennifer and Thomas Fisher (1999) 'Effective NGO Campaigning: A New Economics Foundation Briefing', London: New Economics Foundation.

Chapman, Jennifer and Thomas Fisher (2000) 'The Thoughtful Activist: A Toolkit for Enhancing NGO Campaigning and Advocacy', draft to be posted on the New Economics Foundation website (http://www.neweconomics.org/)

Daily Graphic (1997) 'GINAN deserves support', 15 December 1997.

Government of Ghana (1993) 'Ghana Demographic Health Survey Report of 1993', Accra: Government of Ghana.

This paper was first published in Development in Practice (10/2: 151–65) in 2000.

# Heroism and ambiguity:
## NGO advocacy in international policy

## Paul Nelson

### Heroism and ambiguity

NGO policy activism has been widely portrayed in a heroic light. Campaigns to abolish anti-personnel landmines, restrict child labour, enforce marketing codes for infant formula, protect dolphins and whales, and extend political and civil rights have been covered favourably in the media, studied by a handful of political scientists, and even honoured as Nobel Peace laureates.

These campaigns have mobilised moral outrage into political action on topics where the targets are clear, the cause obviously just, and the abuses graphic. Yet the policy victories of NGOs in these areas (like those of States) are often tenuous and difficult to assess in practice, and securing their implementation generally requires continued political pressure.

Because NGO alliances rely on public participation and the mobilisation of values-based action, they need clearly identified opponents and results in order to motivate public action. But campaigns targeting the World Bank, especially on matters of economic policy, often encounter ambiguity and uncertainty. The Bank affirms that it shares NGOs' agenda of poverty reduction, sustainable development, empowerment, and partnership. Have NGOs made a difference to the Bank's economic policy? How can they know?

In 1997 I evaluated a campaign against orthodox structural adjustment policy, carried out between 1994 and 1996 by the London-based development NGO Christian Aid. The campaign, and the evaluation, offer a chance to reflect on these questions and on other issues of self-governance that face NGOs as they become more prominent political actors.[1] NGO advocates have little record of critically assessing their own impact. Evaluating impact is difficult, and the results are usually ambiguous and debatable, but the process is essential to NGOs' effectiveness and credibility. This essay suggests an approach.

NGO advocacy with the World Bank and the International Monetary Fund (IMF) is, I believe, ethically essential, substantively important, and politically relevant to the relationship between the international financial institutions (IFIs) and national policy. But there is a danger that NGO advocates and friendly observers could be seduced by the heroic image that they and others have created. I am not arguing that the heroic image needs to be erased, but that NGOs need to adjust to their new prominence and to the political–economic environment in which they operate. This involves adopting a second generation of advocacy strategies, one that places greater emphasis on implementation of policy, on institutional changes at the IFIs, and on national-level strategies.

This paper is organised as follows. The second section examines NGO campaigns and the sources of ambiguity in their evaluation, and introduces a campaign entitled 'Who Runs the World?' (WRTW). The third section focuses on the process of NGO advocacy, drawing lessons from some recent criticism, and from WRTW. The final section returns to the question of impact and uncertainty, and suggests an approach to ongoing NGO evaluation.

A note on the IMF: WRTW targeted the IMF as well as the World Bank, but contact and results at the IMF were slender. Information and opinion from the IMF were hard to obtain: an IMF public-affairs officer observed that the Fund is more centralised than the Bank, and that, for the public, 'all roads lead to me'. This officer himself declined to speak on the record about the campaign. Advocacy with the IMF is an important and difficult effort for NGOs, and this article will not attempt to add to excellent papers by Scholte (1998) and Polak (1998) of the Center of Concern.

## Campaigns on economic policy

NGOs have campaigned to influence the World Bank on issues including dam construction, indigenous people's rights, energy policy, micro-credit lending, structural adjustment, human rights, popular participation, gender, and corruption.

Development NGOs have become regular participants in discussions of popular participation and social-sector projects, areas in which they are considered to have special expertise or delivery capacity that makes it necessary to listen to their concerns. Their substantial and growing efforts to influence the Bank are evaluated less fully and frequently than other NGO activities. Foundations and interested observers have however produced some reviews (Nelson 1995; Fox and Brown 1998; Sogge 1996).

The campaigns of environmental NGOs have had the most visible impact. Alliances and networks originating in struggles to modify or stop particular dam and highway projects have pressed for reforms in sector policies, information disclosure, environmental assessment procedures and accountability mechanisms. NGOs have had particular difficulty in influencing the World Bank on the subject of macro-economic policy. Fifteen years of structural adjustment lending has produced strong dissent from NGOs, both North and South, but the principal impact of their criticism at the Bank has been to help to motivate increased investment in compensatory Social Investment Funds.

NGOs' reform agendas have, in general, succeeded when the agenda or strategy calls for the World Bank to do more – to expand, not curtail, the range of its influence. The Bank has responded to criticism on environmental and social issues by accepting new roles in national environmental planning, project planning, managing the Global Environment Facility, financing pollution abatement, providing training and technical assistance, supporting micro-finance lending, poverty assessments, and post-conflict rehabilitation.

The critique of adjustment lending has usually called for a reduction in the World Bank's role (Nelson 1996). But the critique's most tangible success resulted from NGO support for UNICEF's call for social safety-net programmes to accompany adjustment loans. More fundamental criticism of privatisation, export promotion, and the political impact of the adjustment conditions may have helped to persuade Bank staff to promote wider national 'ownership' of adjustment plans. But the critique has not persuaded any major actor to promote heterodox alternative strategies, and the crisis in Southeast Asia does not appear significantly to have weakened the official consensus on neo-liberal economic strategies.

Economic structural adjustment is an inherently difficult policy area for NGOs to influence. Most economists believe that the best evidence of its impact comes from complex economic models that are outside the expertise of NGO advocates. NGO protests are often viewed as exactly the kind of political pressure that World Bank intervention is meant to correct: the ability of interest groups to sustain their claim to entitlements from government.

## 'Who Runs the World?'

Christian Aid's two-year campaign aimed to promote greater accountability and change the nature of structural adjustment policies (SAPs) promoted by the World Bank and IMF, particularly in the Philippines, Jamaica, and Zimbabwe. The campaign coincided roughly with the World Bank's 50th anniversary, and with the appointment of James Wolfensohn as President. Its principal objectives were as follows:

1. to get SAPs changed in some countries and ... influence the design of new SAPs;
2. to make the World Bank and IMF more open and accountable to governments, taxpayers, and the poor;
3. to show that there are people-friendly alternatives to SAPs (Christian Aid 1994).

Many of the campaign's initiatives gained the attention of decision-makers in government or the IFIs. It supported the position of key internal reformers, stimulated the media to pay attention to adjustment and debt issues, mobilised a segment of British public opinion, encouraged parliamentary inquiry and government reporting of its policies and votes in the Bank and the IMF, facilitated other NGO initiatives, and helped NGO and church partners in Jamaica, the Philippines, and Zimbabwe to gain increased access to World Bank officials.

## Ambiguity

But the campaign's actual influence on World Bank policy and practice is obscured by several sources of uncertainty. The organisation is far from static, and has undergone a major change (in style, at least) since James Wolfensohn became President in June 1995. The relatively slow process of developing and financing new projects creates a 'pipeline' of projects in various stages of development, unequally influenced by new policies (Fox and Brown 1998). Interrelations among the Bank, governments, and the IMF further complicate the picture, and Bank staff members have no incentive to acknowledge that confrontational strategies are effective, even if in fact they are.

Most development NGOs encounter another sort of ambiguity as well: even fierce critics of the World Bank support at least the principle of multilateral development finance, and often the continued funding of the Bank itself. Development NGOs may be more affected in this regard than advocates focused on human rights or environmental issues, whose policy agendas are less likely to include support for multilateral lending.

The large number and loose co-ordination of NGO initiatives further complicates the task of distinguishing effects of various initiatives. NGO advocates are not always in agreement or closely co-ordinated, and there is no certain way to differentiate their various effects. Consider the difficulty in assigning 'credit' for institutional and policy changes made by the Bank in Jamaica, including an NGO liaison role in the Bank mission, the creation of the Public Information Centre (PIC), and NGO representation on the board of the Bank-financed Social Investment Fund (SIF). Participants in WRTW note these changes as results of their efforts, but the first two are also tied to larger trends in the Bank's reorganisation, and the Jamaican regional PIC was initiated by an innovative World Bank Resident Representative.

Monitoring the *process* of NGO advocacy is one partial solution to this problem of uncertainty. This is the focus of the third section of this article.

## Process: what can NGOs learn from recent criticism?

Most criticism of NGO advocacy has been aimed at NGOs based in industrial countries, which co-ordinate most network campaigning. The criticism raises the question of how campaigns balance five important sets of variables:

- *choice of political arenas*: balancing national and international advocacy strategies
- *self-governance*: balancing strategic leadership with broad participation
- *mass mobilisation*: balancing mass political strategies with insider approaches
- *strategy*: balancing confrontational and co-operative approaches
- *perspective*: balancing short-term campaign goals and long-term constituency building.

### Balancing national and international strategies

A coalition involving international NGOs and NGOs based in the World Bank's borrowing countries must choose and balance strategies that target national governments and international institutions. When NGOs choose strategies that use international organisations to gain influence over governments, they may contribute to shifting key policy decisions (and authority) into international arenas.

Jordan and van Tuijl (1997) outline several distinct types of inter-national campaigns, and distinguish the international, national, and local political arenas in which the actors operate. They show that some campaigns, particularly in politically volatile situations where local participants are at risk, suffer from inadequate communication, co-ordination, and acceptance of risk and responsibility by international NGO partners. Cleary (1995) argues that international NGOs favoured confrontational strategies in several instances in Indonesia, when local interests might have been better served by negotiation.

But these are relatively well co-ordinated campaigns based on environmental issues, and indigenous people's rights and human rights. In advocacy on economic policy, links have tended to be less tightly formed, and participants' lobbying strategies less tightly co-ordinated. Much of the NGO advocacy on adjustment in the international arena has addressed the issues globally or regionally, rather than at a national level. WRTW continued this approach, linking agendas only loosely with Southern partners. WRTW promoted its own agenda for policy change, but the ties between the campaign in the UK and Washington and NGO partners' national agendas were loose and flexible. Local partners defined their lobbying objectives, so much so that there is some inconsistency between the radical rethinking of adjustment called for in WRTW materials, and the more limited efforts for debt relief and changes in the administration of the SIF that were the substance of the lobby effort in Jamaica and the Philippines.

The international campaign, said one member of Christian Aid's staff, was 'partner-informed', not 'partner-directed'. In the Philippines, the Freedom from Debt Coalition focused on the IMF programme, arguing to government and the public that the country needs not IMF direction but a domestically rooted programme of 'fundamental reforms'. Jamaican partners noted three objectives: lobby the Government to recognise the 'social debt' and pursue debt forgiveness; persuade the World Bank and government to compensate 'losers' in the reform process; and press for expanded citizen involvement in decisions about spending and borrowing. These objectives overlap with Christian Aid's campaign goals, but criticism of the adjustment model itself does not feature in the partners' stated priorities.

## Internationalising economic policy

Do international NGO campaigns assign too much importance to the World Bank? Critics within the Bank and others charge that NGOs blame the Bank for social ills that actually result from bad government policy or global economic change. By doing so, it is charged, NGOs can delay the process of calling governments to account for inept, self-seeking, or corrupt practices.

This criticism was levelled at WRTW from its launch. A commentary in the *Financial Times* faulted the campaign's monograph 'Who Runs the World?' for ignoring African governments' responsibility for their countries' economic and social ills. The criticism is a difficult one for international NGOs based in the industrialised countries, who – with few direct routes to influence the governments that borrow from the World Bank – have seized on donor lending and aid policies as among the most effective approaches. The Bank's institutional self-confidence and influence also seem to have invited attack.

Heavy reliance on international solutions, particularly the Bank, has had an effect on the level at which key political battles are fought. By moving some authority over national policy decisions into the international arena, NGOs could actually reduce the significance of local participation by eroding the policy-setting power of borrowing governments. Some environmental safeguards that were proposed to restrain the World Bank's lending for environmentally questionable projects have also expanded the Bank's influence and justified an increasingly intrusive approach to lending and conditionality (Nelson 1996).

NGOs are only secondarily responsible for this internationalising trend: the increased external influence on national decision-making is a product of larger trends. But NGO advocates should carefully weigh any strategies that increase the leverage of international agencies. Aid donors impose demands for accountability on governments – demands that can reduce their effective accountability to their own citizens. Harrigan (1998) argues that IMF and World Bank influence has had this effect in Jamaica.

Liberalisation and privatisation may often be forced on populations where opposition is broad and unheeded. But adjustment plans are not generally any longer programmes foisted on unwilling governments. Substantial support for liberal reforms has grown in most governments, and much government resistance to the IFIs' macro-policy influence now amounts to delaying implementation of agreed-upon loan conditions.

NGO coalitions should give careful consideration to whether a strategic focus on the IFIs reduces the pressure for government accountability. An ongoing global dialogue between NGOs, governments, and the World Bank offers a possible approach to integrating the national and international dialogue. The Structural Adjustment Participatory Review Initiative (SAPRI) is an experiment with nationally based advocacy co-ordinated at the international level. Growing out of Washington-based negotiations with the Bank, SAPRI now involves governments, NGOs, and the Bank in nationally based discussions and investigations of adjustment policy.

The international effort is co-ordinated by a committee with NGO representation from every region. National reviews in the participating countries are planned and co-ordinated by joint committees involving NGO and government participants. Reviews have begun in Ghana and Hungary, and are planned in Uganda, Zimbabwe, the Philippines, Ecuador, and Bangladesh.

Advocacy with national institutions and by national interests is likely to become more important in promoting NGOs' agendas. Dialogue with responsible Bank staff in country operational departments is increasingly important, as the Bank expands its country offices' responsibilities, and implementation of hard-won policy changes often requires co-operation by the national authorities that implement projects.

## Balancing and integrating mass action and insider lobbying

NGOs, sometimes praised for opening decision-making processes to a flood of popular opinion and local knowledge, also employ strategies that rely more heavily on careful research and documentation, and direct lobbying by NGO staff. Often, advocacy combines strategies that rely on expertise with others that rest on representation. NGOs generally treat these as complementary, and sometimes this is so. But at other times they collide and conflict. Both occurred during WRTW.

Roe (1995) has criticised international NGO advocacy on environmental issues as a debating exercise between members of a 'New Managerial Class', in which NGO professionals debate with other members of the same global class, posted in the international financial institutions. The critique raises the concern that NGO lawyers, scientists, economists, and anthropologists based in the industrial capitals, with class origins and academic training similar to those of the World Bank's staff, can force policy-making processes that are open to their own participation, without assuring access for excluded communities. This charge merits a full review, but my purpose here is solely to touch on how WRTW balanced broad participation with élite lobbying. The campaign relied jointly on staff reporting and lobbying, public actions by Christian Aid's activist members in the UK and Ireland, and initiatives by Southern NGO partners.

Broad-based public advocacy was most effective when it targeted the British government. The grassroots lobby of Parliament won improvements in transparency and accountability, including greater disclosure of the British Executive Directors' work on the boards of the World Bank and IMF. Letters and postcards from constituents appeared to spark a level of interest from MPs that surprised some knowledgeable observers. Christian Aid supporters sent mass mailings of postcards to World Bank and government officials. The strategy benefited in one case from exquisite timing and a bit of luck. British Chancellor Kenneth Clark used a stack of postcards that he received just before a 1996 G-7 Summit to bolster the UK position in favour of IMF gold sales and generous multilateral debt-relief.

At their best, public and high-level approaches are mutually reinforcing. Sustained public pressure may help NGOs to secure access to ranking officials, and a successful report, press release, or public event that draws media attention can inspire further public confidence and action. Public pressure may lead to a point at which high-level negotiation is necessary to secure the political gains made possible by public actions, as in the debate over multilateral debt relief during 1996. Early in his presidency, Wolfensohn called for a study of the needs and options for multilateral debt relief that led, via tortuous negotiations, to the now-adopted HIPC initiative. When an internal initiative emerged within the World Bank, NGOs' principal task was no longer to persuade management to take the issue seriously, but to shape the initiative. Bank staff who had paid little attention to NGOs' concerns were suddenly open to NGO input on the details of the process.

Public pressure remained important, but shaping the details of the initiative called for a new level of knowledge and analytical skills. NGOs were prepared, despite their relative shortage of macro-economic expertise, by having developed and stated in advance their minimum standards for a multilateral debt-relief initiative.

Broad-based public strategies sometimes have unanticipated, positive effects. Before the World Bank/IMF 1995 Annual Meeting in Madrid, Christian Aid circulated a statement calling for changes in the IFIs' governance and their policies on adjustment and debt. The Declaration was adopted by church groups in Canada and the USA, and thousands of religious leaders had signed on before it was delivered in Madrid. The Declaration helped to energise a fledgling Religious Working Group on the World Bank/IMF in the USA.

Christian Aid's presence at official international meetings during the campaign – Annual Meetings of the Bank/IMF, Copenhagen Social Summit, G-7 Summits – appears to have yielded the campaign's greatest successes with the media. Two-person teams of Christian Aid staff, armed with a newly released report on a relevant topic, were among the most successful of the many NGO representatives present in interjecting alternative perspectives into financial and mainstream press coverage of the meetings. Outspoken NGOs attract media attention in such meetings, and particularly so in the British media when the UK Treasury was the leading government proponent of a new debt-relief proposal.

The reports produced for the campaign were timed for release at these summits, and were directed both to the media and to policy makers. They sought to present issues simply enough to motivate campaigners, but with enough sophistication to avoid demonising the IFIs. Within the Bank, however, the reports were generally viewed as lacking rigour, and treated as public-relations problems.

Media advertisements, too, illustrate the tension between public campaigning and insider influence. The campaign used advertisements to reach the British public, through national and local dailies; and to draw attention to the issues at the time of World Bank Annual Meetings in 1994, through advertisements placed in the *Financial Times*. The advertisements are the best example of the many meanings of 'influence' in the campaign. Some within the World Bank say the advertisements earned Christian Aid a reputation as a 'head-banger', and harmed its dialogue with the Bank, but others acknowledge that the advertisements brought a higher level of attention to the campaign. The advertisements also increased reporters' recognition of the issues and of the campaign.

### Balancing and integrating confrontational and co-operative strategies

NGOs have forced the Bank to learn to manage external criticism. Many within the World Bank acknowledge that NGOs' public criticism in the 1980s called the attention of governments and the Bank to serious and neglected issues. But now that NGOs have been admitted to the dialogue, some argue, the high-volume, public critique is at best background noise, at worst a distraction from serious dialogue. Exposure to criticism has raised the threshold of sensitivity: an open letter or public protest that might have attracted much attention at the Bank in 1985 may now be regarded as a routine matter.

Like many public agencies, the World Bank favours dialogue with 'constructive' critics. Balancing confrontational and co-operative approaches involves both co-ordination between different campaigns and initiatives (such as SAPRI and Women's Eyes on the World Bank), and strategic choices. Does confrontational campaigning compromise co-operative approaches, or strengthen them? Can a single organisation be effective and credible in both kinds of discussion? The experience of WRTW suggests that it can. But maintaining the balance requires careful attention, as demonstrated by Christian Aid's involvement in three more cooperative initiatives.

### NGO Working Group on the World Bank

In the early 1990s, Christian Aid was a member of the 26-member NGO Working Group on the World Bank (NGOWG). The NGOWG's meetings with Bank staff have been, since the early 1980s, a forum for its policy dialogue with development NGOs. Discussion is generally collegial and rests on the premise that the NGO and Bank representatives share common aims and need more open discussion to arrive at shared strategies. Some NGO activists have characterised the Working Group as unfocused and unrepresentative.

Christian Aid's representative played a leading role in re-energising the Working Group and encouraging its recent reorganisation, which aims to broaden Southern NGO involvement and facilitate Southern leadership.[2] The experience of the NGOWG suggests that co-operative strategies may be most effective when backed by broad NGO participation and linked to other, more confrontational, campaigns (Covey 1998).

### The Lesotho Highlands Water Project

Christian Aid has worked with the Highlands Church Action Group in Lesotho since 1992 to help to improve the social impact of a major hydro-electric and water-diversion scheme, funded in part by the World Bank. NGOs involved in a global campaign against major dam projects, and against the Bank's role in such projects, are also involved in advocacy.

Christian Aid won high praise from World Bank staff close to the project as a 'credible, professional, engaged critic of the project'. Bank staff implicitly criticise other NGOs whose arguments they characterise as part of a global anti-dam campaign, drawing criticisms from a checklist accumulated elsewhere. Critical campaigning (such as WRTW) may actually increase the effectiveness of such a dialogue. The World Bank's task manager noted that colleagues tended to give attention to measured, 'constructive' comments from Christian Aid, because they thought the NGO had been predisposed to attack the Bank (telephone interview with the author, December 1996).

Appreciation for the 'constructive' dialogue over social policy issues, however, did not prevent the World Bank from proceeding with finance for a new phase of the project, without ensuring that demands for compensation of resettled communities were satisfied.

### The politics of aid: a critical constituency

NGOs are among development aid's most consistent advocates, and, at times, aid's most trenchant critics. This position as a 'critical constituency' for aid is considered untenable by some in government and at least a few in the NGO world. One British official succinctly charges that 'the NGOs' message is: "Aid is terrible! And we want more of it!"' (interview with the author,

November 1996). The issue is a perennial one for NGOs, and, in a period of dwindling aid budgets, WRTW attracted particularly harsh criticism.

Three government and Bank officials told me similar versions of a rather dramatic morality tale of the good and bad NGOs. Oxfam GB and Christian Aid, the story went, held somewhat similar positions on the World Bank before 1994, but Oxfam appreciated the danger that confronted the Bank and particularly IDA (International Development Association), and perceived that NGO advocacy could potentially 'bring down the whole system' (interviews with the author, November 1996). Oxfam emphasised support for IDA as the framework for any criticisms, while Christian Aid launched a highly critical public campaign.

World Bank and British aid officials charged that critical campaigning plays into the hands of opponents of multilateral aid, including those in the US Congress. Officials asserted that criticising adjustment lending undermines efforts, including Christian Aid's own, to build a constituency for aid. (Conversely, one might argue that an NGO's support for aid spending, even when couched in a critique of aid practice, weakens the incentive for official donors to change policy or practice.)

Was WRTW ill-timed, given the perceived crisis of IDA concessional financing? It seems likely that both risks are real: criticism could strengthen opponents of development aid spending, and knowledge that an NGO will ultimately support its government's contributions may weaken an NGO's leverage in pressing for changes. But from the perspective of many NGOs, full, unconditional support for aid spending would be dishonest, while opposition would be counter-productive. Organisations that choose to criticise and conditionally support aid programmes will appear inconsistent at times. They need to be skilful in judging when to emphasise their criticism or support, and they need to cultivate close relationships with more radical NGO critics, in order to avoid undercutting their efforts to press for reforms.

World Bank staff and government officials may not like the criticism, but staff interviewed all affirmed that public campaigning does not diminish their willingness to discuss and learn from an NGO's alternative perspectives.

### Short-term campaign objectives and long-term network or coalition building

Like other political activists, NGO campaigners have both short-term and long-term needs and objectives. Their campaigns are urgent, aiming to relieve immediate human suffering and create opportunity. But they also often give attention to the longer-term processes of coalition- and constituency- building for expanded impact. Christian Aid's work in coalitions during the WRTW period included facilitating and/or hosting roles in the Bretton Woods Project, the Debt Crisis Network, and the NGO Working Group on the World Bank. The early experience of these coalitions suggests three reasons to emphasise such coalition work.

First, coalitions around specific institutions (Bretton Woods Project) or issues (Debt Crisis Network) allow a focus and specialisation by staff that few individual NGOs can afford to maintain. Their specialisation may better equip NGOs for technical discussions with the World Bank when such dialogue is needed. For NGOs in the UK and Western Europe, effective coalition building helps to compensate for the obvious advantages of access that Washington-based NGOs enjoy.

Second, NGOs can hardly afford to forgo potential sources of influence by dividing their efforts. The World Bank is a skilled participant in dialogue with NGOs and the media. The creation of a new office in London was rightly taken as a sign that the campaign had gained the Bank's attention, but it also calls for a new level of sophistication and unity from NGOs.

Third, building longer-term support from public constituencies may sometimes justify campaign strategies that would not be chosen purely for short-term policy change. Press advertisements and published reports that gain press coverage, for example, can bolster the confidence and enthusiasm of a political constituency, even when the advertisements' direct impact is questionable.

## Conclusions and recommendations

The charges that NGOs are not sufficiently reflective and self-critical in assessing the significance and impact of their advocacy (Sogge 1996) have come mostly from sympathetic observers, and should prompt NGOs to more deliberate and consistent assessment of advocacy projects. Results are difficult to discern, but candid self-assessment is important, both to promote effectiveness and to practise transparency. This paper closes with some principles for improved monitoring and assessment.

### *Work with a model of institutional change*

It is difficult to trace and verify impact in a major international organisation. But there is a set of factors that are consistently important for achieving significant policy change, and where change is often at least somewhat easier to monitor and attribute. NGOs can use these factors to sketch a model of the components of change in the target institution. With such a model, advocates can strategise and evaluate their efforts, in part by assessing their impact on the principal factors involved in winning institutional change.

Policy advocates have often noted that there is a process of gaining influence at the World Bank, whose steps include official acknowledgement that an issue is within its scope or mandate; consideration and adoption of new policy; and implementation by staff and borrowers. Recent developments in the debates over debt and adjustment suggest four key strategic factors in motivating significant policy change: support from senior management, initiative by major shareholders, active internal leadership, and external pressure.[3]

- *Support from senior management*: Wolfensohn's direction has opened new opportunities in the debt and adjustment debates. The sometimes embattled President has made common cause with the Bank's NGO critics on some issues, and sought their co-operation in funding discussions. Senior management has in the past been able to block consideration of initiatives on debt and adjustment.

- *Initiative by major shareholders*: NGOs are quick to note their own leadership role in some policy areas, but major changes at the World Bank require action by its Governing Board. The USA has championed environmental initiatives and the information-disclosure and inspection-panel reforms, and the UK's leadership on debt was essential to winning consideration for proposals supported by NGOs. NGOs can help to open new space for innovation by staff who share their concerns and priorities, but such change cannot be institutionalised without the Board's assent, and Board action usually requires leadership by one of its major shareholders.

- *Active internal leadership by individuals committed to change*: Such internal leadership was essential in advancing the popular participation agenda within the World Bank, and in the development of the HIPC debt-relief initiative. When such leadership is present, external advocates may devise a mix of strategies that expand the space for new initiatives internally, while maintaining political pressure on senior management and the Board. (Active staff leadership has not been enough to win rapid change in issue areas such as gender equity and family planning (Siddharth 1995; Conly and Epp 1997).)

- *External pressure from NGOs, other observers, and the media*: The kind of pressure needed may vary with the stages of policy change, and the strength and interest of other actors (management, shareholders, internal leadership). Public political pressure that threatens the image of the IFIs appears to be the key factor in establishing an issue as a concern, and remains important at later stages of a successful effort. At another stage, the pressure may also require analytical and negotiating skills to engage in discussions over the details of new institutional and policy alternatives, as in the debate over multilateral debt relief in 1996.

By holding a model such as this one clearly in mind, policy advocates can plan and assess their own efforts, asking how effectively they advance one or more of the essential ingredients of change.

### Make the terms and agendas of NGO partnerships clear

It is often assumed that NGO coalitions should speak with a single voice on the details of their target issues, and often this is appropriate. But expectations among NGO partners may sometimes be more flexible, as in WRTW, and it is important that these understandings be as clear as possible among participants. Within a campaign on structural adjustment policy, for example, there is room for different priorities between advocates focused on the World Bank in Washington and advocates focused on national policy in Jamaica or the Philippines. What is important is that the agreed, shared agenda is well defined and carefully adhered to, so that the coalition is not easily split if government or the Bank co-operates more readily with one participant than with others. International advocates must also be clear and explicit in stating for whom they speak when they advance a criticism or proposal.

### Focus on changes in practice and on institutional change at the World Bank

Aspects of the NGO agenda (such as participation, gender equity, poverty reduction, sustainability, or energy efficiency) are being accepted into the World Bank's vocabulary and policy apparatus. NGO advocates have been well aware of the gap between policy and practice, but winning institutional changes in practice has proved difficult.

The next generation of advocacy priorities and strategies should shift emphasis from global-level policy to institutional mechanisms and the implementation of policy commitments. Tried and tested methods for winning policy change have been joined by new approaches required at a new juncture. The environment/ infrastructure campaign emphasises institutional changes for accountability and transparency, monitors rule revision in the Bank, and presses for the extension of safeguards to loans for private-sector projects. Campaigners are monitoring country-by-country implementation of new rules for debt relief, and initiating a public campaign for more radical relief. Some adjustment critics are participating in the national-level SAPRI joint review.

## Test the model, and strategies, against experience

Political, intellectual, and institutional commitments have led academics and practitioners to focus on demonstrating NGOs' efficacy as political actors, more than to subject the campaigns to rigorous review. But a more rigorous and candid review of advocacy strategies and impact would benefit NGOs, by helping them to identify effective strategies, and by demonstrating their commitment to the principles of transparency and accountability. As NGOs attract more attention as political actors in international arenas, they can expect more critical review. They will do well to initiate and encourage such studies themselves.

## Be attentive: influence flows both ways

The World Bank has accepted the legitimacy of NGOs' participation in policy discussions and its own obligation to respond to civil-society interventions. The Bank, in turn, uses its liaison with NGOs skilfully to signal its affiliation with aspects of the NGOs' agenda. The Bank now presents itself as the leader among major donors in areas such as public participation, social safety nets during economic reform, debt relief, and involuntary resettlement. Some NGO advocates tirelessly point out the limits of the Bank's practice in these areas, but they have learned that a reputation is sometimes more easily won than substantive change.

NGOs themselves are also influenced through their interaction with major donors. Planned, deliberate co-operation in even a single component of a World Bank-financed project is often a major undertaking for an international NGO or its country or regional office, and for national or sub-national NGOs. Critics of the Bank have long recognised that NGOs which accept major support for project work or participation in a conference or committee may open their priorities and practices to its influence.

But the same is true of participation in a policy dialogue, even when NGOs imagine themselves to be the agent of change and the World Bank the target. The political realities of the institution and its political environ-ment can shift NGOs' agendas towards the politically feasible, and the content of the Bank's contributions to the discussion can influence NGO conceptual frameworks as well. NGOs should ensure that such change is deliberate and in line with their own mission and commitments. Without careful attention, the Bank's expanding 'partnerships' with a variety of civil-society organisations will only accelerate the already rapid homogenisation of organisations and strategies in the development industry.

# Notes

1   This article draws on the author's evaluation report (Nelson 1997), in which references to interviews and personal communications may be found (available from Christian Aid, PO Box 100, London SE1 7RT). I thank Christian Aid for encouraging publication of the results of the evaluation of their WRTW campaign.

2   Christian Aid participated in the NGOWG as a representative of the Association of Protestant Development Organisations.

3   This line of thinking was suggested by Justin Forsyth, then of Oxfam International.

# References

Christian Aid (1994) 'Who Runs the World?', campaign folder, London: Christian Aid

Cleary, Seamus (1995) 'In whose interest? NGO advocacy campaigns and the poorest', *International Relations* 12(5): 9–36

Conly, Shanti R. and Joanne E. Epp (1997) *Falling Short: The World Bank's Role in Population and Reproductive Health*, Washington: Population Action International

Covey, Jane G. (1998) 'Critical cooperation? Influencing the World Bank through policy dialogue and operational cooperation' in Fox and Brown (eds.) 1998

Fox, Jonathan and David L. Brown (1998), 'Assessing the impact of NGO advocacy campaigns on World Bank projects and policies,' in Fox and Brown (eds.) *The Struggle for Accountability: The World Bank, NGOs and Grassroots Movements*, Cambridge MA: MIT Press

Harrigan, J. (1998) 'Effects of the IMF and World Bank on public expenditure accountability in Jamaica', *Public Administration and Development* 18:5–22.

Jordan, Lisa and Peter van Tuijl (1997) 'Political Responsibility in NGO Advocacy: Exploring Emerging Shapes of Global Democracy', unpublished paper, June 1997

Nelson, Paul J. (1995) *The World Bank and NGOs: The Limits of Apolitical Development*, London: Macmillan

Nelson, Paul J. (1996) 'Internationalising economic and environmental policy: transnational NGO networks and the World Bank's expanding influence', *Millennium* 25: 605–33.

Nelson, Paul J. (1997) 'Who Runs the World? A Partial Evaluation of a Two-Year Policy Campaign', London: Christian Aid

Polak, Jacques J. (1998) 'IMF Study Group Report: Transparency and Evaluation', report and recommendations by the Center of Concern, Washington DC: Center of Concern

Roe, Emery (1995) 'Critical theory, sustainable development and populism', *Telos* 103: 149–62

Scholte, Jan Arte (1998) 'The International Monetary Fund and Civil Society: an Underdeveloped Dialogue', paper presented at a Workshop on Global Economic Institutions and Global Social Movements, Centre for Economic Policy Research, London, 26 February 1998

Siddharth, Veena (1995) 'Gendered participation: NGOs and the World Bank', *IDS Bulletin* 26(3): 31–8

Sogge, David (ed.) (1996) *Compassion and Calculation: The Business of Private Foreign Aid*, London: Pluto Press.

*This paper was first published in* Development in Practice *(10/3&4: 478–90) in 2000.*

# Northern words, Southern readings

## Carmen Marcuello and Chaime Marcuello

This paper presents two sides of the same coin: certain words used in the North, and a reading of their effects in the South. First, we summarise the recent evolution of Spanish non-government development organisations (NGDOs), which have gained in visibility and prestige as a response to socio-political changes in Spain. We then present a reading of the work of these NGDOs from the perspective of various Southern actors. We show instances of a kind of perverse inertia that undermines precisely what it is they are seeking to do. Thus, in Central America, recipients of foreign aid identify two extremes which we call *living by the wound* and *the project culture* (also known as 'projectitis'). If NGDOs want to meet their goals, they must guard against these unintended effects.

## Northern words...

### Spanish NGDOs

Like other social movements in Spain, the history of NGDOs is tied up with the country's socio-political evolution. To understand the backgrounds of these social movements, we must take into account the almost 40 years of the Franco dictatorship (1939–1975) and subsequent developments. The dictatorship conditioned the forms, models, and history of social movements, within a highly authoritarian context. Political and social action was thus defined as either conservative, national-catholic, or anti-communist. Following Franco's death, the transition to democracy was marked by great ebullience. Trade unions and clandestine organisations came out into the open, and new ones were born. These became the protagonists and very core of citizen action. As democracy was consolidated, social movements took on new missions and explored previously prohibited possibilities. The predecessors of today's NGDOs first had to survive the dictatorship, then pushed for democratisation, and finally came to occupy second place in terms of citizen action during the first decade of democracy.

We can discern two stages in their evolution. The first is characterised by their *social invisibility*. Neither before nor during the 1980s were NGDOs relevant to Spanish public opinion. Their activities were largely associated with missionary fundraising campaigns. This image began to change only very slowly. In 1982, the Socialist Party came to power. This brought about qualitative changes in the government's development aid policies. The term NGO came into being for the first time, though little attention was paid to NGOs. The second stage is thus marked by the achievement of *social visibility*. This was a gradual process. The '0.7% platform' mobilised many citizens (Marcuello 1996a). At the same time, there was more information about the desperate situations in the South. Social invisibility was thus converted into *social prestige*.

NGDOs acquired this social recognition because of three factors:

First, free advertising in the mass media. Second, the coopting of their language and successes by the politicians. Third, their growing presence as sponsors of the campaigns of private and public companies. These are three spaces conquered not by magic, nor by altruism on the part of the newspapers, the politicians and the companies: if they did not have 'social prestige' nobody would be supporting a concert for Rwanda, for example. (Marcuello 1996b)

NGDOs want this fragile achievement to continue, because they know that it has only just begun and that there is still much to be done within Spain. They know that they have come to represent something within the collective consciousness, and that there has been a qualititative change in how NGDOs are perceived. But more remains to be done.

Thus, Spanish NGDOs now face a kind of adolescent crisis, a time of search, internal discussion, and social consolidation. The challenge is more complex than ever, but Spanish NGDOs now have some experience. Most of them, and certainly those which belong to the federation, want to affirm their identity because they know that their greater social visibility imposes greater precision on their work.

## The collective discourse

The NGDO Committee was founded in 1986 and brings together about 90 organisations in Spain. It has become a major reference point for NGDOs, public institutions, and society. Admittedly, the Committee represents an unstable balance, given the diversity of its members. Nonetheless, it is acknowledged as the leader of 'joint action in cooperation with the peoples of the Third World'. In the Committee's own words: 'our general objective is to increase and to improve international development cooperation and to accomplish common actions in response to the interests of the peoples of the Third World'. Its objective is, 'to change the unbalanced and unjust relationships of dependency of the South on the North and to raise public awareness of the need for change'. [1]

Its members fight for a model of development that is sustainable, endogenous, balanced, and global; *sustainable*, guaranteeing the welfare of the present and future generations, based on the protection of natural resources and of human rights; *endogenous*, based on the direct participation of the beneficiaries, and where foreign aid constitutes a stimulus to the development, but never a new kind of dependency; *balanced*, based on questioning the social, economic, and political conditions that produce inequality among the countries of the North and the South and among the different sectors of the population; *global*, based on the need profoundly to transform Northern development models, being the principal cause of the imbalances and the relationships of dependency between North and South.

On paper, the general perspectives are very clear. It is a Northern discourse, well formulated, well written. It represents years of NGDO experience and summarises the conventional wisdom on overseas development assistance. But how is this discourse seen by the Southern counterparts? How does it translate into practice? How do the beneficiaries read what is done in the name of these high-sounding words?

## Southern effects...

In general, the answers to these questions are positive. But now we focus on the 'perverse inertia' of this Northern discourse. For there are darker sides to all NGDO actions — Spanish NGDOs included. Despite their short experience in the international arena, they have adopted the rhythms and procedures of other Northern NGDOs, repeating once again the same development paradigms and rhetoric about North–South relations.

### Perverse inertias

Effects and tendencies that are the opposite of what was intended are what we call 'perverse inertias'. In this case, these are the effects of Northern-funded development cooperation projects, whether non-governmental or official. We look at this in the light of our own work in El Salvador, Nicaragua, and Guatemala, and on the basis of visits by aid recipients from these countries. Their differences notwithstanding, these three countries serve as a basic reference or model of how international cooperation works.

Our research focused on both quantitative and qualitative issues and was conducted during 1995–1997. Here, we present our partial conclusions on some of the qualitative elements. Our methodology included interviews, discussion groups, and participatory action-research. These techniques allowed us to capture people's actual words. We then analysed what they had said in order to get a sense of the central elements within their worldviews. Here, we offer a selection of the most significant readings of the Northern aid discourse, by some of its recipients in the South.

Translating words into reality is difficult. Often, development projects do not respond to the recipients' felt needs — endogenous development — but to Northern NGDOs' own project repertoire. As the beneficiaries said:

> We need support, and as we want to ask these people for money,
> know that we must request it for certain things. Since we're going to ask
> so-and-so for money, we have to focus on women and ecology ... that's
> the fashion today. Perhaps we don't really need a cattle-raising project,
> but we know that they will fund this or nothing. So we get hold of the
> 25 cows, even though they are going to ruin much of our land.

This happens frequently. The North sets the agenda. The recipients know that neither the rhythms of cooperation nor the cash intended for them are in their hands:

> For example, the European Community gives money for rural
> development, but only for agro-forestry or forestry. So, either you
> request a project for rubber-tapping or to collect plants for tea-
> infusions — to give a silly example — in other words, a project
> which does what they want of you, or you won't get anything.

But it is not only the macro-policies of government institutions that define the scope and funding of international cooperation. Northern NGDOs are also responsible. These have the resources to work with their Southern counterparts, but almost always do so according to their own logic — the plans, standards, and models for action of the Northern NGDOs themselves.

> Look what happened to us. We were thinking about a reconciliation
> project. We wanted to begin very gently. But a First World NGO came
> to say that they, too, were interested in reconciliation, and in a series
> of similar projects. Their ideas seemed very interesting... but then we

had to change everything to fit in with them. Although we did this together and discussed everything,... the point is that they had funding for projects that fitted in with their ideas, and unless we went along with it, the money would not be forthcoming.

Development cooperation projects are meant to be endogenous and focused on the 'beneficiaries', who are supposed to be, or become, the central subjects of their own development: the protagonists. In theory, donors should take second place. But the inertia of almost 50 years of international aid shows us the opposite. It is rare to find cases where the recipients play the leading role. In fact, Northern NGDOs are seen simply as *funders* (to say nothing of the official aid agencies, which are more distant still):

Who decides how the money for projects is to be spent? Basically, the Northern NGDOs. Some may consult [with us] on the real needs — if only because no-one is going to say they didn't do so. But in reality, decisions about how the funds are to be spent are more often made according to plans and budgets established in the North than on the basis of reality in the South.

We must stress here that this inertia is known about and fought against. The Spanish NGDOs know how easy it is to slip into it, which is why they are resisting this trend. They have done good work in terms of establishing priorities, and ensuring that their projects respond to real needs by spending time in the recipient communities. Despite this, however, another perverse inertia appears:

It is true that there are Northern NGO people who come and stay with us, listen to us, examine the projects we are interested in, on the basis of which they draw up projects to present to their governments. They do a good job. But once done, the situation on the ground changes — and our reality does change a lot — and the project on paper no longer fits our needs. They cannot change it, however, because the funds are approved for fixed purposes. Who is going to mess about with funds from the European Community? But if you can't change it in the light of new circumstances, then it's immaterial whether the project has been well-planned.

The bureaucratic, organised, and rigid rationales of most Northern institutions cannot be readily adapted to suit realities that are less structured — or, rather, which are organised in a different way. Most Northern NGDOs replicate the procedures of the institutional donors, which they are indeed concerned to follow. They know that they must answer to external audits, even at the expense of imposing these 'westernising forms of rationalisation':

> For example, when the refugees were returning, we planned for a project that would start immediately, with a second phase three years later. But as time went by, things changed. The reconstruction work was no longer needed. The project was no longer viable. But since not even a comma could be changed in the project document, the project was ineffective ... so that the aid that was intended to help a community to re-build had the effect of dividing it further. I'm painting a very black picture, but this often happens.

The project protocols are pre-defined in ways that do not allow for adjustments in response to changing circumstances. The need for flexibility in the design, follow-up, execution, and evaluation of development projects is one of the things that beneficiaries most demand. They do need collaboration and help, but they need this not like some kind of yoke around their necks, but as agile and effective cooperation. Experience shows that bureaucratic pressure compromises the optimum use of the resources invested.

## The project culture

NGDO action has another kind of impact on the recipient population. Whenever assistance comes from outside, whatever the source, people's way of life is changed. Where aid policies are effected through the design and execution of projects, this compels people to start thinking in terms of projects and international aid:

> You see, people see aid coming in from outside and realise that they must organise themselves if they are to get anything. They see that assistance is given not to individuals but only to groups. So they begin to organise — not only people such as returnees, who are used to it, but also local villagers. In other words, they begin to feel that what they have to do is to formulate projects for funding. They assume that this is why the returnees are better off than they are, for example. So the 'project culture' is generated — 'I have a need, so I must come up with a project to resolve it'. And since neither the state nor the local authorities are doing anything, we have to ask the white foreigners who are the ones with the cash. The result is 'projectitis' — the project culture.

This project culture, which aims to resolve problems through projects funded from abroad — either directly by Northern agencies or via their local 'partners' — tends to demobilise local citizen action, firstly because the State is relegated to second or even third place; and secondly, because people's own efforts are put 'on hold' as their trust is placed instead on the benevolence of the 'friends of international solidarity'.

And that's not all. After years of being involved in projects, other effects emerge — as in the case of refugees and returnees. In extreme cases, self-help is discouraged: as one respondent said: 'People see everything apart from looking after the fields or the home — whether building a house or sinking a well — as something that can only be done via a project'. However, those who receive (or endure) development aid are also aware, especially in El Salvador and Guatemala, that this is a temporary thing, that it will only last for a couple of years, so they must make the most of it. So they invent as many projects as they can — even if they are not needed:

> Let's give them poultry, a dozen hens each. Good. Twelve laying hens that you have to look after, and then you'll get eggs. So the poultry arrive. You have to make a proper coop. But then you have a setting to which the chickens are not accustomed. They get up on the chairs, the tables, they get in the way. They're aren't strong like the local variety, so some of them fall sick and die. But the others are such a pest that the people end up killing and eating them. When the agency representative arrives, the people tell him or her that the tiger ate the chickens. The point is that this was not the right project in the first place.

Projects can be useful. When the circumstances, the people, and the resources are in synergy, and things work as they should: success. But it's quite the opposite when 'perverse inertias' are operating. If the project is ready-made, or pretty well decided beforehand without asking people what they really need, it is unlikely to engage them. Yes, consultation does sometimes take place. But it is also true that the pre-formed plans tend to carry more weight than the local realities. This means two things. Firstly, in a descriptive sense, a popular education process is needed to find out what people want and need: 'People say many things; perhaps some don't make sense, but out of these we can draw up a list of needs and then ask the community to prioritise...' Secondly, and prescriptively, projects should be flexible and able to adapt to changing realities: 'What happens isn't like this. It's obvious that there are some with the money, and others without. There are no two ways about it. It's not that people are stupid, rather they are grateful — and also know that if they are grateful they may get more money. So the project culture is deepened.'

This *projectitis* encourages a mechanical approach to formulating projects: 'People develop the knack of coming up with projects — projects for anything under the sun'. And it also habituates people to the idea that money intended for projects actually gets diverted,

> ...for the war or whatever, or even for corruption ... Someone who used to be honest gets to manage US$100,000 then disappears with US$2,000. So, corruption is generated, along with power struggles, not over how to serve the community, but over access to money.

## Living by the wound

The project culture is intimately bound up with living by the wound. It is both a parallel and a direct result:

> People think that they have suffered so much and that more will be given to the one who suffered the most. Basically, this is not their fault. They have seen that masses of people have come to hear about their history, how they were slaughtered, how they were killed, and so on...and they see that after these testimonies, projects arrive. This has gone on since 1982... There comes a time when people feel very poor after having returned from exile with nothing ... and they automatically tell the first person who arrives how much they have suffered because they believe this is what they have to do to get help. This is what we call 'living by the wound'.

To live by the wound is to use one's personal narrative of suffering (or that of a loved one) in order to leverage resources, especially money, either via projects or gifts, whether as a means of survival or to meet a particular need. It is a vicious circle created by projectitis, and by the bad (or perhaps good!) conscience of the outsiders who come into contact with the reality of suffering.

If we ask what gives rise to that perverse inertia, the answer comes from the people who have lived through it:

> Who is responsible for projectitis and for living by the wound? They are the ones who do it, but they didn't start it. The guilty ones are the international organisations, not only NGDOs, but also UNHCR, the Catholic church and many big agencies that have supported, for example, the Mexican government ... They encourage that kind of dependency, a dependency that has nothing to do with dignity. 'Here's some beans.' And although they are foul, you have to accept them. How can you say you don't want something that has been given to you? But people do recover their dignity at a certain point. 'I don't want any more weevil-infested old beans ...'.

'Right, you obviously aren't in need then, that's why you're turning them down', they say.

The challenge to NGDOs, as seen from the South, is to change these inertias. Procedures need to be clarified, and more flexible mechanisms adopted, so as to give the leading role to the beneficiaries and see how they behave. Donors and beneficiaries alike must distinguish between the various approaches to, and types of, cooperation. They need to get rid of the confusion that generates the situations we have described, and which also tends to undermine traditional community networks and to introduce a certain lack of solidarity, as a precondition for entering into the world of development projects:

> Before, it took no time at all to build a community structure with everyone's input, and without any outside help. Now it is very hard to find volunteers to do any unpaid work. NGOs and international agencies pay for everything, including labour. So people say it is impossible to build a community hall, without having a project and without money: 'we have a lot to do; what will we eat?' and so on. This kind of aid has generated a lack of solidarity where previously people were willing to work for the common good, and were very organised.

True, without NGDOs, many things would not have been possible. But there comes a time when the NGDO reduces people's capacity to make political demands, because everything gets turned into projects. In the past, projects were used to support things like revolving funds. But today, the attitude is 'either you give it to me or I don't want it'. It is not that NGDOs are solely responsible for this change in attitude, but it is, neverthless, a natural consequence of the kind of aid they offer.

In emergency situations, such as those afflicting Central America throughout the 1980s, this loss of values is less obvious. But the same approach to aid continues in the name of development — but a development that is seldom sustainable and often creates dependency:

> These people ... arrived without any project, but with a lot of external help; enough to obtain land and things ... But after that, all the community houses, cooperative centres, the shops, were all built on a voluntary basis... even the runway, which meant bringing earth from several kilometres away. All this without a single project. Now we need to re-build, but no project means no reconstruction. Without a project and wages for the labourers, the runway will not be repaired. The very runway that is used by the tiny aeroplane that

brings us help. Things are out of sync. But people have become innured to it.

## Conclusions

We have explored the dark side of the fine NGDO words. Spanish NGDOs, like all the others, have adopted an impeccable rhetoric. But rhetoric and theory are one thing, practical results are another. Spanish NGDOs repeat the same internationally established development clichés. Development is to be sustainable, beneficiary-led, endogenous, human, participatory — all the best possible attributes. But the interpretation of these claims in practice shows some perverse inertias that should be fought against. The consequences of years of international development cooperation are felt in the two pathological trends explored above; pathological for two reasons. First, because they are an unintended effect of the prevailing discourse. Second, because they embed the intended beneficiaries in a situation that is both alienating and enslaving.

True, development projects have had mixed results. Some beneficiaries will be grateful for generations. But we must recognise that these examples have not helped to improve the living conditions of humanity overall.

The great majority of our interlocutors, who have been on the receiving end of development projects, feel the contradictions of their situation. The clearest among them adopt a bitter-sweet tone: they value others' efforts, their solidarity, but they also claim their dignity as intelligent human beings. Theirs is a fierce critique of the way in which their lives and their expectations of development are taken over by others in the name of international solidarity. They do not need a new set of parents or experts to explain to them how they must develop. The true protagonist is the 'beneficiary' and his or her community, not the intellectual vanguards who seek short-cuts to the 'truth'.

We need to fight against these pathologies, which are both socially demobilising and tend to blunt people's critical capacity — assuming, that is, that NGDOs want to be true to their rhetoric. The staff of Spanish NGDOs are largely aware of these perverse inertias. In trying to turn things around, the question is to participate, cooperate, and help to generate processes in which the recipients of development projects become the subjects of their own history. NGDOs must resist just being bureaucrats, and move towards where they say they want to go: 'To participate as equals with the peoples of the world in the common cause of development.'

# Note

1 From the CONGD 1997 promotional leaflet 'Participate as Equals with the Peoples of the World in the Common Cause of Development'.

*This paper was first published in* Development in Practice *(9/1&2: 151–8) in 1999.*

# References

Marcuello, Ch. (1996a) 'El movimiento 0,7: un pulso colectivo', *Acciones e Investigaciones Sociales* 4: 201–218.

Marcuello, Ch. (1996b) 'Identidad y acción de las organizaciones no-gubernamentales', *Revista de Gestión Pública y Privada* 1: 103–122.

# Menchú Tum, Stoll, and martyrs of solidarity

## Larry Reid

According to the mainstream media, civil society and grassroots campaigns are increasingly affecting foreign policy. Recent events, like the signing of the International Treaty to Ban Land Mines, have opened the media's eyes to the phenomenon of foreign-policy action at the grassroots, but it has been around for a lot longer.

Many such campaigns are in solidarity with some kind of struggle. The causes adopted by solidarity groups are as diverse as society itself. Recent examples include the anti-apartheid struggle in South Africa, the revolutionary governments in Cuba and Nicaragua, the anti-government forces during the civil wars in El Salvador and Guatemala, the Zapatistas in Mexico, and the liberation of East Timor from Indonesian occupation. The common thread of international solidarity groups is that people, primarily in the North, give time, money, and energy to a struggle that benefits people in a different culture, primarily in the South.

Solidarity groups form part of the broader international development community, so it is important to understand them in order to understand the whole development picture. Why do people devote so much to people with whom they have nothing obvious in common? This paper looks at one possible motivating factor for solidarity work: the role of the martyr. It first considers the general concept of the martyr, and then examines a specific case as reflected in two books: *I, Rigoberta Menchú* and *Rigoberta Menchú and the Story of All Poor Guatemalans*. The first presents an account of a well-known activist for social change in Guatemala. The second disputes many of the claims related in the first book, and calls into question the martyr status of its subject. The paper draws on solidarity with Central America and Guatemala, primarily from an English Canadian perspective, but the questions raised should be asked about conflict, social change, and international solidarity elsewhere.

# The impact of solidarity groups

From about 1980 to 1997, solidarity with struggles for changes in Central America was perhaps the most popular foreign-policy issue for Canadians. As measured by the number of groups, their location throughout the country, and the number of people who participated, perhaps only the anti-apartheid struggle in South Africa and support for Cuba have generated as much Canadian grassroots activity. Because of the grassroots nature of many of these groups, it is difficult to find many hard data about participation, but we can make some observations.

Some grassroots solidarity activities were expressed through national campaigns. The two best known were probably Tools for Peace (T4P), which sent material and financial aid to revolutionary Nicaragua, and Project Accompaniment (PA), which sent volunteer observers to accompany the return of Guatemalan refugees to their country. T4P sent a large amount of aid to Nicaragua, raised by people across Canada collecting donations from their own communities. PA sent about 150 individuals to spend six weeks or more (some spent eight months) with returning and returned refugees. Each person paid her or his own way or raised funds in their own communities in order to go live in the heat and rain and insect-infested areas of some of the most remote parts of Guatemala.

Not as easy to identify, but clearly a factor, was the tremendous amount of work done to support the struggle in El Salvador. While solidarity with El Salvador never had a clearly identifiable national organisation in Canada, most people would agree that it was at a comparable level with solidarity for Nicaragua and Guatemala.

In addition to the national campaigns, there were solidarity groups in cities and towns across the country. Typical activities involved raising funds for projects in Central America, educating the Canadian public about conditions in the region, and lobbying the Canadian government, usually by letter-writing campaigns, on refugee, aid, and foreign-policy matters. 'The low level of priority that the Canadian government assigned to Central America before 1980 was challenged, and to some extent altered, by the nation's citizens' (North 1990:211).

Other examples where the grassroots solidarity movement may have had an effect include the following.

- Increased aid to Nicaragua after Hurricane Joan. The Canadian government initially promised a small amount, which it increased after being bombarded by letters and phone calls expressing outrage at its lack of generosity.

- According to McFarlane (1989:151), '[b]y 1978, External Affairs correspondence was displaying a great deal of fretting over the "domestic dimension" to the Central American problem...'. The increased level of solidarity activism meant that External Affairs could no longer claim to be the 'expert' on Central America. Solidarity groups had their own people on the ground reporting on what was happening there.

- Churches and solidarity groups often sponsored refugees to come to Canada. In some cases, these refugees went on to participate in solidarity activities, and some took on other roles within the academic and NGO communities.

Another area of influence exerted by the solidarity movement is the cross-over of solidarity activists to other areas of work on Central America. A number of the new crop of NGO staff working on the region were previously active in solidarity groups, and some Latin American Studies scholars also have a solidarity background.

Most solidarity work was done by volunteers who not only received no material benefit from their work, but often contributed money, transport, lodging, food, and time, to solidarity activities. The few paying jobs in solidarity work generally involved long hours for poor wages.

## Martyr syndrome

A martyr is someone who suffers or dies for a religion or cause. For solidarity communities, martyrdom is often an important part of their awareness and lobbying campaigns. This experience can be collective, like the Dili massacre in East Timor, or personal, like the assassination of Salvadoran Archbishop Oscar Romero. Some don't actually require the death of the martyr, but they do require that this person should have experienced great suffering. The latter category includes Nelson Mandela in South Africa and Rigoberta Menchú Tum in Guatemala. We shall look at Menchú Tum's case in more detail below.

The martyr figure is used in many ways. For example, in the mid-1990s, the English Section of Amnesty International in Canada did several direct-mail campaigns which contained a very graphic description of a torture session. The envelope even carried a warning that what was described inside wasn't for the squeamish. However, just as the warnings of 'mature content' on televised movies guarantees them a good audience of adolescent boys, I couldn't help but wonder if the warning wasn't part of the campaign marketing sizzle.

Some international development NGOs use another type of martyr. Judging by their direct-mail campaigns and other marketing efforts, many seem to think that the way to get donations is to portray the recipients of their aid as the most helpless and pathetic people on earth. This has been called the 'pornography of poverty'. The Canadian Council for International Cooperation (CCIC) has a code of conduct for members, to prevent the worst such cases. The existence of this code and a label for the phenomenon indicate that the problem is a real one.

Witnessing or hearing stories of horror and suffering are very compelling to the majority of human beings. Past generations turned out to see heretics and witches burned at the stake. Nowadays we slow down at road accidents on the motorway, trying to see what happened. The question for solidarity movements is: what is the wisdom of building support for a cause that is based on reactions akin to those of people who turned out to see heretics burned at the stake during the Inquisition? We may have a good turn-out for the burning, but as soon as the killings stop, so does the support.

The level of Central American solidarity activities is now far below what it was in the 1980s, even if Chiapas in Mexico is included under this umbrella. In fact, many people involved in solidarity with Chiapas were also involved in Central American solidarity 15 to 20 years ago. It appears that when one group of people stop being martyrs, some solidarity activists move on to another group who are acquiring this status. But martyrs don't seem to help to build a long-term, grassroots network which supports the people of Central America.

This martyr syndrome has another undesirable effect on the relationship between people in the North and our 'partners' in or from the South. Too often, solidarity activists would allow Central Americans to speak, as long as what they wanted to tell was the story of their suffering. However, if they wanted to speak about other things, they were marginalised and ignored. I am personally aware of a case where Central Americans who wanted to speak at a Canadian government–NGO consultation in 1996 were told by an employee of one of the major solidarity organisations that the Central Americans should not speak, because the NGOs were there to speak for those who had no voice. The obvious irony here is the question of who was denying the Central Americans their voice.

Other Central Americans who cannot or will not tell stories of personal horror are ignored, or even distrusted ('if they don't have a personal story of physical suffering, maybe they're a spy'). Those who do tell their story suffer too. José Recinos, a Guatemalan who walked most of the way across Canada in 1996 to raise awareness about human-rights abuses in Guatemala, said that he often felt the most tiring thing was talking about his torture experience every day.

## The debate about the martyr in *I, Rigoberta Menchú*

The Guatemalan solidarity movement has a well-known martyr figure in the person of Rigoberta Menchú Tum. Menchú Tum won the 1992 Nobel Peace Prize and is an indigenous woman from the K'iche' people, in the department of Quiché, in northern Guatemala. As an indigenous person, she is a member of the majority of Guatemala's population, but a majority which has been margin-alised and exploited since the arrival of Europeans in 1524 (Martínez Peláez 1994).

She first became known to the world after the publication of *I, Rigoberta Menchú*. This became one of the standard texts for solidarity activists who supported the struggle of the Guatemalan people against the domination of the small, economically powerful, mostly European-descended or mixed-blood (*ladino*) élite in Guatemala.

On 15 December 1998, the *New York Times* published an article by Larry Rohter, claiming that some of the incidents related in this book were inaccurate. The article was based on Rohter's own investigations in Guatemala, but it was prompted by, and it quoted from, a forthcoming book by David Stoll, an anthropologist at Middlebury College in Vermont, entitled *Rigoberta Menchú and the Story of All Poor Guatemalans*.

Stoll worked for some years as a journalist before returning to university and obtaining a doctorate in anthropology. His dissertation was later published as *Between Two Armies in the Ixil Towns of Guatemala*. In *Rigoberta Menchú and the Story of All Poor Guatemalans*, Stoll says that he basically stumbled across the fact that no one remembered anyone being burned alive in the town square of Chajul, meaning that one of the best-known stories from *I, Rigoberta Menchú* could not be true. Stoll investigated further and published some papers on the subject. He claims to report what his informants tell him and points out that many of his informants are also indigenous Guatemalans. He had the collaboration of Barbara Bocek, an archaeologist from Stanford University who was working as a Peace Corps volunteer. Bocek speaks K'iche' and was therefore able to learn much from K'iche' women, many of whom speak little or no Spanish.

The first part of Stoll's book presents data based on his attempts to corroborate a number of events from *I, Rigoberta Menchú*. In the second part, Stoll discusses the significance of his findings. One of the issues he raises is the role that the earlier book might have played in prolonging the Guatemalan civil war by helping to generate international support for the Guatemalan National Revolutionary Unity (URNG), the principal guerrilla umbrella group during the civil war.

I shall not venture into the debate about which book is more correct, nor will I speculate on the authors' motivations for writing their respective books, since other sources are available.[1]

## The construction of *I, Rigoberta Menchú*

*I, Rigoberta Menchú* provides an excellent case study for some of the debates that have been raging in anthropology in the last 20 years concerning who should really be considered the author of a book of this kind, and indeed what it means to be the 'author' of an anthropological work.

Most people agree on this much of the genesis of *I, Rigoberta Menchú*. In January 1982, Menchú Tum was in Paris during a speaking tour about Guatemala. Elizabeth Burgos, an anthropologist, was interested in writing a testimony of a Guatemalan indigenous person, and came in contact with Menchú Tum. Burgos recorded 26 hours of Menchú Tum's testimony over the course of a week. Then Menchú Tum left Paris, and Burgos went on to publish the work. Elizabeth Burgos is named as the author, indicating that she thinks it is her book.

Arturo Taracena was at that time the representative in Paris of the Guerrilla Army of the Poor (EGP), then Guatemala's largest guerrilla organisation. In an inteview (Aceituno 1999:1B) in *el Acordeón*, the Sunday cultural supplement to the Guatemalan daily *el Periódico*, Taracena says that four people worked on the book: Menchú Tum, Burgos, Francisca Rivas, and himself. According to Taracena, he and Cécile Rosseau, a Quebecoise who was the representative in Paris of the Revolutionary Organisation of the People in Arms (ORPA), another guerrilla organisation, were the chain that connected Burgos to Menchú Tum. Menchú Tum was staying with Taracena. Rosseau knew that Burgos wanted to write a testimony of a Guatemalan indigenous person, and she knew Taracena. Burgos asked the questions and recorded Menchú Tum's testimony. Rivas, a woman of Cuban origin also living in Paris, transcribed the interviews, because Burgos' Spanish wasn't up to the task. Taracena corrected the Spanish, since Spanish was Menchú Tum's second language, and also wrote the glossary of Guatemalan slang for non-Guatemalan readers of the Spanish edition.

According to Taracena, Burgos proposed that he not be mentioned in the book, in order to forestall accusations that it was a political work, and he 'didn't disagree'.

Menchú Tum has disowned the book: 'I'm the protagonist of the book, and it's my testimony, but I'm not the author' (*Prensa Libre* 1998a:5); but she has also said, 'It's my testimony, and I'll defend it' (*Prensa Libre* 1998b:4).

One important point is usually lost in the complicated story of the creation of *I, Rigoberta Menchú*. Its readers created the Rigoberta Menchú of the book, and it is unlikely that she is the same person as the one who currently heads the Fundación Rigoberta Menchú Tum. Most readers probably remember her demographic details (indigenous woman from Guatemala who speaks Spanish as a second language), but don't know what she has been doing since she won the Nobel Peace Prize. The accidental nature of the creation of *I, Rigoberta Menchú* means that Menchú Tum, Burgos, or Taracena may have been responding to what they knew, consciously or unconsciously, would reverberate with the Northern solidarity activist's own caricature of Guatemalan indigenous people.

## The attempt to discredit *I, Rigoberta Menchú*

Stoll questions six parts of the account in *I, Rigoberta Menchú*.

- The book says that the army burned to death one of Menchú Tum's brothers, Petrocinio, in the town square of Chajul, and forced her and her family to watch. Stoll says that's not true. He reports that seven residents of Chajul say the army never burned anyone alive in the town square. According to Stoll, Petrocinio died in different circumstances, and without the family present.

- It says that another brother, Nicolás, died of hunger. Stoll says that no brother died of hunger in the way Menchú Tum described it. Rohter says Nicolás is alive and well, and that he and a half-sister know that two older brothers died of hunger, but before Nicolás was born, which means at least 10 years before Menchú Tum was born.

- It says that Menchú Tum never went to school and couldn't speak, read, or write Spanish until shortly before giving the testimony on which the book is based. Stoll says that Sister Margarita of the Insituto Belga-Guatemalteco says that

Menchú Tum was a good student, and was in her first year of *básico* (grade seven) in January 1980.

- It says that Menchú Tum's family was involved in a land dispute in Chimel between indigenous families like hers and non-indigenous families who were favoured by the State because of their ethnic background. Stoll says that Menchú Tum's older brother (and other sources in the area) claim that the dispute was between Menchú Tum's father and his in-laws, another indigenous family.

- It says that Menchú Tum's father, Vicente Menchú, was a founder of Committee for Campesino Unity (CUC). Stoll says that Vicente Menchú was not a founder of CUC, basing his claim mainly on circumstantial evidence.

- It says that Menchú Tum was a member of CUC and an organiser and catechist in Uspantán. Stoll says that Menchú Tum was not a member of CUC in Guatemala, nor was she an organiser and catechist in Uspantán, again basing his claim mainly on circumstantial evidence and chronologies, adding that no one recalls her activism in her community.

All the points that Stoll challenges relate to Menchú Tum's status as a suffering 'martyr'. The first three show how she and her people suffer and are deprived. The last three show that the reason they suffer is their status as indigenous people and because they are activists.

## Repercussions

The publication of the *New York Times* article caused a storm in the Guatemalan press. Much of this simply repeated the original report, but the headlines included things like 'Rigoberta lied in her autobiography' (*Siglo Veintiuno* 1998:2). Columnist Alfred Kaltschmitt used the occasion to imply that there had been no human-rights abuses in Guatemala during the civil war, or at least that both sides were equally guilty (Kaltschmitt 1998). At the international level, the people who always maintained that the conflicts in Central America were the result of communist agitation took advantage of the controversy to trot out their arguments again (Horowitz 1999; D'Souza 1998).

Others came to Menchú Tum's defence. Rosalina Tuyuc, an indigenous congressional deputy for a party generally sympathetic to Menchú Tum, said that Stoll's accusations 'originate from the racism against indigenous people that exists even today' (*Prensa Libre* 1998c:5).

In the same article, Aroldo Quej, an indigenous deputy for a party less sympathetic to Menchú Tum, said, 'I don't share many of the positions of Ms Menchú, but that doesn't mean that I don't respect the honour that was bestowed on her, nor the international prestige that she has'.

The *Chronicle of Higher Education*'s website (*Chronicle* 1999) has the following comments that are indicative of one line of response to Stoll's book:

> Allen Carey-Webb, an associate professor of English at Western Michigan University, says readers must put Ms Menchú's work in context. 'We have a higher standard of truth for poor people like Rigoberta Menchú,' he says, adding: 'If we find a flaw in her, it doesn't mean her whole argument goes down the drain.'

> Joanne Rappaport, president of the Society for Latin American Anthropology, has similar worries. Mr Stoll's book, she says, is 'an attempt to discredit one of the only spokespersons of Guatemala's indigenous movement.'

In another interesting point from the same website, Rick Anderson, Head Acquisitions Librarian, UNC Greensboro, asks if:

> ... students will be well served by instruction on this topic that makes no distinction between the truth and falsity of what purports to be eyewitness testimony? Is the case against the Guatemalan government so flimsy that we who oppose its tactics must resort to fabrication in our criticism of it?

Overall, the result of the debate was at least embarrassing to solidarity activists. The credibility of one of our symbols was called into serious question in a number of mainstream media outlets.

## Reaction of English Canadian solidarity activists

In an earlier paper (Reid 1999), I surveyed a number of solidarity activists in order to find out their attitudes towards the debate. The 13 respondents provided some interesting insights.

It is clear that these respondents do *not* do the work they do for Guatemala solely because of *I, Rigoberta Menchú*. All but one said that the disputed accuracy of the book would not change what they believe about Guatemalan indigenous people, while the remaining respondent disputed the use of the word 'biography' in the question. Although respondents did not base their views on Guatemala solely on this book, they seem to think other people might change their views about the situation of Guatemalan indigenous people if *I, Rigoberta Menchú* were shown to be an inaccurate biography. (The remaining respondent again disputed the use of the word 'biography' in the question.)

Despite the fact that almost all respondents said they would not change their views on the basis of the factual accuracy of *I, Rigoberta Menchú*, a majority did rate this book as either 'important' or 'very important' in the formation of their views on Guatemala. Eighty-five per cent had read more than ten books or in-depth articles about Guatemala – not surprising, given the population from which the sample was taken. People inclined to devote a lot of time to solidarity activities will probably also find time to keep up with their reading. Combined with other sources of information available to them (Guatemalan friends living in exile, videos, travel, among other things), the evidence suggests that solidarity activists are reasonably well informed about Guatemala.

The energetic response to Stoll's book in other circles was also apparent in additional comments that a few respondents provided. However, despite the reactions that Stoll's book has aroused in the general solidarity community, most respondents who had not read it resisted the temptation to dismiss it outright. Over two-thirds said they couldn't pass judgement on the accuracy of Stoll's accounts, because they had not read the book. Of the four respondents who found Stoll's book to be an 'unlikely' account of events, two had actually read it. This, too, supports the conclusion that activists analyse what they read, and are not inclined to read just one book and accept it as the truth.

In follow-up interviews, I asked some respondents why *I, Rigoberta Menchú* was important to them. One said that, 'As a young woman, I was horrified by her story and Guatemalan history'. The book motivated increased interest in Guatemala, and probably contributed to other activities, including personal visits, that deepened her understanding of the country. Another respondent indicated that the book was important both for the historical facts, and for the 'human face' that it put on the recent tragedies in Guatemala. Finally, another respondent said that the book '[fitted] in to what I was learning at the time'.

Of those who responded that *I, Rigoberta Menchú* was irrelevant to their views on Guatemala, one respondent indicated that this was because they knew that events like those recounted in the book did happen, even if they didn't happen to Menchú Tum herself. This person went on to say that their opinion of Menchú Tum might change depending on the outcome of the dispute between the two books, but not their opinion of what happened in Guatemala.

The survey suggests that the martyr figure probably motivated activists to learn more and get more involved. However, it also shows that activists have a deeper and broader understanding of the issues than comes from reading one book.

## Conclusion

The martyr is a powerful symbol for solidarity movements. Martyrs attract people to the cause, or at least motivate them to find out more about what is behind the martyr. As people take up a cause and become activists, they increase their knowledge, and this knowledge allows them to evaluate new information critically, including information about their martyr. Activists don't devote time, money, and energy to their cause on the basis of a simplistic understanding of events.

Unless people are taken beyond the initial exposure to a martyr, however, the martyr figure becomes counter-productive. As soon as the events that create the martyrs cease, so does interest in the cause. For movements that are trying to create long-term social change, this means that their support from solidarity groups disappears exactly when they could really start to take advantage of it. Another danger of investing everything in the image of a martyr is that, by discrediting the martyr, the whole cause is also discredited. If a martyr is to be used to generate public support for a cause, then activists have to be capable of taking public understanding beyond the simplistic analysis of that martyr's suffering. Finally, a solidarity movement that is built on people who were attracted to a martyr element will continue to be influenced by its members' attraction to martyrs. Their tendency to see their Southern partners in this way can affect all aspects of their work, and can alienate people who should be their partners. Solidarity activists have to see their Southern partners as something other than suffering people in order to do effective work.

## Notes

1   Two interesting debates are a series of articles and letters in the *Nation* (Grandin and Goldman 1999, Stoll 1999, Grandin 1999, Goldman 1999, Nelson 1999), available at: www.thenation.com. See also the Chronicle of Higher Education's web site (Chronicle 1999).

## References

Aceituno, Luis (1999) 'Arturo Taracena rompe el silencio', *el Periódico* 10 January.

Burgos-Debray, Elizabeth (1984) *I, Rigoberta Menchú: An Indian Woman in Guatemala*, London: Verso.

Chronicle of Higher Education (1999) chronicle.com/colloquy/99/Menchú /background.htm.

D'Souza, Dinesh (1998) 'I, Rigoberta Menchú, Not!', *Weekly Standard* 28 December.

Grandin, Gary and Francisco Goldman (1999) 'Bitter fruit for Rigoberta', the *Nation* 8 February.

Grandin, Gary (1999) Exchange of letters to the editor, the *Nation* 14 June.

Goldman, Francisco (1999) Exchange of letters to the editor, the *Nation* 14 June.

Horowitz, David (1999) 'I, Rigoberta Menchú, liar', *Salon* 11 January.

Kaltschmitt, Alfred (1999) 'Del libro de la Menchú y otros etcéteras', *Siglo Veintiuno* (Guatemala City) 17 December.

Martínez Peláez, Severo (1994) *La Patria del Criollo, ensayo de interpretación de la realidad colonial guatemalteca*, Mexico DF: Ediciones en Marcha.

McFarlane, Peter (1989) *Northern Shadows. Canadians and Central America*, Toronto: Between the Lines.

Nelson, Diane M. (1999) Exchange of letters to the editor, the *Nation* 14 June.

North, Lisa (ed.) (1990) *Between War and Peace in Central America, Choices for Canada*, Toronto: Between the Lines and CAPA.

Prensa Libre (1998a) 'Más críticas a libro de Menchú' 16 December.

Prensa Libre (1998b) 'Es mi testimonio y lo defenderé' 17 December.

Prensa Libre (1998c) 'Ataques a Menchú son racistas' 17 December.

Prensa Libre (1998d) 'La otra versión' 17 December.

Reid, Larry (1999) 'David Stoll and the Story of All Poor Solidarity Activists', paper presented at the Canadian Association of Latin American and Caribbean Studies conference, Ottawa, Canada.

Siglo Veintiuno (16 December 1998a) 'Rigoberta miente en autobiografía'.

Stoll, David S. (1993) *Between Two Armies in the Ixil Towns of Guatemala*. New York: Columbia University Press.

Stoll, David S. (1999) *Rigoberta Menchú and the Story of All Poor Guatemalans*, Boulder, CO: Westview Press.

Stoll, David S. (1999b) Exchange of letters to the editor, the *Nation* 14 June.

*This paper was first published in* Development in Practice *(11/1: 77–85) in 2001.*

# The People's Communication Charter

## Cees J. Hamelink

*The development of the GII ... must be a democratic effort ... In a sense,
the GII will be a metaphor for democracy itself ... I see a new Athenian Age
of democracy forged in the fora the GII will create ... The Global
Information Infrastructure ... will circle the globe with information
superhighways on which all people can travel. These highways — or,
more accurately, networks of distributed intelligence — will allow us to
share information, to connect, and to communicate as a global community.*
(US Vice-President Al Gore)

### Highway Utopias

Development has never seemed so easy to achieve. An abundance of
Utopian scenarios promise sustainable development once digital
highways have been constructed. The deployment of new information
and communication technologies (ICTs) is to usher in a 'new civilisation',
an 'information revolution', or a 'knowledge society'.

This line of thought emphasises historical discontinuity as a major
consequence of technological developments. New social values will evolve,
new social relations will develop, and the 'zero sum society' comes to
a definite end, once ICTs have realised worldwide access to information
for all.

The current highway Utopias forecast radical changes in economics,
politics, and culture. In the economy, the ICTs will create more
productivity and improved chances for employment. They will upgrade
the quality of work in many occupations, and also offer myriad
opportunities for small-scale, independent, and decentralised forms of
production. In the domain of politics, the decentralised and increased
access to unprecedented volumes of information will improve the
process of democratisation. All people will be empowered to participate
in public decision-making. In the cultural field, new and creative
lifestyles will emerge, as well as vastly extended opportunities for

different cultures to meet and understand each other; and new 'virtual communities' will be created which easily cross all the traditional borders of age, gender, race, and religion.

The essential vehicle to make these dreams come true will be the 'Global Information Infrastructure' (GII). The GII was launched by US Vice-President Al Gore in a speech at the 1994 conference of the International Telecommunication Union (ITU) in Buenos Aires. The proposal has received a good deal of international political and corporate support. The meeting of the G-7 in Brussels in February 1995 decided to move ahead with implementing this global infrastructure. Its Final Declaration stated that the global information society is expected to enrich people worldwide by providing, to developing countries and countries in transition, the chance 'to leapfrog states of technology'. Countries such as Canada, Japan, Singapore, and the European Union are intent on the rapid realisation of national information infrastructures.

The developing world has also shown considerable interest, as illustrated by the African region. Interest in ICTs was very prominent during the First African Regional Symposium on Telematics for Development (1995) and also at the 21st session of the Conference of African Ministers responsible for Economic, Social and Development Planning in the same year. The 1995 Cairo Workshop on the Role and Impact of Information and Communication Technologies in Development recommended that 'without proper national information and communication policies, strategies and implementation plans, countries will not be able to partake fully in the global information society'. Although most African countries are not known as hot-spots for ICT development, the United Nations Economic Commission for Africa (ECA) Conference of Ministers adopted on 2 May 1995 Resolution 795, 'Building Africa's Information Highway'. In this, African ministers for economic and social development requested that the ECA set up a high-level working group on information and communication technologies in Africa made up of African technical experts, with a view to preparing a plan of action. The High-Level Working Group (after meetings in Cairo, Addis Ababa, and Dakar) produced Africa's Information Society Initiatives: An Action Framework to Build Africa's Information and Communication Infrastructure. In May 1996, the plan was authorised by the Conference of Ministers meetings at Addis Ababa. The May 1996 Conference on Information Society and Development (ISAD) in South Africa was the venue for launching this initiative, which by 2010 foresees for Africa an information society in which:

Every man and woman, schoolchild, village, government office, and business can access information through computers and telecommunications; Information and decision support systems are used to support decision making in all the major sectors of each nation's economy; Access is available throughout the region to international, regional and national 'information highways'; A vibrant private sector exhibits strong leadership in growing information-based economies; African information resources are accessible globally reflecting content on tourism, trade, education, culture, energy, health, transport, and natural-resource management; and Information and knowledge empower all sectors of society.

Big info-communications business is also taking a growing interest. Companies such as Time/Warner are making massive investments to secure a profitable place on the Information Superhighway. The GII project has a large number of 'computeropian prophets' such as European Commissioner Martin Bangemann, the Chief Executive Officers of companies such as AT&T, IBM, Microsoft, and American Express, media-tycoon Rupert Murdoch, authors such as Alvin Toffler, and US Vice-President Al Gore. The latter stated in his Buenos Aires address that the GII is a prerequisite to sustainable development. It will provide solutions to environmental problems, improve education and healthcare, create a global market-place, and forge a new Athenian age of democracy.

It is obviously true that ICTs can perform tasks that are indeed essential to democratic and sustainable social development. They can provide low-cost, high-speed, worldwide inter-active communications among large numbers of people, unprecedented access to information sources, and alternative channels for information provision which counter the commercial news channels; and they can support networking, lobbying, and mobilising. The 1995 Fourth World Conference on Women held in Beijing, for example, showed the benefits that women's groups could get from using ICTs. The overall experience of those involved in the Beijing electronic networking (despite all the real limitations) was that the low-cost and high-speed communications had improved organisational efficiency and facilitated access to up-to-date information. Southern NGOs indicated that the networks had allowed them to influence the conference agenda, to mobilise lobbies, and to counter commercial press coverage. The participants generally felt that the technology had strong empowerment potential. There are, however, serious obstacles in the way of realising this potential.

## Economic factors

The introduction and use of ICTs do not take place in a social vacuum. This process cannot be separated from the emerging global communication order. The reality of this order is a global info-communications market that has yielded in 1997 over US$1.5 trillion in revenues, and that continues to feature a process of mergers and acquisitions which is very likely to lead to the control of the world's information and cultural supply by some four to six multi-media mega-conglomerates around the turn of the century.

Today's forerunner of the projected GII, the Internet, has begun to attract the attention of the major forces in this global market-place. The Internet, at present a public meeting place where more than 30 million PC users in some 150 countries exchange information, search databases, play games, and chat — and which has been guided by the rule of sharing information for free — has now been discovered as a major vehicle for commercial advertising. This raises the question: will the Internet (the Net) remain an open, free, competitive, egalitarian public space? This is highly unlikely, since it cannot develop outside the current global economic order. It is fast becoming the new global advertising medium.

There is a great battle underway, with the future control of the world's largest network at stake. Money-making on the Net will require it to become an advertising medium. For companies to re-coup their enormous investments, advertising and sales will be essential. The competition to attract advertising dollars is already starting. As a result, a communicative structure that so far has been public, non-commercial, unregulated, uncensored, anarchistic, and very pluralistic may soon turn into a global electronic shopping mall.

It is difficult to understand how this transformation of the Net from a public forum into a commercial vehicle (much as happened in many countries with television) can contribute to the realisation of the empowerment potential of ICTs. In any case, if the GII project is predominantly driven by the search for profits, it is highly improbable that current inequalities in access to and use of ICTs will go away.

## Political obstacles

An important political obstacle to the creation of open, public networks is the current global trend towards deregulatory policies. Their bottom line is that the introduction and use of ICTs should be largely, if not totally, a matter of market relations. The G-7 and the EU governments have reiterated that the GII will have to be constructed primarily through private investments.

Global and regional policy-making (primarily) addresses the removal of all obstacles in the way of the unhindered operation of the major ICT-investors on markets around the world. The policies of the World Trade Organisation (WTO) and International Monetary Fund (IMF) are instrumental in supporting the global commercial media system. They are not particularly helpful to the democratisation of the world's info-communications sector. A landmark in deregulatory policies is the 1997 WTO telecom agreement. This requires signatories (68 countries, representing 98 per cent of the US$600 billion telecom trade) to liberalise their markets to foreign competition. According to various governments, this will strongly facilitate the global Super-highway, but most probably as an infrastructure for transnational business, rather than necessarily as platform for public debate on social development.

The agreement has seriously compromised the chances for universal network access, since national policies may be considered anti-competitive if governments intervene in the market to guarantee universal service. According to industry spokesmen, the agreement will speed up the search for global alliances.

## Info-telecom disparity

There seems to be general agreement in the scientific literature and in public policy statements that the gap in access to ICTs between the developed and developing countries in widening, and that this hinders the integration of all countries into the Global Information Society. The seriousness of the gap is clearly demonstrated by the figures for the world distribution of telephony.

- There are one billion telephones in the world and approximately 5.7 billion people. Today some 15 per cent of the world population occupy 71 per cent of the world's main telephone lines. Low-income countries (where 55 per cent of the world population lives) have fewer than 5 per cent of the world's telephone lines.
- High-income countries have 50 telephone lines per 100 inhabitants. Many low-income countries have less than one telephone line per 100; this ranges from Cambodia with 0.06 to China with 0.98 in 1992 (according to figures provided by the ITU/BDT Telecommunication Indicator Database).
- More than half the world's population have never even used a telephone!

- Fewer than 6 per cent of Internet computers are in Eastern Europe, Asia, Africa, the Middle East, Latin America and the Caribbean. Fewer than 4 per cent of World Wide Web users are in the Third World.
- In India there is one telephone line and 0.2 PCs for 100 people, compared with 49 lines and 15 PCs in Japan, and 63 lines and 21 PCs per 100 people in the USA.

The reality of the widening gap in ICT capacity raises the serious concern that the poorer countries may not be able to overcome the financial and technical obstacles which hamper their access to the new technologies. An obvious question is whether the international community is ready to provide the massive investments needed for the renovation, upgrading, and expansion of networks in developing countries. To illustrate the scope of funds involved: it would take some US$12 billion to get half of the Philippines population on the Internet. To increase tele-density from 0.46 lines per 100 inhabitants to one per 100 in sub-Saharan Africa would require an investment of US$ 8 billion.

A particular funding problem also arises if the Internet is to be transformed into a global inter-active electronic highway. This demands a radical expansion of current band-width to transport all these signals. Simply to provide broad-band capacity to all US citizens would demand investments of several hundreds of billions of dollars.

In response to the challenge of the info-telecom gap, many public and private donor institutions have proposed plans to eliminate the disparity. Concern about the gap has inspired the World Bank, for example, to establish in early 1995 the Information for Development Program, charged with assisting developing countries in their integration into the global information economy. In 1995, the ITU established WorldTel: an ambitious project to generate private investments to bridge the global telecom gap by developing basic infrastructures. WorldTel aims to establish some 40 million telephone connections in developing countries in the next ten years, with an investment fund of at least US$ 1 billion.

AT&T plans that its Africa One project should have a fully operational optical fibre cable around the whole continent by 1999 to provide connections for all the major coastal cities. Siemens and Alcatel also have designs (Afrilink and Atlantis-2 respectively) to provide telecom connections, especially to West Africa. Both the International Satellite Organisation (IntelSat) and the Regional African Satellite Organisation are actively promoting the expansion of e-mail services for the continent.

Apart from the mismatch between these plans and the funds that are really required, there is also the critical issue of the appropriateness of the technologies to be transferred, and the capacity of the recipient countries to master them. Current discussion on 'the gap' provides no convincing argument that the technology owners will change their attitudes and policies towards the international transfer of technology. Hitherto, the prevailing international policies have erected formidable obstacles to the reduction of North–South technology gaps. Today, there is no indication that existing restrictive business practices, the constraints on the ownership of knowledge, and the rules on intellectual property rights that are adverse to developing-country interests are radically changing. There are as yet no realistic prospects that the relations between ICT-rich and ICT-poor countries will change in the near future.

The key actors in international ICT policy-making have expressed a clear preference to leave the construction of the Global Information Society to 'the forces of the free market'. It would seem that under the institutional arrangements of a corporate-capitalist market economy, the development of an equitable information society remains a very unlikely proposition.

An any rate, it may be questioned whether within the realities of the international economic order there *can* be any serious reduction of the disparity. It may well be an illusion to think that ICT-poor countries could catch up or keep pace with advances in the North, where the rate of technological development is very high and is supported by considerable resources. This is not to say that poor countries should not try to upgrade their ICTs. They should not, however, do this in the unrealistic expectation that those who are ahead will wait for them. The situation may improve for the poorer countries, but the disparity will not go away.

## What should be done?

The most immediate political challenge today is the fact that the use of ICTs for sustainable development will be determined not by technology, but by politics. The realisation of their potential requires a re-thinking of the wisdom about current deregulatory policies, a re-thinking of the role of public funding, and a massive effort in training and education for the mastery of ICTs.

This political agenda is unlikely to be taken seriously if ICT policies are left to Princes and the Merchants alone. If market-driven arrangements are — for some time to come — the standard environment within which ICTs will be deployed, then the only force that could make a real difference are the ordinary people who buy on the market, and who have the (often unused and rarely recognised) power to say 'no'.

The realisation of the empowerment potential of ICTs should, therefore, primarily be the concern of civil-society organisations. They need to mobilise and lobby for and with the ordinary men and women whose lives will be affected by the digital futures that are currently envisaged. Today there is only a very modest beginning of a global civil activism in the info-communications sector, connected with the People's Communication Charter, described below. These movements must urgently extend their reach by attracting the support of large public-interest organisations (labour unions, educational institutions, religious bodies) and intergovernment organisations such as UNESCO and ITU.

Since our cultural environment is as essential to our common future as is the natural ecology, it is time for people's movements to focus on the organisation and quality of the production and distribution of information and other cultural expressions. Mobilising the users' community, and stimulating critical reflection on the quality of the cultural environment, is a tall order. However, it can be done, and it is actually being done. An increasing number of individuals and groups around the world are beginning to express concern about the quality of media performance. A start has also been made with the creation of a broad international movement of alert and demanding media users, based upon what has been called the *People's Communication Charter*.

## The People's Communication Charter

This Charter is an initiative of the Third World Network (TWN) in Malaysia, the Centre for Communication and Human Rights in The Netherlands, the Cultural Environment Movement in the USA, and AMARC — the World Association of Community Radio Broadcasters — based in Peru and Canada. In the early 1990s, academics and activists associated with TWN and its affiliated Consumers' Association of Penang (CAP) initiated a debate on the feasibility of a world people's movement in the field of communication and culture.

The TWN and CAP had already an impressive record in developing people's movements in such areas as reforming international trade and conservation of the tropical rain forest. They had proved capable of bringing the concerns of grassroots people in the South to the diplomatic negotiations of the Uruguay GATT multilateral trade round, and UNCED in Rio de Janeiro.

An obvious problem is that information consumers are seldom organised in representative associations. They are a diverse community, geographically dispersed and ideologically fragmented. The *People's Communication Charter* was seen as a first step in creating a constituency for concerns about the quality of the cultural environment. It provides a common framework for those who share the belief that people should be active and critical participants in their social reality, and capable of governing themselves. The Charter may help to develop a permanent movement concerned with the quality of our cultural environment. One idea is to organise an International Tribunal which would receive complaints by signatories to the Charter, and invite the parties involved to submit evidence and defence upon which the Tribunal could come to a judgment.

The Charter is not an end in itself. It provides the basis for a permanent critical reflection on those worldwide trends that will determine the quality of our lives in the third millennium. It is, therefore, important to see it as an open document which can always be updated, amended, improved, and expanded. In fact, since the Charter was presented on the Web (http://ww.waag.org/pcc), new ideas and suggested changes have been proposed and discussed. A critical moment in the history of the Charter was the founding convention of the Cultural Environment Movement in March 1996, when the first public ratification of the text took place. In June 1997, the governing body of the World Association for Christian Communication (WACC) endorsed the Charter, following much discussion by WACC members in its eight regions; and important amendments proposed by its central committee.

In 1998, the Charter will be on the agenda of the General Assembly of AMARC and of the Paris Convention of the Cultural Environment Movement. For the celebration of the 50th anniversary of the Universal Declaration of Human Rights (UHDR) in December 1998, initiatives are being developed to secure some form of acclaim for the Charter from the international political community.

Most important, however, is the goal of soliciting more support for the ideas that the Charter embodies from individuals and institutions worldwide. In August 1996, for example, it was displayed at the famous Dokumenta exhibition at Kassel in Germany, and was discussed and signed by many visitors. The web-site of the Charter is where such events and progress in widening support for it are publicised.

Beyond the text itself and its endorsement, the most critical element for the future of the Charter is obviously its implementation. In an open, democratic, people's movement this cannot be organised by some central governing body. Implementation is very much the concern of local and national groups, either newly formed or already established for other (or similar) purposes. The realisation of the people's right to communicate cannot be an homogeneous project, but will take different forms in different socio-cultural and political contexts. In one country, this may be the institution of an ombudsman's office to be responsible for the quality of the cultural environment; in another a national award may be given to the TV programme found most in violation of the Charter's principles; in some places a civil-society campaign to rescue public broadcasting may be necessary; elsewhere the focus may be on protecting children or defending the media interests of people with a disability.

This is really the business of ordinary people. It is also the ultimate test-case for the meaning of the People's Communication Charter. It only makes sense if people themselves eventually begin to be concerned about implementing it.

*This paper was first published in* Development in Practice *(8/1: 68–73) in 1998.*

# Annotated bibliography

*Development-related advocacy – from high-level lobbying to development education to efforts to make local government accountable to local citizens – is increasingly an integral part of how development and relief NGOs go about their work. Since the early 1990s, there has been a growing literature from within the aid community outlining the intellectual underpinnings of this aspect of what was then referred to as 'scaling-up' NGO impact, and of external accounts and critiques of specific campaigns. More recently, in their focus on corporate social responsibility and on new (often transnational) social movements, scholars and activists have addressed the actual and potential role of advocacy by NGOs and other civil-society organisations in helping to achieve development goals or to redefine what these should be. We have sought to reflect these broad areas in this annotated bibliography.*

*While their goals and ways of working differ, there are also many development organisations for whom advocacy is their primary* raison d'être; *we have selected some of these in order to illustrate something of the range of organisational approaches to issues of major relevance to development, such as debt, employment, the environment, food, housing, human rights, indigenous peoples, and trade; as well as giving examples of innovative approaches to collaboration across the North–South divide and other major divides.*

*The bibliography was compiled by Nicola Frost with Deborah Eade, Reviews Editor and Editor respectively of* Development in Practice.

**Sanam Naraghi Anderlini**: *Women at the Peace Table: Making a Difference*, New York: UNIFEM, 2000.
Although the particular effects of armed conflict on women have been recognised in recent years, the implications for women's involvement in advocating for peace have yet to be fully accepted, despite numerous international commitments. This cross-regional study highlights the activities of women who have organised to resist militarisation and to influence peace negotiations. Examples from prominent activists in Burundi, Northern Ireland, and Cambodia, among others, show how women's participation in all stages of peace negotiations is crucial for establishing a peace which is sustainable, equitable, and inclusive. The book aims to share individual

experiences and strategies, and to examine some of the challenges facing women working for peace. Full text available online at www.undp.org/unifem/

**Alan Barker, Firoze Manji et al**: *Writing for Change: An Interactive Guide to Effective Writing, Writing for Science and Writing for Advocacy*, Fahamu and IDRC, 2000, CD-ROM.

An interactive resource to help fundraisers, researchers, and campaigners to develop effective writing skills. The section on advocacy includes hints on how to adapt material for specific lobbying and campaigning needs. It includes practical examples and exercises, some of which can be used by people training writers, and links to relevant websites.

**Sharon Beder**: *Global Spin: The Corporate Assault on Environmentalism*, 2nd edn., Carlton North, Australia: Scribe Publications, 2000.

The author examines the techniques employed by global corporations to manipulate public and political opinion about environmental issues. Beder argues that 'corporate activism', emerging in the 1970s, and assuming new importance in the 1990s, has enabled the commercial sector to dominate the environmental debate to an alarming degree. The book explains how corporations fund civil-society 'front groups', or PR-generated grassroots responses, and promote issues that are in the interests of business; it illustrates how a similar relationship exists between corporations and some right-wing think tanks. It also considers corporate influence on the media.

**Manuel Castells**: *The Information Age: The Rise of the Network Society* (Vol. 1), 1996 and *The Power of Identity* (Vol. 2), Oxford: Blackwell 1997.

*The Information Age* is concerned with trends of globalisation and identity, in the context of the information-technology revolution and the restructuring of capitalism, which have given rise to 'the network society'. Characterised by the pervasive power of global capital, and interconnected media systems, networking is a growing form of global social organisation, and has been accompanied by expressions of collective identity which challenge globalisation and cosmopolitanism. The nation-state is thus called into question, while powerful technological media are now used by various contenders to amplify and sharpen their struggle, as for example in the *Zapatistas'* use of the Internet.

Volume 2 examines networks of identity such as religious communalism (including Islamic and Christian fundamentalism), and ethnic and territorial collective identity, which are elaborated into the broader theory of the Information Age. It also covers social movements against the New Global Order, the environmental movement, movements centred on issues of family and sexuality (such as some forms of feminism, and the US gay community), the relationship between States and social movements, and the role of the media and 'electronic popularism'.

**Jennifer Chapman and Amboka Wameyo**: *Monitoring and Evaluating Advocacy: A Scoping Study*, London: ActionAid, 2001.

A growing amount of NGO activity falls under the rubric of 'influencing and advocacy work', but there are as yet very few tools with which to measure and evaluate its impact or worth. This study is an overview of existing approaches to advocacy and frameworks for evaluating it, for example by Christian Aid, CIIR, NEF, Save the Children, and USAID. It includes a useful guide to recent publications and grey literature.

**Seamus Cleary**: *The Role of NGOs under Authoritarian Political Systems*, Basingstoke: Macmillan, 1997.

Drawing on his experience in Indonesia, South Africa, Sri Lanka, and the Philippines, the author challenges claims by Northern NGOs to represent the most vulnerable people in society, through their links with the grassroots. In Indonesia, for example, he shows how British NGOs, establishing themselves as interpreters of others' needs, actually exceeded local people's demands, and sacrificed accountability to serve institutional ends. The book draws general conclusions about whose interests are served by such representation, making distinctions between operational development organisations and advocacy-based NGOs. It also highlights the importance of domestic capacity for presenting advocacy cases as a crucial element in their success. See also 'In whose interest? NGO advocacy campaigns and the poorest', *International Relations* 12(5) 1995.

**David Cohen, Rosa de la Vega, and Gabrielle Watson**: *Advocacy for Social Justice: A Global Action and Reflection Guide*, Bloomfield CT: Kumarian, 2001.

Building civil society and nurturing democracy has become part of mainstream development discourse. But while some NGOs are taking the lead in this work, others still lack the skills needed to assume new roles in policy advocacy for social and economic justice. This book is a direct and interactive response to this growing need. The result of a collaboration between the Washington-based Advocacy Learning Institute and Oxfam America, this resource is the first comprehensive guide for worldwide advocates of social and economic justice. It explores the elements of advocacy and offers a toolkit for taking action, comprehensive case studies, training materials, and resource listings. A website supports the published resource with expanded directory material and background information.

**Robin Cohen and Shirin Rai (eds)**: *Global Social Movements*, London: Athlone Press, 2001.

While global economic forces, led by transnational corporations, shape the nature of globalisation from above, social movements in a variety of fields are influencing the new global consciousness from below. This activity indicates the shift into a new era of transnational social action which is more participatory and more focused. This book undertakes a wide-ranging and systematic analysis of the activities of social movements in areas such as human rights, religion, labour, environmental issues, and women's rights.

**Preecha Dechalert**: *NGOs, Advocacy and Popular Protest: A Case Study of Thailand*, International Working Paper No. 6, London: Centre for Civil Society, 1999.

Through examining a series of popular anti-government protests in Thailand in 1997, in which many local NGOs became involved, the author seeks to understand why public protest has become part of their advocacy work. The author argues that NGOs serve as 'resources', rather than full actors, by providing access to solidarity networks, and that they therefore can be seen as 'social movement organisations'. Full text available online at www.lse.ac.uk/Depts/ccs/

**Denise Deegan**: *Managing Activism: a Guide to Dealing with Activists and Pressure Groups*, London: Kogan Page, 2001.

Written by the head of a PR agency which deals with pharmaceutical companies, this book considers the issue from the perspective of the companies, governments, and organisations vulnerable to the 'threat' of activist activity. It covers approaches to communication with activists, and gives guidance on how to deal with hostile groups who are unwilling to negotiate. It offers strategies for managing community and media relations, and advice about planning a proactive communications programme.

**Michael Edwards and John Gaventa (eds)**: *Global Citizen Action*, Boulder CO: Lynne Rienner, 2001.

With contributions from a number of leading writers on civil society and global action, this book attempts to represent the cutting edge of thinking about non-State participation in international affairs. It examines the different agendas encompassed within 'civil society' and explores the nature of the engagement with international institutions. Chapters assess the potential for a Southern constituency for global advocacy movements, discuss the relationship between civil society and global financial institutions, and explore the possibilities for transnational advocacy networks.

**Jonathan A. Fox and L. David Brown (eds)**: *The Struggle for Accountability: The World Bank, NGOs, and Grassroots Movements*, Cambridge MA: MIT Press, 1998.

This book analyses reforms within the World Bank to adopt more rigorous environmental and social policies, and the subsequent conflicts over how and whether to follow them in practice. It asks how the Bank has responded to NGO/grassroots environmental critiques, with case studies to assess degrees of change, how far advocacy campaigns (often led by NGOs) represent those most directly affected by Bank projects, and to what extent NGOs are accountable to their own partners. The Bank is shown to be more publicly accountable as the result of protest, public scrutiny, and their empowering effect on inside reformers. Transnational NGO networks are also gradually becoming more accountable to their local partners – partly because of more vocal and autonomous grassroots movements, and partly in response to the Bank's challenge to the legitimacy of its NGO critics.

**Colin Fraser and Sonia Restrepo-Estrada**: *Communicating for Development: Human Change for Survival*, London: I.B. Tauris, 1998.
The authors argue that the substantial shift in human attitudes and behaviour needed to realise sustainable global development is best achieved through a focus on communication processes as a way of facilitating change. This book is full of lively illustrative examples, including observations of communication within and between institutions, as well as between 'developers' and 'developed'. The authors also consider the role of communications policies at the level of national government and conclude with a 'framework for action', which fits communication into a holistic strategy for sustainable development.

**Dan Gallin**: *Trade Unions and NGOs: a Necessary Partnership for Social Development*, Geneva: UNRISD, 2000.

This paper, prepared for Copenhagen Plus 5, argues that trade unions and NGOs are distinct from other actors in civil society in that they have 'specific agendas for the improvement of society', but it also emphasises the differences between them – most notably that NGOs can choose whether and how to become involved in labour-related issues. The author, head of the Global Labour Institute, reviews the history of their alliance, and considers new areas of co-operation, for example on environmental issues and gender equality.

**Sara Gibbs and Deborah Ajulu**: *The Role of the Church in Advocacy: Case Studies from Southern and Eastern Africa*, Occasional Papers Series No.31, Oxford: INTRAC 1999.

In this review of the involvement of churches and church organisations in advocating for human rights, democracy, and poverty alleviation in Africa, the authors consider what opportunities exist for mutual support from similarly involved NGOs in Europe. They examine the church's role in advocating specific issues such as human rights and democracy in Kenya; transition to a multi-party democracy in Malawi; and economic issues related to improving the basic standard of living in Zambia. The study focuses attention on the strength of national and international links as a crucial factor contributing to successful advocacy work, even at a grassroots level.

**Gustavo Gutiérrez**: *The Density of the Present: Selected Writings*, Orbis Books, New York: 1999.

Presenting the work of one of the intellectual architects of Liberation Theology, this anthology offers his account of a century of social teachings on the 'preferential option for the poor', and describes the political journey of Catholicism from Pope John II's encyclical on work, to the landmark 1968 Conference of Latin American Bishops at Medellín, and the 1992 Conference at Santo Domingo. This radical interpretation of Christian teaching inspired a continent-wide popular movement for change throughout the 1970s and 1980s, in which many of its proponents were persecuted. See also *A Theology of Liberation: History, Politics and Salvation* (1988) by the same author; *The Violence of Love* (1998) a posthumous work by Msgr Oscar Romero; and *2000: Reality and Hope*, edited by Jon Sobrino and Virgilio Elizondo.

**Richard Heeks**: *Information and Communication Technologies, Poverty and Development*, Development Informatics Working Paper No. 5, Manchester: Institute for Development Policy and Management, University of Manchester, 1999.

This paper looks at whether new information and communication technologies (ICTs) might contribute to poverty alleviation in developing countries, particularly through their application to small and micro-enterprises. It concludes that, since there are serious restrictions on access to ICTs, and to relevant data, their role is most likely to be one of facilitating communication and information sharing, making poor people 'information providers rather than information recipients'. The wider goal will be achieved only when the tendency to fetishise ICTs is overcome, and the true opportunity costs of investing in this area rather than others are understood. Full text available online at: www.man.ac.uk/idpm

**Institute for Development Research**: *Building Knowledge and Community for Advocacy*, Boston MA: IDR, 1999.

This report on a workshop on North–South advocacy partnerships explores the theory and the practice of advocacy work. Among the topics discussed are: measuring impact, advocacy models and assumptions about power, the challenges of North–South collaboration, capacity building in both Northern and Southern organisations, and building constituencies for advocacy initiatives. It offers a practical resource for anyone interested in fostering a local, national, or international community of advocates.

**Lisa Jordan and Peter van Tuijl**: *Political Responsibility in NGO Advocacy: Exploring Shapes of Global Democracy*, Washington/The Hague: World Bank Information Center/NOVIB, 1998.

NGOs have become a political reality as they mobilise, articulate, and represent people's interests or concerns in many decision-making arenas. However, the authors argue, the relationships among NGOs that engage in advocacy across geographical and institutional boundaries are highly problematic. Such dynamics determine the quality of NGO advocacy, both as a channel for differing goals and expectations of development as well as in effectively shaping new forms of democracy. This paper uses the concept of political responsibility to describe representation and accountability in transnational NGO networks. Based on case studies of NGO advocacy campaigns, the paper identifies four types of relationship which may develop among NGOs, each leading to different levels of accountability: the hybrid campaign, the concurrent campaign, the disassociated campaign, and the competitive campaign.

**Margaret E. Keck and Kathryn Sikkink (eds.)**: *Activists Beyond Borders: Advocacy Networks in International Politics*, Ithaca, NY: Cornell University Press, 1998.

The contributors to this volume examine pressure groups which take the form of networks of activists that coalesce and operate across national frontiers. They sketch the dynamics of emergence, strategies, and impact of activists from diverse nationalities working together on particular issues, such as violence against women. See also 'Transnational advocacy networks in international and regional politics', *International Social Science Journal*, 1999, 51(159): 89–101.

**Robin Mansell and Uta Wehn (eds.)**: *Knowledge Societies: Information Technology for Sustainable Development*, Oxford: OUP, 1998.

Commissioned by the United Nations Commission on Science and Technology for Development, this comprehensive study examines the potential risks and benefits for developing countries of the dramatic advances in the development of information and communication technologies. It considers how these new technologies can be used to promote development goals at a national level, through the strategic development of an inclusive 'knowledge society', including sections on developing indicators of participation, improving access and capacity with regard to information technology, and issues of intellectual property.

**Phil McManus and Gerald Schlabach (eds.):** *Relentless Persistence: Nonviolent Action in Latin America*, New Society Publishers, Philadelphia, 1991.

Introduced by the Brazilian priest Leonardo Boff, a leading proponent of Liberation Theology, this volume illustrates in human terms diverse social movements inspired or supported by the radical Catholic church – from Christian Base Communities to human-rights workers, from indigenous and landless people's organisations to popular resistance to military dictatorship. Through case studies and personal testimonies, this collection explores the relationship between faith and politics, and demonstrates the dynamic integration of reflection, strategy, and action that has given many thousands of ordinary people the courage to work for social transformation. See also Boff's 1997 work on the destruction of the Amazon and the oppression of Brazil's indigenous population, *Cry of the Earth, Cry of the Poor.*

**Carol Miller and Shahra Razavi (eds.):** *Missionaries and Mandarins: Feminist Engagement with Development Institutions*, London: IT Publications in association with UNRISD, 1998.

Contributors document various strategies adopted by women working within development bureaucracies to advance a feminist agenda – so-called 'femocrats' – and women's movements pushing for the adoption of progressive policies, with examples from Australia, Canada, Morocco, and New Zealand. Other contributions consider in a more generic fashion organisational behaviours and the way in which gender policies are often simultaneously promoted and undermined, both in State and intergovernment institutions and in the NGO sector. The overview essay by Shahra Razavi, 'Becoming multilingual: the challenges of feminist policy advocacy', is particularly relevant.

**Valerie Miller and Jane Covey:** *Advocacy Sourcebook: Frameworks for Planning, Action and Reflection*, Boston MA: IDR, 1997.

Aimed at advocates and trainers, this sourcebook offers analysis and practical advice to organisations wishing to expand their advocacy capacity. The result of joint-learning projects between Southern and Northern NGOs, the book draws upon the growing body of collective NGO knowledge and experience around the world. Containing a broad range of frameworks and concepts, as well as case studies of successful advocacy efforts, it provides strategies for assessing public-policy systems, increasing organisational capacity building, and measuring the impact of individual advocacy campaigns. Valerie Miller is also author of *Policy Influence by Development NGOs: A Vehicle for Strengthening Civil Society* (*IDR Reports* 11(5), 1994) and *NGO and Grassroots Policy Influence: What is Success?* (1994) in *NGOs In Policy Influence: A Selection of IDR Reports* (1997) Collection IV. (See IDR entry for more information.)

**Andrew A. Moemeka (ed.):** *Development Communication in Action: Building Understanding and Creating Participation*, Lanham, Maryland: University Press of America, 2000.

Moemeka's vision of development communication is one of dialogue, discussion, and exchange rather than persuasion. This book begins by tracing the changing communication roles that have accompanied the paradigm shifts in development in the last 50 years. It examines the cultural implications of the 'new world communication order', where access to information is recognised as a critical index of power. Although the book has a strong conceptual and theoretical element, contributors also consider the role of the mass media and religion in development communication, and there is a reminder of the importance of effective intra-household communication with regard to issues such as domestic violence.

**Paul Nelson:** *The World Bank and NGOs: The Limits of Apolitical Development*, London: Macmillan, 1995.

Drawing on academic study and activist research, the author explores the growing NGO involvement with World Bank activities, both as partners in programmes to mitigate the social cost of structural adjustment, and as promoters of an 'NGO agenda' in policy dialogues. He examines the implications for global development of the Bank's apparently more informal, pragmatic approach, and asks whether NGOs' engagement with its policy and practice compromises their own legitimacy in developing civil-society institutions. He concludes that strategies of engagement and collaboration have more often resulted in NGOs becoming vehicles for service delivery than instruments for evaluation and scrutiny. Hence, the rapprochement is changing NGOs more than the Bank. Nelson concludes that dialogue and monitoring are critical.

**Andy Norrell:** *Bridging Gaps or 'A Bridge Too Far'? The management of advocacy within service providing NGOs in the UK*, International Working Paper No.3, London: Centre for Civil Society, LSE, 1999

NGOs' greater involvement in advocacy has resulted in changes to their organisational structures and strategies, with implications for internal and external relationships. This study includes a literature review on the links between NGO growth, the emergence of different organisational forms for advocacy and collective action, and organisational change. Advocacy management differs from that of service-provision, and a structural approach makes it easier to see how the integration of an advocacy function could strengthen organisational links. A survey of 17 British NGOs allows the author to suggest how NGO service-providers can combine appropriate organisational structures and strategies for managing advocacy. Full text available online at www.lse.ac.uk\depts\ccs

**Peter Nwosu, Chuka Onwumechili, and Ritchard M'Bayo (eds.):** *Communication and the Transformation of Society: a Developing Region's Perspectives*, Lanham, Maryland: University Press of America, 1995.

The contributors to this book cover an exceptionally wide range of topics relating to the theory and practice of communication for development across Africa. The book opens with a theoretical framework for considering the function of communication policy in promoting and supporting social and economic development. Contributors then consider the role of the media in African history, and contemporary use patterns, in order to contextualise the application of development communication to sectors such as health care and agriculture. Case studies illustrate this application, and the book ends with some potential future directions. Although the world of communication technology is changing very quickly, the book's sound conceptual focus means that it is less likely to date than other similar works.

**Robert O'Brien, Anne Marie Goetz, Jan Aart Scholte, and Marc Williams:** *Contesting Global Governance: Multilateral Economic Institutions and Global Social Movements,* Cambridge: Cambridge University Press, 2000.

This book examines the relationship between global social movements (GSMs) and the multilateral economic institutions (MEIs) over the last two decades. Do the GSMs play a significant role in global governance? What influence have they had over the internal structures and practices of the economic institutions? The authors argue that an understanding of this relationship is the key to comprehending the form and nature of global governance. The case studies used to unpack these interactions include the World Bank and the women's movement, the WTO and labour, the IMF and civil-society groups, and the contrasting approaches of the Bank and the WTO in engaging with environmental groups. The conclusion is that the current situation is best described as a concept of 'complex multilateralism', a hybrid model of interactions, but one which results in only minor reform of the economic institutions.

**Molly Reilly and Margaret Schuller (eds.):** *Becoming an Advocate Step by Step: Women's Experiences in Central and Eastern Europe and the Newly Independent States,* Washington DC: Women, Law and Development International, 2000.

With contributions from human-rights activists from many countries in Central and Eastern Europe, this book seeks to describe the incremental process of learning and participation experienced in the development of human-rights advocacy in these States, as much as it documents the achievements of policy change. The papers give some insight into the particular problems facing advocates in a region with weak civil society and legal systems, and considerable social and economic dislocation.

**Judith Richter:** *Holding Corporations Accountable: Corporate Conduct, International Codes, and Citizen Action,* London: Zed Books, 2001.

As large transnational corporations have an increasing impact on many aspects of social and economic life, this book asks whether it is sufficient to continue to rely of industry self-regulation alone. The author argues that the most successful method of fostering a global political climate amenable to practical regulation of TNCs is to attend closely to their adherence to such regulation as currently exists. She also explores the roles of citizen groups, national governments, and international agencies.

**Amory Starr:** *Naming the Enemy: Anti-Corporate Social Movements Confront Globalization,* London: Zed Books, 2000.

A systematic survey and analysis of the social movements that oppose the way in which multinational corporations exploit the legal mechanisms of globalisation to the detriment of human rights and national sovereignty. The author suggests a three-part typology of these movements: those that use existing democratic institutions, State structures, and direct action to constrain corporate power; those that build new transnational democratic frameworks for a more populist and participatory approach to social justice; and those seeking to de-link communities from the global system in favour of small-scale local economies.

**Henk Thomas (ed.):** *Globalisation and Third World Trade Unions*, London: Zed Books, 1995.

Addressing the crisis in which the Southern organised labour movement has found itself, the author finds that as a result of globalisation, and transnational corporate management strategies, trade union membership has been eroded, and labour is increasingly casualised. Structural adjustment has reduced the ability of the State to intervene in labour issues, just as the informal sector grows in importance, and many women, often unorganised, enter the workforce. He examines these challenges in Africa, Asia, and Latin America, and considers some potential strategies which trade unions might use to protect standards of living and labour rights in the South.

**UNESCO:** *World Communication and Information Report 1999–2000*, UNESCO Publishing, Paris, 1999.

This report offers an overview of the development of information and communication technologies and their socio-cultural impacts, particularly on human development and on the role of government. Freedom of the media, the role of public-service broadcasting, editorial independence, the use of the Internet in education, cultural pluralism, worldwide access to information resources, challenges to intellectual property, and censorship on the Internet are discussed by eminent specialists from all origins. Regional chapters examine to what extent telecommunications, computers, and the Internet reach developed and developing countries, urban and rural areas, literate and illiterate, the rich and the poor.

**Jim Walch:** *In the Net: A Guide for Activists*, London: Zed Books, 1999.

Written for activists, this book is a practical guide to progressive uses of information and communication technology for social and political change. However, it also gives an overview of the history of the Internet, in particular the way in which computer networking has moved from being an exclusive instrument of State and business, to being a tool for 'global humanisation'. The argument is supported by case studies from a variety of political and social contexts worldwide.

**Lawrence Marshall Wallack et al:** *News for a Change: An Advocate's Guide to Working with the Media*, London: Sage, 1999.

Written by seasoned activists with long experience of media advocacy, this guide provides step-by-step instructions for working strategically with the media to promote social change. It includes sections on using advertising as well as the more obvious avenue of news media and internet channels, to achieve visibility, gather support, and challenge established positions. There is also advice on how to evaluate media work.

**Thomas G. Weiss and Leon Gordenker (eds.)**: *NGOs, the UN, and Global Governance*, Boulder CO: Lynne Rienner, 1996.

Based on a special issue of *Third World Quarterly*, this book discusses the implications of the 'NGO phenomenon' – particularly the growing influence of transnational NGOs in promoting a principle of decentralised, collaborative 'global governance'. Contributions examine a range of NGO activities and relationships, including NGO interaction with the UN on issues such as the environment, HIV/AIDS, and the international women's movement. The conclusion is that the UN–NGO relationship is characterised by ambiguity: issues of accountability became more urgent as NGOs become more influential, yet continued NGO pressure and scrutiny is needed to ensure that the UN's rhetoric of transparency and participation is put into practice.

**Peter Willetts (ed.)**: *'The Conscience of the World': The Influence of Non-Governmental Organisations in the UN System*, London: Hurst, 1996.

Taking a deliberately broad definition of NGOs, this book aims to trace the history of their growing involvement with the UN, and the development of transnational NGO advocacy networks. There are portraits of NGO relations with various UN agencies, especially with relation to human rights and the environment, with chapters written by staff of Amnesty International and Save the Children. The conclusion, which may sound slightly dated today, is optimistic about the growing potential for NGO influence at the UN.

**Anne Winter**: *Is Anyone Listening? Communicating Development in Donor Countries*, Geneva: UN NGLS, 1996.

Drawing on a series of consultations on communication for development, the author focuses on how communicators might help to formulate new and more nuanced understandings of development and gain broad public support for an international agenda of support for and solidarity with people living in poverty. She examines the phenomenon of 'donor fatigue', but finds that the general public is rightly sceptical about the relationship between aid and development, weary of being patronised by aid agencies who over-simplify the issues in order to raise funds, and confused by limited and generally negative coverage of poverty-related issues in the mass media.

**World Vision** has produced a number of thought-provoking titles on NGO advocacy, in addition to its own position papers. See, in particular, the multi-authored *African Voices on Advocacy and Transnational NGOs and Advocacy* (Discussion Papers 4 and 5), both published by World Vision UK in 1997.

# Journals

*(Few journals are dedicated to this subject; see author entries for individual articles.)*

**Development in Practice**: published five times a year by Carfax, Taylor & Francis on behalf of Oxfam GB. ISSN; 0961-4524. Editor: Deborah Eade.

A multi-disciplinary journal of practice-based analysis and research concerning the social dimensions of development and humanitarianism, which acts as a forum for debate and the exchange of ideas among practitioners, policy makers, and academics worldwide. The journal seeks to challenge current assumptions, stimulate new thinking, and shape future ways of working. Other relevant titles in the *Development in Practice Readers* series include: *Development and Social Action* and *Development, NGOs, and Civil Society*. www.developmentinpractice.org.

**The Ecologist**: published monthly. Editor: Zac Goldsmith.

The world's longest-running environmental magazine, *The Ecologist* covers a broad range of both topical and broader debates, such as the implications of globalisation for employment, health, and the environment; farming, and ecological protests of all kinds. The website has details of related campaigns events around the world. www.theecologist.org/

**Global Networks**: published quarterly by Blackwell. ISSN: 1470-2266. Editor: Alisdair Rogers.

This new journal (launched in January 2001) approaches transnationalism and globalisation from a social scientific perspective. It looks at cultural, economic, and political networks with bases in international business, family relationships, or social organisations, and considers how these new forms of transnational association can 'enable the imagination and construction of innovative forms of human solidarity and citizenship', which can include resistance and alternatives to the prevailing model of globalisation. www.globalnetworksjournal.com/

**The International Journal of Children's Rights:** published quarterly by Kluwer, ISSN: 0927-5568. Editor: Michael Freeman.

Edited by lawyers, this journal provides an explicitly interdisciplinary perspective on the policy and practice of furthering children's right in all parts of the world. Recent issues have included papers on relevant UN conventions, labour issues, and religion.

**Gazette: The International Journal for Communication Studies:** published six times a year by Sage. ISSN: 0016-5492. Editor: Cees J. Hamelink.

Publishing articles on the full range of communications and technology issues, the journal focuses on the role of communication in world politics and world trade, and the relationship between communication and development processes. As well as covering more theoretical fields, it explores the legal, social, and ethical implications of new communications technologies, and in particular the implications of international human-rights standards for communications policy and planning.

**New Internationalist:** published monthly.

Edited in rotation by members of the NI cooperative, each issue takes a theme relating to an aspect of poverty and social injustice, with extensive lists of 'action groups' campaigning on the issues covered. Recent topics include global governance, fair trade, torture, and sustainability. The website has some useful search engines, allowing searches by theme, author, or date. The entire magazine, plus back issues, is available online. http://oneworld.org/ni/

**Nonprofit and Voluntary Sector Quarterly:** published quarterly by Sage. ISSN: 0899-7640. Editor: Steve Rathgeb Smith.

The journal publishes articles which report on research on voluntarism, citizen participation, philanthropy, civil society, and non-profit organisations.

# Organisations

**Amnesty International** is a worldwide campaigning movement which works to promote all the human rights enshrined in the Universal Declaration of Human Rights (UDHR) and other international standards. In particular, AI campaigns to free all prisoners of conscience; ensure fair and prompt trials for political prisoners; abolish the death penalty, torture, and other cruel treatment of prisoners; end political killings and 'disappearances'; and oppose abuses of human rights by opposition groups. With around one million members and supporters in 162 countries and territories, AI is possibly the world's largest organisation that advocates on behalf of others. Address: International Secretariat, 99–119 Rosebery Avenue, London, EC1R 4RE, UK. E-mail: amnestyis@amnesty.org. Web: www.amnesty.org

**Association for Progressive Communication** is a global network of NGOs whose mission is to empower and support organisations, social movements, and individuals in and through the use of information and communication technologies to build strategic communities and initiatives in order to contribute to equitable human development, social justice, participatory political processes, and environmental sustainability. APC advocates for and facilitates the use of information and communications technologies (ICTs) by civil society, defends and promotes non-commercial on-line space for NGOs, and seeks to ensure that these concerns inform telecommunications, donor, and investment policies. The *APC Toolkit Project: Online Publishing and Collaboration* is developing and adapting software tools to meet the unique needs of activists and non-profit groups. Address: APC Secretariat, Presidio Building 1012, Torney Avenue PO Box 29904, San Francisco CA 94129, USA. E-mail: apcadmin@apc.org. Web (in English and Spanish): www.apc.org

**The Bretton Woods Project** circulates information, undertakes research, and monitors and advocates for change in the Bretton Woods institutions. Issues addressed include structural adjustment programmes, conditionality, and controversial large projects. Its bulletin, *Bretton Woods Update*, is available in print, e-mail, and web versions. *New Leaf or Fig Leaf? The challenge of the new Washington Consensus* (2000), by Brendan Martin, was co-published with Public Services International (PSI). E-mail: info@brettonwoodsproject.org. Web: www.brettonwoodsproject.org

**Catholic Institute for International Relations (CIIR)** is a UK-based agency with current advocacy programmes on civil society, advocacy and trade, and social justice and human security. CIIR has been a long-term supporter of the struggle for freedom from oppression in East Timor, and has published widely on the topic. Relevant publications include: Rolando Modina, *Democratising Development: Civil Society Advocacy in South East Asia* (2000). Address: Unit 3 Canonbury Yard, 190a New North Road, London N1 7BJ, UK. E-mail: ciir@ciir.org. Web: www.ciir.org/

**El Comité de América Latina y el Caribe para la Defensa de los Derechos de la Mujer (CLADEM)** is a women's rights network made up of individuals and women's organisations throughout Latin America and the Caribbean region. It undertakes and encourages a wide range of initiatives in order to defend and promote women's rights: legislative reform, legal casework, training, university teaching, publications, and solidarity work. In order to avoid a centralised or hierarchical structure, CLADEM is made up of semi-autonomous national chapters; its coordinating committee is currently based in Argentina. www.eurosur.org/CLADEM/

**Development Alternatives with Women for a New Era (DAWN)** is a network of women scholars and activists from the South who engage in feminist research and analysis of the global environment and are committed to working for economic justice, gender justice, and democracy. DAWN's global advocacy is aimed at influencing mainstream development thinking and policy, securing the gains made at UN conferences, working for greater accountability and radical restructuring of international financial institutions, and mainstreaming gender analysis in development organisations. Address: DAWN Secretariat, The University of the South Pacific, Suva, Fiji. Email:<dawn@is.com.fj>. Web: www.dawn.org

**The Development Group for Alternative Policies (Development GAP)** assists Southern organisations to engage with international development-policy debates, and to ensure that Southern concerns and opinions inform decisions made in the North about global economic and environmental issues. It helps to develop NGO coalitions in the North which work in partnership with Southern counterparts on economic and environmental issues. Its analysis and advocacy centre in Washington helps to formulate development alternatives, and to encourage and support Northern policy makers with an interest in promoting economic development rooted in local realities and priorities. Address: 927 Fifteenth Street NW, 4th Floor, Three McPherson Square, Washington DC 20005, USA. E-mail: dgap@developmentgap.org. Web: www.developmentgap.org.

**FoodFirst/Institute for Food and Development Policy (IFDP)**: IFDP, better known as FoodFirst, is a member-supported, non-profit think tank and education-for-action centre. Its work identifies root causes and value-based solutions to hunger and poverty. Regarding food as a fundamental human right, FoodFirst produces books, reports, articles, films, electronic media, and curricula, plus interviews, lectures, workshops and academic courses for the public, policy makers, activists, the media, students, educators, and researchers. The FoodFirst Information and Action Network (FIAN) is the action and campaigning partner of the Institute. Contact details: 398 60th Street, Oakland, CA 94608 USA. Email: foodfirst@foodfirst.org. Web: www.foodfirst.org/

**Freedom from Debt Coalition (FDC)** is a broad-based coalition of organisations, individuals, and political bodies advocating debt relief, economic reform, and the adoption of a pro-poor development model in the Philippines. It does this by a combination of grassroots popular education and mobilisation, high-level lobbying, and focused research. FDC was launched in 1988, in the wake of the popular uprising that led to the overthrow of the Marcos dictatorship. It has since grown into an internationally respected voice on economic issues and is a model of how to develop an issue-based alliance. Address: 34 Matiaga Street, Central District, Quezon City, Philippines. Email <mail@fdc.org.ph>.

**Global Policy Network** links policy and research institutions connected to trade-union movements worldwide. Its members feel that the neo-liberal policy regime being pursued by international and national institutions fails the test of social legitimisation and protects the interests of multinational investors, while undercutting the living standards and bargaining power of workers. The Network aims to foster international solidarity and share research and ideas on the common challenges of globalisation. www.globalpolicynetwork.org/

**Greenpeace** is an international environmental campaigning organisation with a strong local presence, which combines high-level lobbying with headline-grabbing direct action. The central website includes the opportunity to join more than 7000 existing 'cyberactivists' through the site's chat rooms, and there are plans to establish more focused action groups, which would also act as a self-categorising directory of members. International office: Keizersgracht 176, 1016 DW Amsterdam, The Netherlands. Web: www.greenpeace.org

**Habitat International Coalition** is an international alliance of 350 CSOs and NGOs from 70 countries working primarily on housing rights, forced evictions, and human settlements, and concentrating on the recognition, defence, and realisation of the human right to adequate housing. Its three committees work at various levels through training, alliance-building, using the UN system, and research: the Housing and Land Rights Committee (India), the Women and Shelter Network (Tanzania), and the Housing and Environment Committee (Senegal). E-mail: <hic@mweb.co.za>.

**Human Rights Watch (HRW)** is dedicated to protecting the human rights of all, standing with victims and activists to prevent discrimination, to uphold political freedom, to protect people from inhumane conduct in wartime, and to bring offenders to justice. Its extensive network of expert staff and local collaborators investigate and expose human-rights violations worldwide, basing their work on universal rights as embodied in international laws and treaties. Through its authoritative reports and press and advocacy work, HRW seeks to challenge governments, multilateral bodies, and other powerful institutions to end abusive practices and respect international human-rights law. In addition to reports and briefings, HRW produces an overview of human-rights abuses in its annual world report. It has four offices in the USA, as well as representation in Brussels and London. Its website contains information in Arabic, French, Portuguese, Russian, and Spanish. Address: 1630 Connecticut Avenue, N.W., Suite 500, Washington, DC 20009, USA. Web: www. hrw.org

**Institute for Development Research (IDR)** is a non-profit research, education, and consulting organisation dedicated to increasing the capacity of civil-society groups

**uris**

ia House, Bloomsbury Square,
n WC1B 4DZ, UK.
@ibtauris.com>

**CO**

de Fontenoy, F-75000, Paris,
. <www.unesco.org>

**M**

st 45th Street, 15th floor,
ork, NY 10017, USA.
n@undp.org>

**LS**

les Nations, 1211 Geneva 10,
land. <ngls@unctad.org>

**D**

les Nations, 1211 Geneva 10,
land. <info@unrisd.org>

**ity Press of America**

ston Way, Lanham, Maryland
USA.
vrl@rowman.com>

**, Law and Development**
**ional**

nnecticut Ave. NW, Suite 1100,
ton, DC 20036, USA.
ld.org>

**nk Public Information**

Street NW, Washington DC,
@worldbank.org

**s**

Street, London N1 9JF, UK.
edbooks.demon.co.uk>

to advance just and sustainable development. IDR believes that new knowledge should directly affect practice as well as policy making and theory building, and dissemination is therefore integral to its work. A wide range of resources, from *IDR Reports* to practical guides and thematic collections are available in print form and on-line, free of charge. Address: 44 Farnsworth Street, Boston MA 02210-1211, USA. Web: www.jsi.com/idr

**International Committee of the Red Cross (ICRC)** might seem an unlikely candidate for inclusion in this bibliography. However, much of its work is involved both in developing and promulgating international humanitarian law, and in the quiet diplomacy which allows it to work in highly charged situations. See S. Davey and J.L. Blondel (1999), 'The International Red Cross and Red Crescent Movement's involvement in public advocacy campaigns', *International Review of the Red Cross*, 81(833):149–81. Address: 19 avenue de la Paix, CH 1202 Genève, Switzerland. Web: www.icrc.org

**International Federation for Alternative Trade (IFAT)** is a global network of producers and alternative trading organisations (ATOs) which aims to improve the livelihood and well-being of disadvantaged people in developing countries; and to change unfair structures of international trade. In IFAT, producers of handcrafts and food products from the South work directly with buyers and managers of ATOs in a spirit of mutual trust. IFAT was formed in 1989 in response to the growing need to strengthen the ATOs to co-operate on an international level, to lobby on international issues, and to become more influential on the international stage. Address: IFAT Secretariat, 30 Murdock Road, Bicester, Oxon, OX26 4RF, UK. Web: www.ifat.org/

**Jubilee Plus** is the successor to Jubilee 2000, the debt-campaign coalition, operating under the umbrella of the New Economics Foundation (see separate entry). It will continue to link with debt campaigners worldwide in order to sustain momentum in global popular campaigning and education, while preparing to shift the campaign towards a focus on the causes of international debt. Jubilee Plus will continue Jubilee 2000's programme of analysis and research, and will add to existing capacity-building work in the South the aim of embedding more elements of the core campaign in the South. Web: www.Jubileeplus.org

**Movimento dos Trabalhadores Rurais Sem Terra (Brazilian Landless Rural Workers'** **Movement)** is the largest social movement in Latin America. MST's success lies in its ability to organise, to articulate a socio-economic development model which puts people before profits (for instance through organising food co-operatives and primary schools), and to capture the imagination of other farmers' movements and activist groups worldwide. MST has the support of an international network of human-rights groups, religious organisations, and labour unions. It is the Brazilian affiliate of La Via Campesina (www.agronor.org), a global peasant farmers' network which campaigns internationally on food and land-rights issues. MST has a multilingual website at www.mst.org/

**The New Economics Foundation (NEF)** is a UK-based think tank, committed to advancing models of a new economy centred on people and the environment. NEF works to promote participatory democracy and has a long-standing interest in enhancing corporate accountability. Relevant publications include Jennifer Chapman and Thomas Fisher (1999), *Effective NGO Campaigning: A New Economics Fou* *Briefing*. www.neweconomics.org/

**Oxfam International** believes that the causes and effects of poverty re global response and cannot be solved through project work alone. The OI A Office co-ordinates the development of joint strategies and policies fc members and for partners in the South. Through targeting influential pl governments and institutions such as the World Bank, the IMF, and the UN, C to influence the policies which affect the lives of millions of poor people. Thi co-ordinated, simultaneous lobbying in the countries where members ar lobbying with Southern partner organisations, and direct lobbying of institutions. Address: Suite 20, 266 Banbury Road, Oxford OX2 7I Email: information@oxfaminternational.org. Web: www.oxfaminternatio

**Self-Employed Women's Association (SEWA)** has more than 2 million men co-operatives, savings and credit schemes, and advocacy organisations. home-workers, manual workers, and small business owners, who are trad unprotected and unorganised. SEWA aims to improve its members' ba power, and to encourage recognition of their economic and social cont As well as organising at the local level, SEWA runs public campaigns in of its work. SEWA Reception Centre, Opp. Victoria Garden, Bhadra, Ah 380 001, India. E-mail: mail@sewa.org. Web: www.sewa.org.

**Survival International** supports the rights of tribal peoples worldwide supporters in 82 countries. Its advocacy work includes advising on the d international law and informing people of their legal rights. Educational pro in the North promote respect for tribal cultures and explain the conte relevance of their way of life. Survival believes that public opinion is the mos force for change which, if mobilised, will eventually make it impossible for gov and companies to oppress tribal peoples. Address: Survival Internati 11-15 Emerald Street, London WC1N 3QL, UK. Web: www.survival-interna

**The Third World Network (TWN)** is an international network of organisa individuals which conducts research on economic, social, and environmen publishes books and magazines; organises seminars; and provides a platform fo interests at international forums. Publications include the daily bulle (South–North Development Monitor), the fortnightly *Third World Econ* the monthly *Third World Resurgence*. TWN is a member of the World B Committee. Its international secretariat is based in Malaysia, with regiona Latin America and Africa. Address: 228 Macalister Road 10400 Penang Email: twn@igc.apc.org. Web: http://www.twnside.org.sg

**The Transnational Institute** is an independent fellowship of resear activists worldwide who work on issues of poverty and injustice, focusing on the global economy, peace and security, and democratisation. TNI advocacy work on behalf of Southern associates among Northern poli Address: Paulus Potterstraat 20, 1071 DA Amsterdam, The Netherlan tni@tni.org. Web: www.tni.org.

**Kogan Page**
120 Pentonville Road, London N1 9JN, UK. <kpinfo@kogan-page.co.uk>

**Lynne Rienner**
1800 30th Street, Suite 314, Boulder CO 80301, USA.
<questions@rienner.com>

**Macmillan (now Palgrave)**
Houndmills, Basingstoke, Hampshire RG21 6XS, UK.
<bookenquiries@palgrave.com>

**MIT Press**
Five Cambridge Center, Cambridge, MA 02142-1493, USA.
<mitpress-orders@mit.edu>

**New Internationalist**
Tower House, Lathkill Street, Market Harborough LE16 9EF, UK.
<newint@subscription.co.uk>

**New Society Publishers**
PO Box 189, 1680 Peterson Road, Gabriola Island, BC, Canada V0R 1X0.
<webmaster@newsociety.com>

**Orbis Books,**
Box 302, New York 10545–0302, USA.
orbisbooks@maryknoll.org

**Oxford University Press**
Walton Street, Oxford OX2 6DT, UK.
<enquiry@oup.co.uk>

**Sage Publications**
6 Bonhill Street, London EC2A 4PU, UK.
<info@sagepub.co.uk>

**Scribe Publications**
ACN 005 403 823, PO Box 287, Carlton North Vic 3054 Australia.
<scripub@ozemail.com.au>

**I.B. T**
Victo
Lond
<mail

**UNES**
7 plac
Franc

**UNIFI**
304 Ea
New Y
<unife

**UN NO**
Palais
Switze

**UNRIS**
Palais
Switze

**Univer**
4720 B
20706,
<custse

**Women**
**Internat**
1350 Co
Washing
<wld@w

**World B**
**Center**
701 18th
USA. pi

**Zed Bool**
7 Cynthi
<sales@

to advance just and sustainable development. IDR believes that new knowledge should directly affect practice as well as policy making and theory building, and dissemination is therefore integral to its work. A wide range of resources, from *IDR Reports* to practical guides and thematic collections are available in print form and on-line, free of charge. Address: 44 Farnsworth Street, Boston MA 02210-1211, USA. Web: www.jsi.com/idr

**International Committee of the Red Cross (ICRC)** might seem an unlikely candidate for inclusion in this bibliography. However, much of its work is involved both in developing and promulgating international humanitarian law, and in the quiet diplomacy which allows it to work in highly charged situations. See S. Davey and J.L. Blondel (1999), 'The International Red Cross and Red Crescent Movement's involvement in public advocacy campaigns', *International Review of the Red Cross*, 81(833):149–81. Address: 19 avenue de la Paix, CH 1202 Genève, Switzerland. Web: www.icrc.org

**International Federation for Alternative Trade (IFAT)** is a global network of producers and alternative trading organisations (ATOs) which aims to improve the livelihood and well-being of disadvantaged people in developing countries; and to change unfair structures of international trade. In IFAT, producers of handcrafts and food products from the South work directly with buyers and managers of ATOs in a spirit of mutual trust. IFAT was formed in 1989 in response to the growing need to strengthen the ATOs to co-operate on an international level, to lobby on international issues, and to become more influential on the international stage. Address: IFAT Secretariat, 30 Murdock Road, Bicester, Oxon, OX26 4RF, UK. Web: www.ifat.org/

**Jubilee Plus** is the successor to Jubilee 2000, the debt-campaign coalition, operating under the umbrella of the New Economics Foundation (see separate entry). It will continue to link with debt campaigners worldwide in order to sustain momentum in global popular campaigning and education, while preparing to shift the campaign towards a focus on the causes of international debt. Jubilee Plus will continue Jubilee 2000's programme of analysis and research, and will add to existing capacity-building work in the South the aim of embedding more elements of the core campaign in the South. Web: www.Jubileeplus.org

**Movimento dos Trabalhadores Rurais Sem Terra (Brazilian Landless Rural Workers' Movement)** is the largest social movement in Latin America. MST's success lies in its ability to organise, to articulate a socio-economic development model which puts people before profits (for instance through organising food co-operatives and primary schools), and to capture the imagination of other farmers' movements and activist groups worldwide. MST has the support of an international network of human-rights groups, religious organisations, and labour unions. It is the Brazilian affiliate of La Via Campesina (www.agronor.org), a global peasant farmers' network which campaigns internationally on food and land-rights issues. MST has a multilingual website at www.mst.org/

**The New Economics Foundation (NEF)** is a UK-based think tank, committed to advancing models of a new economy centred on people and the environment. NEF works to promote participatory democracy and has a long-standing interest in enhancing corporate accountability. Relevant publications include Jennifer Chapman and Thomas Fisher (1999), *Effective NGO Campaigning: A New Economics Foundation Briefing*. www.neweconomics.org/

**Oxfam International** believes that the causes and effects of poverty require a global response and cannot be solved through project work alone. The OI Advocacy Office co-ordinates the development of joint strategies and policies for its 11 members and for partners in the South. Through targeting influential players in governments and institutions such as the World Bank, the IMF, and the UN, OI works to influence the policies which affect the lives of millions of poor people. This entails co-ordinated, simultaneous lobbying in the countries where members are based, lobbying with Southern partner organisations, and direct lobbying of relevant institutions. Address: Suite 20, 266 Banbury Road, Oxford OX2 7DL, UK. Email: information@oxfaminternational.org. Web: www.oxfaminternational.org

**Self-Employed Women's Association (SEWA)** has more than 2 million members, in co-operatives, savings and credit schemes, and advocacy organisations. They are home-workers, manual workers, and small business owners, who are traditionally unprotected and unorganised. SEWA aims to improve its members' bargaining power, and to encourage recognition of their economic and social contribution. As well as organising at the local level, SEWA runs public campaigns in support of its work. SEWA Reception Centre, Opp. Victoria Garden, Bhadra, Ahmedabad 380 001, India. E-mail: mail@sewa.org. Web: www.sewa.org.

**Survival International** supports the rights of tribal peoples worldwide and has supporters in 82 countries. Its advocacy work includes advising on the drafting of international law and informing people of their legal rights. Educational programmes in the North promote respect for tribal cultures and explain the contemporary relevance of their way of life. Survival believes that public opinion is the most effective force for change which, if mobilised, will eventually make it impossible for governments and companies to oppress tribal peoples. Address: Survival International UK, 11-15 Emerald Street, London WC1N 3QL, UK. Web: www.survival-international.org

**The Third World Network (TWN)** is an international network of organisations and individuals which conducts research on economic, social, and environmental issues; publishes books and magazines; organises seminars; and provides a platform for Southern interests at international forums. Publications include the daily bulletin *SUNS* (South–North Development Monitor), the fortnightly *Third World Economics*, and the monthly *Third World Resurgence*. TWN is a member of the World Bank–NGO Committee. Its international secretariat is based in Malaysia, with regional offices in Latin America and Africa. Address: 228 Macalister Road 10400 Penang, Malaysia. Email: twn@igc.apc.org. Web: http://www.twnside.org.sg

**The Transnational Institute** is an independent fellowship of researchers and activists worldwide who work on issues of poverty and injustice, focusing especially on the global economy, peace and security, and democratisation. TNI undertakes advocacy work on behalf of Southern associates among Northern policy makers. Address: Paulus Potterstraat 20, 1071 DA Amsterdam, The Netherlands. E-mail: tni@tni.org. Web: www.tni.org.

# Addresses of publishers

## (addresses for organisations are listed under individual entries)

**ActionAid UK**
Hamlyn House, Macdonald Road,
Archway, London N19 5PG, UK.
<mail@actionaid.org.uk>

**Athlone Press**
1 Park Drive, London NW1 7SG, UK.
<athlonepress@btinternet.com>

**Blackwell Publishers**
108 Cowley Road, Oxford OX4 1JF, UK

**Cambridge University Press**
The Edinburgh Building, Shaftesbury
Road, Cambridge CB2 2RU, UK.
<information@cup.cam.ac.uk>

**Carfax Publishing, Taylor & Francis Ltd**
Customer Services Department,
Rankine Road, Basingstoke
RG24 8PR, UK.
<journals.orders@tandf.co.uk>

**Centre for Civil Society**
London School of Economics,
Houghton Street, London WC2A 2AE,
UK. <ccs@lse.ac.uk>

**Cornell University Press**
512 E State Street, PO Box 250, Ithaca
NY 14851, USA.
<cupressinfo@cornell.edu>

**The Ecologist**
PO Box 326, Sittingbourne, Kent
ME9 8FA, UK.
<theecologist@galleon.co.uk>

**Fahamu**
38 Western Road, Oxford OX1 4LG, UK.
<info@fahamu.org>

**Hurst**
38 King Street, London WC2E 8JZ, UK.
<info@hurstpub.co.uk>

**Institute for Development Policy and Management**
University of Manchester, Crawford
House, Precinct Centre, Oxford Road,
Manchester M13 9GH, UK.
<idpm@man.ac.uk>

**Institute of Development Research**
44 Farnsworth Street, Boston MA
02210-1211, USA. <idr@jsi.com>

**Intermediate Technology Publications**
103–105 Southampton Row, London
WC1B 4HH, UK. <itpubs@org.uk>

**INTRAC**
PO Box 563, George Street, Oxford
OX2 6RZ, UK. <intrac@gn.apc.org>

**Kluwer**
PO Box 17, 3300 AA Dordrecht,
The Netherlands. <Services@wkap.nl>

**Kogan Page**
120 Pentonville Road, London N1 9JN,
UK. <kpinfo@kogan-page.co.uk>

**Lynne Rienner**
1800 30th Street, Suite 314, Boulder CO
80301, USA.
<questions@rienner.com>

**Macmillan (now Palgrave)**
Houndmills, Basingstoke, Hampshire
RG21 6XS, UK.
<bookenquiries@palgrave.com>

**MIT Press**
Five Cambridge Center, Cambridge,
MA 02142-1493, USA.
<mitpress-orders@mit.edu>

**New Internationalist**
Tower House, Lathkill Street, Market
Harborough LE16 9EF, UK.
<newint@subscription.co.uk>

**New Society Publishers**
PO Box 189, 1680 Peterson Road,
Gabriola Island, BC, Canada V0R 1X0.
<webmaster@newsociety.com>

**Orbis Books,**
Box 302, New York 10545–0302, USA.
orbisbooks@maryknoll.org

**Oxford University Press**
Walton Street, Oxford OX2 6DT, UK.
<enquiry@oup.co.uk>

**Sage Publications**
6 Bonhill Street, London EC2A 4PU, UK.
<info@sagepub.co.uk>

**Scribe Publications**
ACN 005 403 823, PO Box 287,
Carlton North Vic 3054 Australia.
<scripub@ozemail.com.au>

**I.B. Tauris**
Victoria House, Bloomsbury Square,
London WC1B 4DZ, UK.
<mail@ibtauris.com>

**UNESCO**
7 place de Fontenoy, F-75000, Paris,
France. <www.unesco.org>

**UNIFEM**
304 East 45th Street, 15th floor,
New York, NY 10017, USA.
<unifem@undp.org>

**UN NGLS**
Palais des Nations, 1211 Geneva 10,
Switzerland. <ngls@unctad.org>

**UNRISD**
Palais des Nations, 1211 Geneva 10,
Switzerland. <info@unrisd.org>

**University Press of America**
4720 Boston Way, Lanham, Maryland
20706, USA.
<custservrl@rowman.com>

**Women, Law and Development
International**
1350 Connecticut Ave. NW, Suite 1100,
Washington, DC 20036, USA.
<wld@wld.org>

**World Bank Public Information
Center**
701 18th Street NW, Washington DC,
USA. pic@worldbank.org

**Zed Books**
7 Cynthia Street, London N1 9JF, UK.
<sales@zedbooks.demon.co.uk>